"*Amusing, entertaining, and definitely helpful! This book will give future thru-hikers an idea what to expect on the trail. Experienced hikers will see themselves and perhaps have a laugh at the fears, questions, and rookie mistakes we share on the trail and on our page.*"
—Bunny Kramer, administrator of the 15,000-member Facebook page, Appalachian Trail: Women's Group

"*I was so excited for Jane to take on this adventure—and what great stories she has to tell!*"
—Jaimie Matzko, Lead Trail Guide for A Walk in the Woods and REI Adventures; one of 6 guides worldwide honored with REI's Top Guide award in 2017

"*A thoroughly excellent read! Funny, and fascinating; there is something intriguing about knowing another's thoughts, an opportunity to compare them to our own. I was in her head, and that added dimension and color to Jane's intriguing experience. Treat yourself to this fabulous book!*"
—Aura Imbarus, Ph.D., Founder / CEO, *Beyond Magazine* and author of the critically acclaimed Amazon best-seller, *Out of the Transylvania Night*

"*This is storytelling at its best! Back again for her 3rd book, Jane Congdon gives us a witty account of—after retiring as an editor in a large publishing company—following a strange compulsion to hike the Appalachian Trail. Her transformation from rookie to seasoned hiker occurs over 1,195 miles of mountain trails and promises adventures along the way. A thoroughly excellent read! Funny, fascinating, and fabulous!*"
—Sharon Babineau, author of *The Girl Who Gave Her Wish Away*

"In a world of trail books, few have this much heart and reflection. Jane Congdon gives us an unflinchingly honest account of her amazing journey: the good, the bad, and everything in between. Her tale is delivered with authenticity and an easy sense of humor, and somewhere between "Hot Pants" and "April Ice," I knew she had a hit on her hands."
—Anna Huthmaker, Founder of Trail Dames, Inc.

"Jane's descriptions of the trail made me feel as if I were walking along with her. Thank goodness I could experience the beauty and the reality of the trail without really hiking! Jane also gives you a glimpse of her unique sense of humor. So pick up a copy, reserve a day, sit down, and enjoy a great read!"
—Jackie Burnett, avid reader and 20-year veteran of book clubs

"You don't have to be a hiker to appreciate this well-written account of a woman's sudden desire for adventure. Jane Congdon's decision to hike the Appalachian Trail in her 60s upended her quiet life and sent her on an inner journey that accompanied the outer one."
—Jenn Granneman, author, blogger for *Psychology Today* and founder of the website: Introvert, Dear

"I read memoirs to see how the main character approaches difficulty and what he or she learns; how the person changes as a result of those experiences. I also like to read about worlds and situations I may not encounter myself. This book is full of good lessons."
—Cyrus Webb, President at Conversations Radio Network and host of Conversations LIVE

HOW THE

WILD EFFECT

TURNED ME INTO A HIKER AT **69**

An Appalachian Trail Adventure

Jane Congdon

BETTIE YOUNGS BOOKS

Disclaimer: This is a true story, and the characters and events are real. Some names and attendant facts have been changed for privacy and storytelling purposes. The overall chronology is an accurate depiction of the author's experience.

About the cover: The boots and socks are the author's; taping of the boots was recreated to reflect the original application of tape to the toes after several hundred miles on the Appalachian Trail. In the background photo: the walkway and arch marking the approach to the AT in Amicalola Falls State Park, Georgia.

Cover design: Tatomir Pitariu
Arch photo credit: Jane Congdon
Boot photo credit: Brian Phillips Studio, Cincinnati
Stylist: Joseph Barnett
Typesetter: Beau Kimbrel
Map of the Appalachian Trail: Mapping Specialists, Limited

BETTIE YOUNGS BOOK PUBLISHERS / BURRES BOOKS IMPRINT
www.BettieYoungsBooks.com
info@BettieYoungsBooks.com

Bettie Youngs Books are distributed worldwide. If you are unable to order this book from your local bookseller or online, you may order directly from the publisher: www.BettieYoungsBooks.com. For BRAILLE, DAISY, and DYSLEXIE editions, go to www.ReadHowYouWant.com.

Library of Congress Control Numbers available upon request.

ISBN Book: 978-1-940784-63-2
ISBN eBook: 978-1-940784-64-9

Printing 1 2 3 4 5 6 7 8 9

What would you do if you weren't afraid? —Spencer Johnson, *Who Moved My Cheese?* ©1998

Make the most of today. Get interested in something. Shake yourself awake. Develop a hobby. Let the winds of enthusiasm sweep through you. Live today with gusto! —Dale Carnegie

OTHER WORKS BY JANE CONGDON

- *It Started with Dracula: The Count, My Mother, and Me*

- *Mr. Joe: Tales from a Haunted Life*
  (co-authored with Joseph Barnett)

Contents

Acknowledgments vii
Map of the Appalachian Trail ix
Part 1: Rookie! 1
Chapter 1: Possessed 3
Chapter 2: We Need to Talk 7
Chapter 3: Unlikely Candidate 13
Chapter 4: Camping 101 19
Chapter 5: Countdown 25
Chapter 6: *"Alone?"* 31
Chapter 7: The Flip 39
Chapter 8: Unadorned 43
Chapter 9: Into the Woods 47
Chapter 10: First, There Is a Mountain 53
Chapter 11: Springer Mountain 57
Chapter 12: Good to Know 61
Chapter 13: Meltdown 65
Chapter 14: Woody Gap 69
Chapter 15: If This Is Morning, Then I'm in a Nightmare 73
Chapter 16: Neel Gap 77
Chapter 17: Shakedown 83
Chapter 18: A Place for Everything 87
Chapter 19: Gimme Shelter 91
Chapter 20: When It Rains 95
Chapter 21: Grandma in Hot Pants 99
Chapter 22: Beasts of Burden 103
Chapter 23: Changes 107
Chapter 24: A Pack of Trouble 111
Chapter 25: North Carolina 115
Chapter 26: Franklin 119
Chapter 27: Sliding In 123
Chapter 28: Miles to Go 129
Part 2: None On 135
Chapter 29: Watch Me Pull a Rabbit Out of My Pocket 137
Chapter 30: Stay or Go? 143
Chapter 31: Out of the Woods 147
Chapter 32: April Ice 151

Chapter 33: Don't Fence Me In 157
Chapter 34: Whoops! 161
Chapter 35: Strike Up the Band 165
Chapter 36: Hot Springs 171
Part 3: The Return 175
Chapter 37: Together Again 177
Chapter 38: A Breaking-in Period 181
Chapter 39: Trail Days 189
Chapter 40: After Damascus 193
Chapter 41: Do Unaka? 197
Chapter 42: Ash Gap 201
Chapter 43: Turtle 205
Chapter 44: The Sisterhood of the Fair Ladies 209
Chapter 45: Signs of Sinus 213
Chapter 46: Virginia Rain 217
Chapter 47: The End of the Up 221
Chapter 48: Cobwebs for Breakfast 225
Chapter 49: Mind Control 229
Chapter 50: Eh? 235
Chapter 51: Hey, Wild Bill! 239
Part 4: Winds of Change 243
Chapter 52: At a Crossroad 245
Chapter 53: Now I Lay Me Down to Fight Bugs, Smell Chickens,
            and Worry About Being Murdered 249
Chapter 54: Three Months 257
Chapter 55: Waynesboro 261
Chapter 56: One More Mountain 265
Chapter 57: After-Effects 271
Chapter 58: A Priest, a Bear, and a Handyman 275
Chapter 59: Oh, Shenandoah! 281
Chapter 60: The Apology 287
Epilogue 291
Author's Comments 295
Questions for Discussion 297
About the Author 299
Reading List 301
Other Books by Jane Congdon 305

Acknowledgments

First, thanks to Cheryl Strayed, my inspiration, for her 1995 hike on the Pacific Crest Trail and her subsequent memoir, *Wild*. She and I have never met except briefly on Facebook, though our paths cross over time and distance in my mind and the pages of this book.

My publisher, Bettie Youngs, is extraordinary for her publishing and marketing knowledge and her willingness to share that knowledge. Thanks, Bettie Youngs Book Publishers, for bringing this and my previous two memoirs to print.

Thanks to everyone who contributed to the publishing process. Turning a manuscript into a book is a journey of art and words that has fascinated me for more than 40 years.

Thanks to our typesetter, Beau Kimbrel, and our cover designer, Tatomir Pitariu.

I always appreciate Amy Cole, Assistant on Call, for expertly formatting my manuscripts and catching the occasional typo I missed.

Many folks supported me while I was on the trail. Special thanks to Joseph Barnett, Charles and Becky Peveler, Judy and Larry Gerow, Jennifer Buff, Sarah Hollier, and Anita Skeen.

Thanks to my very early readers whose comments on individual chapters got me on track: Diane Tarantini, Daleen Berry, Judy Foster Gerow, and Joseph Barnett.

Early readers (entire manuscript): Joseph Barnett, Mary Noschang, Debbie Sebastian; book club members Jackie Burnett, Lennie DeMania, and Becki Wellbrock; Bunny Kramer.

The authors whose books I read in preparation for the AT, listed in the back pages of this book; Jenn Granneman, whose book *The Secret Lives of Introverts* and other writings clarified my knowledge of introversion and extroversion after my hike.

A tip of the trekking poles to every hiker from Earl Shaffer (who in 1948 was the first to complete the entire Appalachian Trail) to Grandma Gatewood (who hiked the AT three times, the first at age 67 and the last at 75) to Jennifer Pharr Davis (2011 AT speed-record holder) and to all the unknowns like me. To every trail angel, hostel owner, and hiker-friendly town: Thank you.

Thanks to the Appalachian Trail Conservancy, whose mission is to conserve and manage the trail. The ATC provides information and services to hikers; maintains pertinent records; and works with volunteers, government agencies, and others to preserve the priceless beauty of the trail for future generations.

Thanks to the volunteers who maintain the AT from end to end. Thanks to all of those who work with pride in our parks and on our trails to protect our natural resources and provide guidance to those who use them.

A pronunciation note: You will read the word *Appalachian* many times in this book. We who grew up in the Appalachian Mountains pronounce it "Appa-latch-un," and we think we are correct; however, many people say "Appa-lay-shun." Whichever way you pronounce *Appalachian*, welcome.

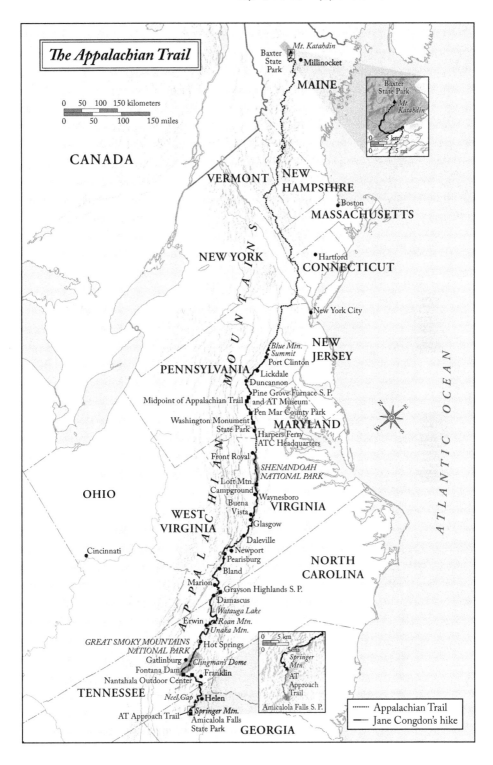

The Appalachian Trail

0 50 100 150 kilometers
0 50 100 150 miles

CANADA

Baxter State Park

Baxter
State
Park

Mt. Katahdin

Millinocket

MAINE

VERMONT

NEW
HAMPSHIRE

Boston

MASSACHUSETTS

NEW YORK

Hartford

CONNECTICUT

New York City

PENNSYLVANIA

Blue Mtn.
Summit
Port Clinton

NEW
JERSEY

Lickdale
Duncannon

Pine Grove Furnace S. P.
and AT Museum

Midpoint of Appalachian Trail

Pen Mar County Park

Washington Monument
State Park

MARYLAND

Harpers Ferry
ATC Headquarters

Front Royal

SHENANDOAH
NATIONAL PARK

OHIO

Loft Mtn.
Campground

Buena
Vista

Waynesboro

VIRGINIA

WEST
VIRGINIA

Glasgow

Daleville

Cincinnati

Newport
Pearisburg

Bland

NORTH
CAROLINA

Marion

Grayson Highlands S. P.

Damascus

Watauga Lake

Erwin

Roan Mtn.
Unaka Mtn.

GREAT SMOKY MOUNTAINS
NATIONAL PARK

Hot Springs

Gatlinburg

Clingman's Dome

Fontana Dam

Franklin

Nantahala Outdoor Center

TENNESSEE

Neel Gap

Helen

AT Approach Trail

Springer Mtn.

Amicalola Falls
State Park

GEORGIA

ATLANTIC OCEAN

Baxter State Park

Mt.
Katahdin

0 5 km
0 5 mi

0 5 km
0 5 mi

Springer
Mtn.

AT
Approach
Trail

Amicalola Falls S. P.

········· Appalachian Trail
——— Jane Congdon's hike

PART 1
ROOKIE!

Chapter 1
Possessed

Didn't you ever hear of a person with a compelsion complex?
. . . Listen, you find compelsion nuts all over.
—TV Deputy Barney Fife to Sheriff Taylor in an episode
of "The Andy Griffith Show," 1962

The sales clerk put 30 pounds of weight in the backpack I'd seen online, so I could walk around and get the feel of it. Wow, it was heavy! Carrying a pack had seemed just fine in the abstract, but in reality, it was hard. I don't have the best posture, which may have added to the feeling of carrying a bag of cement through the store.

Some things look better from a distance. Take the Appalachian Trail, the famous footpath also known as the AT that follows more than 2,000 miles of the Appalachian Mountain Range through 14 Eastern states from Georgia to Maine. After more than a year of reading and planning, I was hiking that trail. My pack had exceeded its test weight. I slept in a tent or a crude three-sided shelter, filtered stream water, and cooked my supper in foil bags. I wore the same clothes every day, clothes that acquired a distinct stench known as "hiker funk" that defied their weekly encounter with laundry soap. I had given up makeup and accepted that my hairdo would become a "don't."

According to the Appalachian Trail Conservancy, I was one of 1,868 hikers who passed through its headquarters that year—a record number partially attributed to the popularity of *Wild* and *A Walk in the Woods*, best-selling books recently adapted for the big screen.

I'd left the comforts of suburbia to climb mountains alongside other grubby thru-hikers, pray the wild animals would let me live, and hear those three little words behind me: "Let's pass Grandma." It wasn't what I was used to. I was an indoor type on an outdoor adventure, and I knew exactly why.

For my presence in the current class of thru-hikers, those intending to walk the entire trail in good weather and bad despite sore feet or muscles or bones, I could cite one thing. It was the *Wild* Effect. I'd found a used copy of Cheryl Strayed's best-selling memoir of hiking the Pacific Crest Trail (PCT) in Half Price Books. I'd read *Wild* twice and was living proof of its power to lure a growing population of women from our cozy homes to the out-of-doors. Strayed had hiked the PCT in 1995 at age 26. It was now 2015 and I was 69. Even so, I imagined her experience would guide me through the wilderness of the Appalachian Trail. In Cheryl I could see myself, and I didn't feel so dumb or crazy. Maybe I could learn from her mistakes, now 20 years in the past and 2,500 miles west of Georgia.

Prior to my obsession to hike it, I had not thought of the Appalachian Trail in years, if ever. I couldn't have pointed to it on a map. I was afraid of animals and prone to being easily chilled. Considering the capriciousness of Mother Nature along the trail, I might be a fair-weather hiker at best. Early on I wondered if I had the stamina or, more important, the necessary mental attitude.

My doubts proved academic as my planning accelerated. As part of my preparation, I bought an insurance policy. "Congratulations on your new Accidental Death and Dismemberment certificate," the letter read. At my age my thoughts regularly drifted to morbid topics, but here was a menu of unfortunate outcomes in case I forgot any.

When this adventure started, I was five months from my 70th birthday. My doctor had pronounced my body a finely tuned machine. I wore glasses and used two hearing aids, but that meant my obvious difficulties had been corrected. I was thankful for my health, but what was next? My brother called it being in the back row, as in a photograph when the generations line up: kids sitting cross-legged in front, parents in the middle row—some with babies on their laps—and then the grandparents standing in back, their eyeglasses reflecting light and hiding their eyes, giving them the expressionless countenance of the walking dead. Ours was the oldest generation now.

I had begun a bucket list. It swung heavily toward travel, but *hiking*? I'd never had a burning desire to explore the woods with a pack on my back. The longest time I'd spent outdoors was a weekend, and no one but a couch potato would have called me a hiker. At that point most of my enthusiasm and trail knowledge came from books.

After *Wild*, I began ordering other hiking books from Amazon. The first two were *Don't Get Sick* and *Don't Get Eaten*. The list had grown to 43 by the time I left for the trail. In addition to collecting practical advice, I read the stories of men and women who hiked the trail. I knew the history of the AT and the names of towns and shelters all along it. Sometimes I felt like I'd already walked "the Roller Coaster," "the green tunnel," "the Presidents," and all the PUDs (pointless ups and downs) in the 14 states. Through my reading I'd hiked alongside Bill Bryson, Earl Shaffer, Jeff Alt, and the Barefoot Sisters. I'd answered the call of the mountains with Brownie, Badger, Skywalker, Odyssa, and others whose trail names I've forgotten. They had walked the 5,000,000 steps to support charities, forget wars, set records, channel grief, make life decisions, or simply appreciate nature.

I wasn't doing it for any of those reasons. My reason, "Possessed by *Wild*," was one I hadn't seen in a book, but the Appalachian Trail Conservancy was on target with its attribution of growing numbers. I knew the *Wild* Effect was real.

I felt a change coming, a new chance. It was inevitable, as with all travel, and I was curious to see how the AT would affect me.

I wasn't hiking alone. That was a relief to my loved ones, every one of them shocked by my intent to tackle the AT. Considering my lack of experience and low level of interest in either exercise or nature, they wondered why I—a retired book editor who spent most of her life indoors without even a pet—would want to gear up and head for the back country on the Appalachian Trail.

American environmentalist John Muir said, "The mountains are calling, and I must go." His famous declaration became a poster and a T-shirt message popular with those living the outdoor life. I hadn't bought the T-shirt. The mountains were calling me, thanks to *Wild*, but were they calling a wrong number?

The AT is open to anyone who can travel it on foot. A blind man named Bill Irwin completed the trail with a seeing-eye dog. People with artificial limbs have walked it, along with senior citizens and children as young as five. I figured correctly that I would be older than most thru-hikers, many straight out of college and hiking to postpone their entry into the real world. I was older than Grandma Gatewood, who put on a pair of sneakers in 1955 and at 67 became the first woman to hike the Appalachian Trail alone.

The AT lay a world away from my condo in the Midwest, but I was *out there*, meaning *on the trail*. Some might argue for the more popular interpretation—*nut case*—but I thought I could succeed. After all, I had grown up in West Virginia, the Mountain State. I had the equipment, the clothes, and a trail partner; and let's not forget the 43 hiking books.

I didn't know anything.

Chapter 2
We Need to Talk

Maybe our mistakes are what make our fate.
—Sarah Jessica Parker

I'm Early Bird. My hiking partner was Miles. Those are trail names—nicknames hikers use when we leave our regular lives behind to spend weeks or months in the woods. Taking on a trail name allows us to live another life for a while, one that is different from the life we are used to. Instead of being defined by our histories, we are seen in a new way. Our real names, hometowns, and occupations become irrelevant unless we choose to share them. It's a step past pretend, a freeing experience. *Me, but not me.*

I'd expected to hike the trail alone—a grim prospect for someone who has been described as "scared of everything that moves"—and then, two months before I left, Miles asked to come along. Though we hadn't spent time together in years, we lived near the same city and had mutual friends. She was an experienced hiker, having done trails in the United States and abroad with professional guides and a group of like-minded companions. She could tell stories of trails I'd never heard of, but she had not hiked the AT.

The two of us began in Georgia on the 30th of March, heading north. We crossed mountains, rock-hopped creeks, and slept in the woods. We marched through days of rain and black mud. We saw the gradual greening of the forest as spring warmed the South. We had come 137 miles together, crossing into North Carolina over a week ago. Now, three weeks into our thru-hike—a venture we estimated would pair us for the next six months—something was wrong.

"We need to talk," Miles said one morning after we'd come off the trail for a night.

Is there a more ominous statement in any relationship? I had no idea what was to come, but the body knows. I had the feeling one gets clickety-clacking up the first hill of a roller coaster. I was sitting on a bunk in a hiker hostel 350 miles from home, absorbing the news.

My partner was threatening to leave the AT. Because of me. According to Miles, I was a bad trail partner—inexperienced and over-confident, thus untrustworthy and disappointing. We were supposed to have each other's backs, but I did not have hers.

Though I was stunned to hear myself described that way, I knew it was true.

Despite the books I'd consumed on the subject, I didn't know how to hike; I couldn't pace myself. I was afraid of wildlife. Though I had grown up among mountains, I was surprised the Appalachian Trail consisted of them: up and down, up and down, every day. I had missed a white blaze—the standard AT trail marker—on a mountaintop, causing Miles to head in the wrong direction toward thin air. I'd fallen multiple times. I'd run out of food and toilet paper our third day out, 16 miles from the next resupply point and flush toilet. I'd struggled to keep pace because under my 30-pound backpack my shoulders were killing me. I started each day with three tablets of Ibuprofen, known on the trail as Vitamin I, and fed myself a steady dose until we stopped for the night. I became lethargic, neglecting my camp chores to crawl into my sleeping bag long before dark. I hadn't been good company.

"I want to leave," Miles said.

My trail dreams were crashing against reality. I hadn't expected to be perfect—starting out, Cheryl Strayed was as green as the hillsides—but this wasn't what I planned.

I realized with horror that I personified the *Wild* Effect in the worst way. I was the stereotype, the clueless novice unprepared for the trail, the one who would join a stampede of other clueless novices and be the bane of those who watched over our parks and forests. Would we, the clueless, behave irresponsibly? put ourselves in danger? wreck the environment? Maybe not all of that, but in three weeks on the trail I had screwed up to the point my partner was saying she wanted to hop on the nearest bus and go home.

What was I going to do if she left? I could leave too, but I had been planning this hike for months. People knew about it. Did I want to return home after three weeks? It was a decision I might have to make.

Things happen on the trail. People leave every day. We heard about packs being abandoned on top of Springer Mountain, the southern terminus and official northbound (acronym, NOBO) starting point of the trail. Two female hikers told us their companion, whose backpack was loaded with cosmetics, lasted two days. We met a man whose hike was interrupted at the beginning when he fell and damaged a knee. Only 25 percent of thru-hikers finish, according to statistics. I didn't want to be in the other 75 percent, but that morning I would have liked to be somewhere else.

What *was* I doing there?

I'd wondered since feeling the first stirrings if my attraction to the trail was delusional. Though my decision to hike the AT was surprising to others, it wasn't sudden. I had labeled myself a curable romantic as I wavered back and forth, one month being enchanted with the idea of being a thru-hiker and the next turned off and scared at the prospect. Now my feet, imagined from home as somehow floating above the earth, had made contact with the dirt and mud and rocks of Georgia and North Carolina. I had peed behind trees and slept next to strangers. I knew the ripe smell of my own sweat.

"What am I doing here?" is a normal question for someone making a cultural transition that no amount of preparation can duplicate. It's a version of "Am I crazy?"—the question that haunts most of us when we take on something monumental and new. It is a natural question for beginning thru-hikers to ask themselves. I had worked through my reasons for being on the trail before I left home, but I'd done that work with the heat turned on, electronics at my disposal, a stove and refrigerator steps away, my bed nearby, and laundry facilities in the basement. Now it was April, still chilly in the mountains.

Miles and I had spent the night at the Nantahala Outdoor Center, a recreational facility located along the trail. With its restaurants, outfitter, and humble hiker lodging, the NOC was our current taste of civilization among the mountains of North Carolina. We'd slept wrapped in our smelly sleeping bags on mattresses the thickness of sofa-bed ticking. The room held three sets of bunk beds, but the only other occupant that night was a young woman interning at the resort.

Miles and I were alone the next morning as we faced one another across a span of concrete floor for our heart-to-heart. We sat on the bunks we'd slept in—bottom bunks. I chose beds closer to the floor after losing my grip on the ladder to a top bunk in a Georgia hostel, grabbing on with one hand while my body swung outward and connected unpleasantly with a stone wall.

I hated confrontation. The quiet, matter-of-fact way Miles discussed my shortcomings was a relief, but it hurt me and brought back the doubts that plagued me from the beginning. *Poor Miles*, I thought, *to get stuck with me*. I thought I knew about the trail—what to do, how to hike it—but I must have been wrong.

Despite my failures, I knew one thing. Thanks to *Wild*, I'd succumbed to the lure of the trail. In so succumbing, I became part of popular culture, joining hundreds of others. I was there. So what if I was 69? So what if I was more tame than wild? So what if I hadn't mastered the trail in three weeks? I'd hiked and camped and read books in preparation for it. Those walks and overnights and the book knowledge were no comparison with Miles' expertise, but I was determined to succeed. I wanted to finish, but it was more than that.

I liked being on the trail.

Despite its challenges and the fact that I had not yet gained my "trail legs," I liked seeing the Appalachian Trail in person and walking it. Some days it was love-hate, but I was learning to appreciate the peace and beauty of the woods as well as the simple obligations of a long-distance hike. It was a retreat with a physical workout built in. I liked being part of the trail culture, meeting other hikers and stopping in the little towns along the way.

I glanced at our backpacks on the floor of the hostel. How many times had we put them on in unison, bracing for the weight? "Ready?" one of us would say, and we'd hoist our packs, strap them on, and go.

Next to Miles' pack, the trash can overflowed with our mingled discards: used baggies, trail trash, food wrappers, and the remains of my new wool shirt. Shelter mice had eaten holes in it two nights before as it hung on a nail to dry, reducing it to a scrap. I could put a hand through the biggest hole.

Despite the negative report I was digesting, I knew I was capable of hiking the Appalachian Trail. If Miles left, I could walk alone and figure everything out. I'd get lost and cold and exhausted and afraid, but I'd make friends along the way. I could do it, but I didn't want to. I dreaded seeing her go. It was the rejection as much as anything else, but was it too late to fix this giant rip in our plans? If she left now, would we forever be estranged? Could I change the course of this day?

We were scheduled to hike out that afternoon. She had made her case for leaving, and I had to act. If I could demonstrate the desire to change, would it keep my partner on the trail? If I found a way to lighten my pack and relieve my shoulder pain, would that break my string of misses?

There's a saying, "Hike your own hike (HYOH)." I had to think beyond the next few hours if I wanted to stay on the trail; I wouldn't be making changes just for her. Whether Miles caught a bus for home or didn't, I had to shape up.

Chapter 3
Unlikely Candidate

Indecision may or may not be my problem.
—Jimmy Buffett

The first time I mentioned hiking the AT to anyone was a feeler long before the fact. I was standing in our community swimming pool with my brother and another friend, explaining my new fascination with the trail.

"It goes from Georgia to Maine," I said. "You start in March and finish in September, hiking through fourteen states. If it rains, you hike. If it snows, you hike. You don't wash for days or weeks. You carry your own food, water, and shelter in a pack on your back. Sometimes you go for long periods without seeing anyone. It's just you and the wildlife—ticks, snakes, bears, and more."

My brother said, "It's everything you don't like."

Was that true? The woods were part of my childhood in West Virginia, and I entered them unafraid. I hiked and climbed without a care, didn't mind getting dirty, and gave no thought to wild animals. But something happened between that rural childhood and my current life. The short answer is "55 years."

The woman I had become, the one considering a thru-hike, was far removed from the girl who had swung on grapevines and played in the woods all day in West Virginia. None of my current friends or neighbors knew that girl. They knew the former textbook editor who lived near a city of 300,000 people. Thanks to glaciers that removed its ruggedness 10,000 years ago, the land in my county is flat, most suitable for farming. After retirement I spent my days at home, many of them sitting at the computer. When I traveled it was by car, whether to the market or to another state.

Around 1980, during my second marriage, our family geared up and spent weekends in the woods with a group. I liked hiking the trails in daylight, but the nights were long; every sound was a threat. I could not sleep until I saw the first light of day creep into our tent and heard the sweet chirping of birds, known as "the dawn chorus."

I liked hearing birds but couldn't identify them the way some people do, for instance, announcing "It's a pileated woodpecker" upon seeing a flying dot in the sky. I had the same lack of success with identifying plants. In *Wild* the novice backpacker Cheryl recognizes Joshua tree and juniper and sage along the Pacific Crest Trail. I've never been eager to know the names of trees or flowers. Maybe it runs in our family. Mom was in a garden club, but only two types of flowers—marigolds and zinnias—graced our yard.

I liked the *idea* of being in the woods—the clean air, the lovely wildflowers, the quiet—but my appreciation ended when the sun went down. I was petrified in the dark when the forest creatures began their nightly roving and calling.

One night after my interest in thru-hiking caught fire I turned out my bedroom lights and imagined myself alone on the AT. The first image in my mind was that of a big, black bear. A poisonous snake came second; but if the bear got me I wouldn't need to fear the snake, would I?

I had nothing against animals, but I had no relationship with them either. Growing up, I was forbidden to have a dog or cat though I asked many times. We lived between a road and a set of railroad tracks, not the best location for a pet. Mom was terrified of cats, so they were out of the question. Joe and I had small turtles, goldfish, and Easter chickens dyed with bright colors. My baby chick "went to a farm" and we buried Joe's on the hill above the tracks, victim of a neighbor's boxer. Survival of the fittest: I got it. Animals can be alarming with their sudden ways and inbred survival instincts— even when no harm results. The sudden movements of a ruffled grouse in the bushes can startle a person into heart-pounding fear. I know.

The planners of my present community included greenbelt areas around the homes when the town was built. I can look out a window and see a rabbit on the lawn at dusk, families of geese feeding beside the lake out back, or a fluffy squirrel scampering up a tree. It sounds like a Disney movie, but over the years squirrels and raccoons invaded my attic. A mama raccoon had babies in my chimney. Something got under my deck and could not get out. All of them had to be professionally removed. I will kindly omit the details, but aspects of those incidents were chilling and disturbing. I liked forest and woodland creatures best in the abstract.

I also liked the *idea* of sleeping outside. As kids Joe and I used to make tents in the back yard using a hobnail bedspread. We would take a stack of comic books into our tent, intending to spend the night there, and would read until it got too dark. Then, even though we had set up the tent a few feet from the back-porch steps, we would be scared back into the house.

Considering my tentative relationship with nature and my typical thought process, I was enamored with becoming a thru-hiker but pre-conditioned to worry and wonder why. It was a strange combination, but even Cheryl Strayed had her doubts. She expressed them in *Wild* as wanting to "Quit, quit, quit." But that was later, after she'd had a taste of the PCT.

I made my swimming pool announcement to hike the Appalachian Trail in August of 2013. By then I was two months into my own plans. I was reading *Wild* for the second time. I had embarked on a path of wellness that spring, taking medical tests I'd skipped for years. I bought a Vitamix blender to make nutritious smoothies, started taking vitamins, and regularly walked the indoor track and worked out in the fitness room at our community center. I went on a few hikes with friends and even took dance classes to get into shape. In those early days I would work out, dance, hike, or swim, and then come back and eat myself out of house and home before falling asleep.

I researched gear and made my first visit to the outdoor store REI, a wonderland where I could see and touch items I had found on the internet. I took classes at REI to learn more about the AT while continuing to order an avalanche of books and read about what it was like to be on the trail.

I loved adventure and survival stories, but did I really want to act one out? There was one way to know. After taking a few classes in the store, I signed up for a guided group backpacking weekend in the mountains of northern Georgia, sponsored by REI. We would not be on the Appalachian Trail, but the terrain would be similar, and I could rent everything but boots.

Before hiking fever infected me, I had cleaned out my bedroom closet. There on a shelf were my old leather hiking boots from 1980, so I tried them on. *Why did I keep these gunboats?* I wondered, throwing them onto the Goodwill pile. Size 10 indeed. After I signed up for the Georgia trip, what was the one thing I needed to buy? Boots. Technology had made hiking equipment lighter, but it hadn't shrunk my feet. The new ones were size 10½.

Feet are transportation on the trail, so foot pain or injury can mean the end of a hike, and I'd read too many tales of blisters and lost toenails to let vanity guide my choice. The folks at REI helped me choose boots that would keep my heels from slipping and my toes from banging against the insides of the shoes going downhill.

The trip instructions specified that our boots be broken in. I wore mine around the house for a couple days, but the way to break hiking boots in is to go on actual hikes. I decided to visit Sharon Woods, a park near my home, and hike one of the nature trails. Alone, the way I would have if I'd been getting on the AT.

All my fears congealed that afternoon and I was a nervous wreck to be going on a solo hike—even if it was in broad daylight in one of our county parks. What should I take? What should I wear? Would there be animals? Ticks? I realized I had no day pack, no walking stick, nothing to hold my water bottle except my hand, and a serious lack of pockets for what I wanted to carry. You don't take a purse on a hike.

It would have been easy to resist putting my boots in the trunk and heading out. However, I popped my bottle of water into one of the holders between the front seats and started the car. On the way to the park I turned on the radio to a prophetic chorus from "The Reverend Mr. Black," something about having to walk a lonesome valley by yourself. I did feel lonesome—lonesome and brave at the same time.

The sun was bright and warm as I chose the Gorge Trail, a gravel trail .7 miles long. I passed other hikers, some with dogs. At times only a chain-link fence and a few trees separated the trail from a golf course. Men's voices invaded the quiet of the woods, but I was still afraid, casting my eyes left and right. I completed the 1.4-mile round trip that afternoon and emerged with a new sense of confidence.

Hiking the park trail alone was a victory, but I was no more ready than the Queen to step onto the AT. I was months away from having to make that decision, but I would need to accelerate my training and buying if I expected to become a thru-hiker. Maybe I should set a deadline to make up my mind. After all, I wasn't hiking for fun; I was hiking with a purpose. I was trying out for the AT.

My next test was coming up: the guided group backpacking weekend in the mountains of Georgia.

Chapter 4
Camping 101

Camping 101:
1. Go outside.
2. Stay there until morning.
—**Camping poster seen on Facebook**

The most expensive gear for my group hike in Georgia was included in the price; I was going to rent it from REI for the weekend. No way was I going to begin buying costly equipment for a thru-hike I was not sure I would ever take.

At home I had nothing but the old gear from 1980 I'd kept after my divorce. The external-frame pack, two-person tent, sleeping bag, lantern, stove, and cooking pans that had been state of the art 35 years ago were too heavy now. Dry rot had ruined the tent, but the remaining items were in good condition. Perhaps Hercules could carry them for 2,000 miles, but I knew I would have to replace everything if I committed to hiking the Appalachian Trail.

Every ounce carried makes a difference because the ounces add up to pounds. Distance is a factor, too; what we can do for the short term, e.g., make a quick trip into the house with groceries, would be unbearable mile after mile. Some hikers shorten the handles of their toothbrushes to save weight.

The trip was set for Labor Day weekend. Even though my backpack, tent, and sleeping bag—known as the big three—were provided, I needed additional gear and food. My love of gear was rekindled as I bought a set of trekking poles; a rain jacket; a fleece; a warm hat; two dry (waterproof) sacks; a synthetic T-shirt ("We highly advise against cotton . . ."); a plastic mug and bowl; bug wipes; bath wipes; and snacks. The selection of shirts was not wide, so I hoped no one would care that my clothes didn't match.

Each participant was to bring snacks and personal items. I bought the recommended dried fruit and beef jerky at REI and repacked the snacks in zip-style baggies at home to divide them over the two hiking days. When I got into the car to leave, I could smell my snacks! The scent was overwhelming. If I hiked with that food, every bear in Georgia would be snuffling after me. I had to discard all of it and re-buy the snacks in Atlanta. That time I left them in their original packaging—designed to be odor proof.

I drove to my son's house northeast of the city on Friday. The next day I drove north to Black Rock Mountain State Park, where our group gathered in a picnic shelter to receive equipment from our guide and pack for the hike. There were seven of us, plus the guide.

I was the oldest hiker in the group. Part of my purpose in being there was to evaluate my physical ability to endure the trail. Emma "Grandma" Gatewood hiked the AT three times, beginning when she was 67. Could I do it once?

My dry sack of personal items was heavy with "what ifs." What if I got poison ivy? Calamine lotion to the rescue. What if I started sneezing from all the flora? Kleenex and anti-allergy pills would fix that. I had Spenco 2nd Skin in case I got hot spots or blisters, Ibuprofen for pain, something for diarrhea; bug wipes, bath sheets . . . the list went on. My Swiss Army knife was a whopper, and I had a Steripen for purifying water. As I recall, the only one on REI's "Mandatory Items" list was a knife.

My long underwear defied the "no cotton" rule at 50 percent, but I couldn't buy everything new for one night in the woods. Fortunately, I had rainwear, as we had a sudden shower before leaving the shelter. Everyone pulled on rain pants and rain jackets, but we suited up for nothing. In a few minutes the sun emerged, and we left for the trailhead.

I was teamed with another single female for the camping part. We split up the tent pieces, one carrying the cloth and the other, the poles. The group hiked two miles, mostly downhill, before pitching our tents in a clearing. As soon as we got the tents up it rained buckets.

"Get in your tents," our leader said. "If lightning strikes, crouch on your sleeping pad, touching it with only the balls of your feet."

We were not forced into the survival position; however, rain pelted our campsite. "Do you feel that?" I asked my tent-mate. "Our sleeping pads are moving."

The floor of the tent was undulating beneath our legs.

"It's like a waterbed," she said. "We're floating!"

Outside the rain flap, my trekking poles lay in a growing puddle. I pulled my backpack into the tent, but that wouldn't save it. We had pitched our tent in a low spot—a rookie mistake—and now we had to move it to level ground in the rain.

The storm put off dinner for a while, and by then the sun was gone. Our guide said, "Everybody put on your headlamps. We might be cleaning up in the dark." We sat around a campfire listening to katydids, and it was indeed dark behind us. I kept thinking of those tigers in India, the ones that steal into villages and snatch people out of their huts. I saw one of the men get up and slip behind me. No one else seemed to notice until his wife let out a yelp when he intentionally scared her.

We went en masse into the woods to brush our teeth, and then it was bedtime. I slept soundly except for having to pee, but I did not get up.

The two-mile return trip was straight uphill, and the ground was wet from last night's rain, making the hiking arduous. I wanted to keep up—it was important—but I also wanted to throw my gear over the nearest cliff and have someone serve me a tall glass of iced tea under a ceiling fan.

I was not done with my ambivalence.

It wasn't a perfect trip and shouldn't have been; it was a test. They all are. Mother Nature is unpredictable, gear is unpredictable, and we're unpredictable. A thousand things can happen even to the well prepared. I was glad I spent a night in the Georgia woods. Maybe I'd give backpacking another whirl, now that I could boast that I'd hiked four miles.

In the spring I accepted an invitation to camp over Easter weekend on friends' property in the country a few hours' drive from my home. It would be another chance to do an overnight alone, and by then I had a backpack, a sleeping bag, and a one-person tent I needed to field test.

I now owned the "big three" pieces of gear needed for a thru-hike plus some smaller items. I had not committed to hiking the AT, but I should have for the money I was spending. The months were passing. What was I going to do? I gave myself a deadline of June 1, 2014 to decide whether the next spring I was in or out.

My plan for the weekend at my friends' place was to pitch my tent in a flat area away from their house, sleep there overnight while they slept inside, and hike the hills of their property the next day wearing my new backpack. That was a good plan in daylight. When the sun began to sink and shadows fell across the valley floor, it wasn't so appealing. I talked my friends into setting up their tent and camping next to me.

Ten minutes after I snuggled into my sleeping bag, I had to pee but didn't want to get up. As I lay there in misery, my mind did a soft-shoe to the tune of "Me and My Shadow": *"Me . . . and My Blad . . . der. . . ."* In between choruses I pictured every possible creature wandering or slithering out of the woods to get me if I left the tent. Finally, at 5:00 a.m. I went into the house to use the bathroom. Only then could I sleep.

For my next outing I registered for a Road Scholar program titled "Hike the Appalachian Trail in Four States!" I saw it in a catalog that came in the mail. The program was a series of guided day hikes on the AT. How could I resist? I had most of the gear I needed, but not a daypack, so another trip to REI was in order.

This trip, at the end of May, would be the last one before my decision deadline.

Road Scholar (formerly Elderhostel) offers educational trips for men and women ages 50 and older. There were 24 of us. The activity was rated "Challenging," but what did that mean? How fit did I have to be in order to hike the trail in a group of senior citizens?

"Hike the Appalachian Trail in Four States!" was a cushy way to do the trail. Each day a van took us to a trailhead and from there we hiked six to ten miles and then were driven back to our headquarters at a conference center. We had breakfast before departing, lunch on the trail, and dinner back at headquarters.

We hiked in Maryland, Pennsylvania, Virginia, and West Virginia. The days were rough on me, and I didn't have to prepare meals, sleep in the woods, go without bathing, or carry a heavy backpack. Seeing the Appalachian Trail in person was a thrill, but I also had a glimpse of how exhausted I could be if I hiked every day, fixed food, set up a tent, and carried my supplies on my back.

After a day of hiking, I was impatient for a hot shower, foot powder, and food. We were treated to a program every evening after dinner. By then paying attention was agony. One night I sneaked out when the speaker turned away. I was afraid I would drop off to sleep and fall out of my chair.

As my June decision deadline approached, I was feeling a sense of urgency about my life and life decisions. At home my days were too long. The danger lurked that I would fill them with empty pursuits, leading to inertia and depression. Mom had spent years on the couch in her last apartment before she developed Alzheimer's. She ate peanut-butter crackers for lunch and watched reruns of *Law & Order* on TV. I told myself I could not fall into that habit, but I was. In her 80s Mom weighed 90 pounds and was so physically weak she carried her groceries from the car over a period of hours or days. After a meal she would implement her plan to gain weight, which involved lying on her back on the couch to read or watch TV—a move that did little for her lack of girth but inevitably led to a nap. I was liking TV and naps too much myself. All I needed was a TV tray and one of those pockets for the remote that you tuck under a chair cushion. Living alone and having few visitors, it was easy to fall into a pattern of low productivity. I could dust the furniture today, tomorrow, or next month. It didn't matter.

It wasn't just my sedentary lifestyle that bothered me. Too many people I knew were dying. Friends, mentors, and former colleagues were leaving this world. My teen-age idols were old. I was about to enter a new decade. With every year that went by, I felt time slipping away.

By June I was eager to change my routine, and thru-hiking the AT seemed like the ideal plan to shake it up. I committed to the hike. I would start April 1, 2015 in Georgia and see how far I got. I hoped I could get to Mt. Katahdin, the end of the trail in Maine. My preparation was sure and deliberate, but my thoughts would continue to be marked by wild swings of emotion.

Chapter 5

Countdown

Strength is a matter of the made-up mind.
—American poet John Beecher

Now that I was committed to a thru-hike, I felt a new urgency about the trail and my preparation for it. Should I be joining the Sierra Club? Shouldn't I be out hiking right now? What trails should I hike? I discovered on the internet that Ohio has a trail running all around the state. It's called the Buckeye Trail. I'd lived in Ohio for 37 years and hadn't heard of it. I suddenly understood those residents Cheryl Strayed encountered out west who didn't know what the Pacific Crest Trail was.

In the wake of my decision to hike the AT, my mind flew apart like a scattering of birds. Suddenly I was overwhelmed with things to do. Never mind that I had spent a year collecting and reading books about the trail, buying gear, and signing up for practice experiences in the woods. I felt the weight of the preparation that was still to come.

Planning my hike would be logistically complicated until I hit the trail and began to live simply. The first order of business was to organize my growing collection of backpacking gear, books, and clothing. The items were stashed in different locations around the house, making me crazy when the time came to go hiking. I forgot something every time. Once it was my water supply—not a good thing to leave at home.

I was keeping not only the gear, but also the packaging for each item in case I had to return it or remember some fact about it, for example, its weight. I kept the sales receipts in a separate place but the cardboard boxes, sock sleeves, and instruction booklets were piled in boot boxes and shopping bags.

I needed a nerve center!

As opposed to a place to work up my nerve, this nerve center would be a location in my home for all my hiking paraphernalia. I wanted to see all my gear and my full range of clean outfits at once so I could dress quickly and fill my packs from memory as I prepared for every practice hike and then the Big Hike. The goal was efficiency; I wanted my movements to become automatic on the trail. Out there, I might have to dress and assemble my pack in the dark.

My nerve center had to be large enough to accommodate packs, boots, a puffy sleeping bag, a tent, clothes on hangers, and dozens of other items from eating utensils to my collection of hiking books. I chose my linen closet, a double-wide with sliding doors. It was one of two closets in my bedroom, the other being a walk-in for my clothes and shoes. Several years earlier I'd had the linen closet customized. Except for a narrow section for hanging clothes, the space was divided by adjustable shelves. It was perfect.

Out came the bedding, towels, placemats, folded curtains, and suitcases to find another home; into the closet went the hiking gear, books, and outdoor clothing. I had a shelf for my tent, one for my sleep system, another for footwear. There were dedicated spaces for stuff sacks, trekking poles, cooking and hydration gear, and smaller items—socks, whistle, bug net, emergency blanket, Strike Anywhere matches, and so on.

There was one little hitch. After my double-wide nerve center was done and I stood back to admire it, I turned to see a room that resembled a scene from the TV show "Hoarders." My bedroom was full of the items I'd removed from the closet. Extra curtains, comforters, scatter rugs, placemats, shower curtains, and beach towels were piled high on my bed. Suitcases and garment bags littered the floor. I had reversed my storage solutions; now I had no choice but to stash the linens all over the house.

That summer I returned to Sharon Woods, the park where I'd first hiked alone. I tried the trails at other parks in the area. I joined the Cincinnati Nature Center and hiked there a few times a week wearing my backpack. The nature center trails crossed hills and creeks; they were the closest in terrain to the AT. Each trail was named and marked, but they intersected in the woods and I usually got lost. Wherever I started, I would end up on another trail, guaranteeing a longer hike back to the visitor center. Hiking those trails was great practice, but it beat me to a pulp.

I took more classes at REI, one on camping and another called "Women Traveling Solo." In September I went on a guided two-night group hike in the Smoky Mountains called "Women in the Wilderness." In October I spent a weekend backpacking with friends in the Red River Gorge Geological Area of the Daniel Boone National Forest in Kentucky.

Unlike the previous year, I didn't hibernate for the winter. I was months away from my April start date, and there was much to do. I knew I had to be in shape for the trail and prepared for cold weather once I was on it. One day I read a blog by "Dr. Grump," who lives in Maine and observes many thru-hikers. He said the only preparation for the AT is to get out in the cold, wet weather and hike with a pack on your back. I discovered I fell into the group he described negatively as those who might be looking out their windows thinking, "Good golly, Miss Molly, I'm sure glad I am inside today." But I didn't give up.

How do you train to be cold? I bought a puffy jacket that was both lightweight and warm, along with a pair of hiking gloves. I ordered a wool Buff to keep my neck warm and replaced my 50-percent-cotton long undies with a polyester base layer. I began walking every morning before dawn in my neighborhood. It was January. My eyes watered, and my nose ran. I had to stuff my pockets with tissues. Some days it was so cold I found myself projecting it onto the AT: *If I'm freezing now, what if I were on the trail? What if I had to get up, take down a tent, pack a backpack, and start walking to get warm?*

When reality intruded, as it did when I wondered how I would handle backpacking in cold weather, I didn't want anything to do with it. Besides my dread of cold, physical tasks had taken on a new level of difficulty in recent years. When I had to climb onto a kitchen stool to get a bowl from the cabinet, I was slow at it, causing me to wonder if I was too old or too frail for a thru-hike. I knew I was not as agile as I liked to think.

In addition to walking, I was plotting my AT hike. That January I sat at my desk with a long map of the trail, a copy of the book *Appalachian Trail Thru-Hike Planner*, and a legal pad for my scribbles. I worked with a calculator and a NOBO calendar I made on my computer from a blank Microsoft Word calendar. I used the

A.T. Guide, Northbound and the internet to create a detailed daily itinerary that included stops in trail towns, nights in shelters, and the mileage from one stop to the next. As I worked my way through the months, I found a picture of every shelter online. More than 250 had been built along the trail, and many were so similar I lost track of which ones I'd seen before. After that exercise, I was weary of shelters before going near the trail.

By mid-January I had planned as far as Palmerton, Pennsylvania. That translated to July 19 on my hiking calendar. In addition to being a risky pursuit—I had no real idea how far I could hike in a day—the planning was so detailed it was a challenge to stick with it. By Palmerton I was getting reckless, choosing shelters that were too far apart. Did I really expect to make that much progress?

One of my resources for estimating my daily miles was the trail journal of 74-year-old Nan Reisinger ("Drag'n Fly"), one of the oldest women to complete a thru-hike. In addition to narrative, Nan's trail journal gave the dates she and her friend Freckles hiked each section of trail. They started out in the "bubble"—large group—of March/April NOBOs, as I would, but were quickly passed by many of the other hikers. *That would be me*, I thought. I also followed the pace of a male hiker who took lots of breaks because he had trouble with his feet. His hiking progress was about even with the 74-year-old's.

Another winter project was buying food and personal supplies to put in resupply boxes I would mail to myself to be held at various points along the trail—e.g., post offices—where food would be needed but was limited or unavailable. I joined a wholesale club, so I could buy in bulk: Clif bars, Ibuprofen, Pop-Tarts, hearing aid batteries, M & M's, Quaker oatmeal packets, and Via coffee singles were among my purchases.

From a list of suggested mail drops between Georgia and Maine in *Appalachian Trail Thru-Hike Planner*, I determined I needed 14 resupply boxes. After getting free, flat Priority Mail boxes from the Post Office, I put them together and brought all my supplies into my living room. I packed gallon-size baggies with products for breakfast, lunch, dinner, and snacks. I put the meal and snack bags into each mailing box with toilet paper, batteries, sections of the *A.T. Guide* I had taken apart to save weight, and replacement clothing for a different season or location.

In addition to all the prep for my time in the woods, I had to manage what I was leaving behind, including the 14 packages. I needed someone at home to mail my packages, over time, to points along the AT. That someone had yet to be identified, though a few friends volunteered to help me however they could.

I worried about keeping things going back in Ohio while I was hiking the trail. How could I manage my "real life" from the AT? Unlike those hikers who would have parents or spouses at home, I had no automatic backup.

Few of us are carefree, even in retirement. I had mail—including bills—arriving every day. Now I needed to make sure those bills would be paid in my absence and that nothing important that came in the mail would be ignored. The system had to be foolproof.

In order to be away for six months, I paid a few bills ahead and switched the others to automatic payments. I arranged for my water supply to be turned off at the main when I left home and turned back on when I returned from the trail. My brother agreed to watch the house and to get my mail every week, sifting through it for important letters or notices.

As part of my financial planning, I listed my discretionary expenses and realized I would not be spending that money on the trail: no hair appointments, no workouts with a trainer, and no manicures or pedicures. I might be buying replacement gear or clothing, but I would not be shopping for fun. My grocery needs would change as well, from stocking a pantry and refrigerator to buying meals suitable for cooking with boiled water. I would not be putting gasoline into my car.

I could save serious money being in the middle of nowhere! Of course, I could. I'd grown up in a town of 600 people in West Virginia. We didn't spend money every day. What would we spend it on? Unless I count the one-room grocery store in our Post Office building, we had nowhere to shop. New clothes, haircuts, shoes, and everything else beyond white bread and other food basics required trips to other towns. My life was simple then and would be simple again.

What I learned during my practice hikes and subsequent planning days at home confirmed my earlier decision hike the AT.

I realized that (1) hiking the AT always looked better from inside my house; but (2) if I waited a year or two I'd only be older; nothing would have changed with regard to either my fascination or my fears. There was no point in waiting.

My desire was stronger than ever. I was not keen to get out into nature alone, but who would go with me? Considering the cost of gear, the time investment, and the hardships inherent in backpacking 2,000-plus miles, I knew the answer to that: nobody I knew.

Chapter 6

"Alone?"

"Alone (Why Must I Be Alone)"
—**Title of a hit song by the Shepherd Sisters, 1957**

"You're not going *alone*, are you?" asked everyone I knew.

It was the number-one question I heard from family and friends after I told them I was preparing to hike the Appalachian Trail in 2015. According to an article I saw in *Backpacker* magazine, data on crime against female solo hikers doesn't exist; but I will guess that *someone* poses that question to every woman who plans to hike the trail alone.

Some friends asked if I was going with a group. Others advised me to take a dog. A few wanted to know if I planned to pack a weapon. Another one said, "If you camp, do it off the trail." Would I really pitch my tent where the bears and foxes and big cats hang out? Not a chance.

I knew my friends were concerned for my safety, but their questions put me on the defensive. Was I helpless? Was I a child? Was I entering the Appalachian Trail without the prior knowledge of 43 books? No! I could have replied with another question—"Would you like to go with me?"—but I already knew the answer. Most of my friends preferred their creature comforts. I wasn't going solo as a scientific experiment to see which wild animal would eat me alive; I was doing it because I had no hiking partner.

I had mentally gone through my list of friends and had even posted on social media to ask if any had hiked on the AT, but I had dim hopes of finding a companion. The obvious obstacles for most people were money and time. Thousands of dollars could be required if the person didn't have equipment. Time off from work was an issue for many, even at my age. Fitness might be an obstacle, and what about interest? What about the right attitude, the number-one requirement for a long hike? You have to want to be out there in the woods, in survival mode, your body aching, with little to do but put one foot in front of the other day after day.

Maybe going alone would be better. I was used to my own company. I had family nearby, but I spent large chunks of time by myself. I had my routines and set my own schedule. When I wanted to go somewhere, I went. I didn't need others the way some people do. Had I ever been highly social? Some days I didn't even open the front door. When my cell phone rang, I was surprised.

On the other hand, I was not—and never would be—comfortable alone in the woods.

People didn't scare me the way they do some women. Statistics show that 2.5 to 3 million people visit the Appalachian Trail every year. At the time of this writing, only nine known murders had been committed there since 1974, with four of the victims men, and five women. Jennifer K. Wesely, Ph.D., professor of criminology and criminal justice at the University of North Florida, has said women are much more likely to be assaulted by someone they know than by a strange man lurking behind a boulder. "The fear is what's holding women back," she said, "not the reality. Women are not in more danger in wild spaces."

I could see other complications of solo hiking. One morning in the shower, shortly after I'd conceived my idea to hike the AT, I started thinking about ticks. How would I check for them in places I couldn't see or reach? The answer was a mirror. What would I do if I examined my body in a mirror the way the books tell you to and found a tick burrowing under my skin? I don't mean "what would I do" in the usual sense; instructions are available. I mean, how would I cope? I might not be able to touch the thing, even with a pair of tweezers.

More seriously, what if I fell or got lost or developed hypothermia? I had a million reasons to want a partner, yet part of me didn't. Could I hike my own hike with someone else?

Ultimately, we're all alone; there's no other way to say it. People can break your heart. We raise our children to become independent and leave us. Families don't always get along. I was not good in relationships. Having a trail partner 24/7 on a long-distance hike would have some similarities to a marriage, and I'd been divorced twice.

If I entered the trail in Georgia in March, I'd have plenty of company even without a hiking partner. The trail would be crowded then, before 75 percent of the hikers dropped out. Cheryl Strayed hiked the Pacific Crest Trail by herself. She started out feeling sad and empty, with little to lose. Cheryl expected to dispel grief on the trail, but she became so focused on the day-to-day that she didn't grieve or dwell on her problems. Maybe that should be a goal of mine—to come to terms with myself. Living alone all these years I thought I had, but maybe not.

For a time, I considered inanimate objects as potential companions. Many hikers take favorite possessions such as musical instruments or stuffed animals on the trail. I thought Alphie, my portable writing keyboard, would fill the empty place. It would be a way to share my feelings. However, Alphie would also be filling space in my backpack, and at 1.75 pounds was a poor choice, too large and clunky.

To move ahead with my plans, I had to accept the fact that I was going on my backcountry adventure alone. I would set out from home by myself without knowing anyone. My attitude as I got ready was not excitement or joy, but grim inevitability.

The word was out months before I was to leave. I had told a few people I was considering a thru-hike, but when my message evolved to "I *am* going to hike the Appalachian Trail," my friends and family wanted to know more.

My grown son initially said, "Wow! That's exciting!" but later he worried that I was jumping in without enough research and thought. "Why would you skip to a thru-hike after only a few real experiences in the woods?" he wanted to know.

I said, "I'm sixty-eight."

I realized no one had said, "At your age?" Plenty had asked if I was going alone, but not one person had expressed concern about my age. Maybe they didn't know my age.

As my preparation continued, I had to face another missing element: I had not spent the night alone, outdoors, in my tent. After all, that was the plan for my thru-hike. I would sleep in shelters some of the time, but with so many hikers on the trail the shelters could be crowded. Some days I might not make it from one shelter to the next, depending on the weather, terrain, and distance.

What was I waiting for? I considered going to a park near my home that offers backcountry campsites, but the thought of sleeping there by myself was too scary. I couldn't do it. Instead, I took my gear to my friends' country place and set it up in the front yard. That counted; I was alone all night. Though I was not in the middle of the forest, I got to test some of my gear. It rained the whole night but I stayed dry, proving my tent did not leak. The foam sleeping pad I'd bought was a tad too thin for my aging bones, so the next day I traded it for an inflatable model.

As my plans jelled, the nay-saying turned to encouragement. People assumed I was going to succeed. They told others, "She's going to hike the Appalachian Trail." Posts on social media reflected support—"You'll never know until you try"—and admiration. There are many ways to say, "You go, girl!" My friends were applauding me for rising to my full potential and taking on challenges beyond my comfort zone.

I was glad when the "Alone??!!" comments tapered off, but I became skittish as the time drew closer. The hike was real in the sense that it was known, and I was going. Thanks to those last-minute nerves, I became open to having a trail partner; I could see the comfort in it. With no candidates in the wings, I asked the Universe: "If I'm supposed to have a trail partner, please send me one." And then I let it go.

In November I heard from a hiking friend I'd met on the Smoky Mountains outing "Women in the Wilderness." We made plans to meet and hike the Smokies together when I reached Fontana Village, North Carolina, on the AT. She and I exchanged excited e-mails and possible schedules. I blithely agreed to 8- to 12-mile days, having no idea how much ground I could really cover. In the end it was academic; her plans fell through before the month was over. What a letdown that was.

My restless nights and worrying increased. I was plagued with thought-racing in the wee hours about all I had to do. I mangled the blankets every night thinking about my fears. One night I snuggled down into the covers and wallowed in being home. I told myself: *You're safe here. You're in a warm bed. There are no bears. There are no snakes. There are no mice. There are no people snoring, farting, stinking, or blowing their foul breath in your face. You don't have to go to the bathroom; if you did, you would not have to turn on your headlamp and find your way outside with God knows what waiting in the trees. You could walk a few feet on soft carpeting and pee in the toilet instead of a crude privy or the bushes.*

In December of 2014 I took a few local hikes with a woman I'd worked with 15 years earlier. She had heard about my plans through mutual friends and contacted me.

"I hear you're planning to hike the Appalachian Trail," she said on one of our outings.

"I am, and I also plan to write a book about my hike."

"Hiking the AT has been a dream of mine for years."

I knew she and her husband enjoyed hiking together.

"He doesn't want to do it," she said, "this year or next year or ever." It was the camping her husband disliked; besides his refusal to sleep in primitive conditions, he was still working. She was retired.

In my mind we were having conversations. I didn't see them as feelers, but that's exactly what those early meetings were. One day in February I opened my e-mail and found a message from her asking if I would want her company on the AT. I was excited, and my immediate answer was yes, but I tried to contain my elation. I didn't want to be disappointed again if it didn't happen.

Less than two months before my start date she came on board, complete with a trail name I'll change to Miles. It would have been challenging, if not impossible, for someone with less experience and gear to prepare for a thru-hike in just a few weeks, but Miles could be ready.

Having a hiking partner was a gigantic turning point. It would affect all my plans going forward. For the first time, I wasn't trying to work out the details alone; I had input from an experienced hiker. In addition, Miles' husband, whom I'll call Mr. M, volunteered to be our main support at home. He would mail our resupply packages (remember my 14 boxes?) and track credit-card expenditures we would later split.

Miles and I and talked about every aspect of backpacking—topics fascinating to us but of little interest to most of my other friends and family members. I showed her my nerve center full of gear and she showed me her spare bedroom stacked with what she would take to the AT. We gave each other little presents, for instance a packet of foot powder to try or a sample of some new snack food we might want to pack.

At last I had validation: Miles was not going to ask silly questions or try to talk me out of going. She was taking me, my resolve, and my intentions literally. I didn't even take myself literally.

"Neither of us will defer to the other," she said one day. That statement was significant because, at the company where we worked, I had been her boss. I didn't think I'd been a great boss, however, it was 15 years later and we were in a different situation. Neither of us brought up the past. For my part, I wanted old memories to stay outside the bubble of our new adventure. I'd asked the Universe for a trail partner, and the Universe had sent me Miles.

She was 65. Both of us were mothers of grown children who lived away. We talked about our granddaughters; Miles has two and I have one. Physically, both of us were fit and weighed the same at the start—around 135 pounds—but I'm a few inches taller. Each of us looked forward to working off extra pounds and gaining muscle once we were hiking at our peak and burning thousands of calories every day, but we were starting out fit for our years. Miles had medical issues, two being a weak back from prior surgery and a bad left knee. She was smart and goal oriented, so I knew she would address them appropriately. They would not stop her unless . . .

"If my leg goes numb, I'll have to leave the trail," she said one morning as we sat in her kitchen.

We had made a T-chart to illustrate the risks we were willing to take on our hike. On the top left of the T was "Unpleasant" and on the right, "Life-Threatening." "Unpleasant" didn't change any plans; "Life-Threatening" did. Rain was an example of unpleasant; climbing boulders could be life-threatening.

"On the scale of unpleasant to life-threatening," Miles said, "if my leg goes numb, that will be life-threatening.

"Also, both my husband and I have elderly parents. If anything should happen to one of them, I will come home."

I had an issue, too, but I didn't disclose it to Miles until I saw my doctor. I felt weak and light-headed after hiking a few miles. Twice when I was driving home from the nature center I began to black out. The second time I knew that if I didn't get off the road I would have a wreck. I managed to exit the highway and pull into a shopping center until I felt I could drive again, but I was afraid. I didn't need another thing to worry about, especially so close to our departure date, and fainting would not play well on the AT.

"What did you have to eat?" my doctor asked.

"A Clif bar," I said. "I got lost in the snow and had to hike longer than I planned."

"I see this problem in teen-age girls," she said. "They don't want to gain weight, and they eat so little that they faint.

"When you're on the trail, you will need to stop and eat something. You'll be burning lots of calories, and you must replace them. If you feel light-headed, stop. Sit down, rest, and eat."

I was good to go.

Neither Miles nor I intended to give up once we were on the trail; when faced with obstacles, we expected to find alternatives. We had the same goal—to complete a thru-hike—but different concerns. She had no fear of wildlife, which was wonderful; I was afraid of anything that had four feet or slithered. Miles was more wary of people. She suggested a code word we could use to communicate our uneasiness with anyone suspicious that we met. The word we chose was one Miles had used before: *vomit*. As seldom as *vomit* is needed in one's vocabulary, it was a good choice to minimize chances of a false alarm. However, I wondered privately how I could work it into a sentence and hoped I wouldn't have to find out.

I planned to carry a small pink container of pepper spray just because. Miles bought the same one. They were nothing compared to the 10-inch can of bear spray I intended to strap to my waist with a belt every morning to quell my worst fears.

My friends and family were thrilled to know I was not going into the deep, dark woods alone. They knew I had an experienced trail partner in Miles; Wonder Woman couldn't have elicited a stronger endorsement. As for me, I had gone from being scared to being prepared. I was eager for the adventure we were about to take together, and I liked being able to say "we."

Chapter 7
The Flip

*If we sit down and put a list of things we're going to do
on a piece of paper, they almost never work out right.*
—Norman Mailer (on the challenge of plotting a novel)

Now that we were going to be trail partners, Miles and I would
need to meet several times a week until we left for Georgia. Naturally,
scheduling our hike was an important topic.

I had completed a detailed plan for the first three and one-half
months, but now we would have to revisit it together. There was no
other way; the schedule had to work for both of us. We also had to
discuss the rest of our hike—the portion I had not planned beyond
July 19: Palmerton, Pennsylvania. I knew one thing: I expected to
hike northbound all the way to Maine.

We sat down with a calendar, a calculator, a copy of David
"AWOL" Miller's *A.T. Guide, Northbound,* and the existing partial
schedule. I was glad to provide what I hoped was not merely a
starting point.

That first day, Miles suggested we consider a flip-flop hike, one
of several types common on the AT. A "flip" entails hiking to a
predetermined point on the trail and then traveling to the other end
and reversing direction. For example, Miles thought we might start
at the southern terminus of the trail in Georgia as I'd planned and
hike north only as far as Harpers Ferry, West Virginia.

"And then what?" I asked.

"Mister M would drive us to Maine," she said. "The three of us
could have a vacation there. He would climb Mount Katahdin with
us to start our southbound (SOBO) hike and then drive home. You
and I would stay and keep hiking south."

"I've read about flip-flopping," I said. "I know what it is, but what
would be the point?"

"Two advantages. One: The deadline imposed by the October
fifteenth closing of Baxter State Park won't apply to us. We won't

have to rush to get into the park and summit Mount Katahdin. Two: The temperatures in New England in July and August should not be as harsh as they'll be in the fall.

"Your transportation will be provided. Mister M can bring anything we need from home—supplies, warm clothes—when he meets us in Harpers Ferry."

Mr. M was key; otherwise, I would never have considered "flipping" to Maine. It changed my hike. However, I understood the advantages. Eliminating the constant pressure of time would be a plus, especially to me as a rookie. Avoiding fall in the northern states also had its appeal. If he was going to take us, I didn't see any harm in changing the plan from a NOBO hike to a flip, but that was not something I was ready to say to Miles without more processing time.

"Why Harpers Ferry?" I asked, and then answered my own question. "Oh, the Appalachian Trail Conservancy." Stopping at the ATC headquarters on Washington Street is a rite of passage for hikers.

"Yes, and Harpers Ferry is the psychological halfway point of the AT," Miles said. The actual midpoint of the trail was farther north, in Pennsylvania. I had been there on one of my day hikes with Road Scholar the previous year.

Everything cannot be my way, I thought later. *Doesn't having a hiking partner outweigh the inconvenience of a few changes?*

If I agreed to a flip, what would I have to change? I thought about my 14 resupply boxes. The ones to be sent between Georgia and Harpers Ferry would be fine, but I'd have to re-label the others to fit a SOBO hike. That meant determining where Miles and I would be.

I had no *A.T. Guide, Southbound* with which to work out a schedule, let alone calculate resupply stops. At $20.93 with shipping, it wouldn't break me to order one from Amazon. Was it a sign I was committing to the flip? More likely it was the mind of Early Bird at work; like the Boy Scouts, I had to be prepared. The timing was pure luck: I snagged the last Southbound guide in stock.

One day I asked Miles if she realized that, by hiking the AT with me, she was putting herself in this book. It could have been a deal-breaker, but it wasn't. And I could not promise her anything except that I would not use her real name.

"What would you do if *I* wrote a book?" she asked. I would do nothing. Anyone has the right to write a book, and maybe she would.

Twelve calendar days passed before Miles and I finalized the decision to flip. I was happy with the logic of it, and I liked the idea of going toward the South rather than farther and farther away from it. My roots were stuffing the ballot box.

We managed to come away with an acceptable SOBO schedule as well as a NOBO plan that made it through inspection No. 2 with minor revisions. The re-labeling of drop boxes proved easier than I had expected.

The time was flying by. In another few weeks we would be heading for Georgia. With our schedules settled, Miles went away on vacation and I turned to more personal matters, making beauty appointments before my temporary exit from civilization.

Chapter 8

Unadorned

"Trail Faces"
Women's are bare
Men grow hair
—Early Bird

Before I made one footprint on the AT, I knew my beauty habits would have to change. No, they would have to *disappear*.

"If you have to look bad, do it in the woods." Was that Debbie, my nail technician, projecting ahead to the swift and sure demise of my manicure and pedicure? It could have been Tina, my hairdresser, on the occasion of my last haircut and color before leaving home. Either way, the experts agreed.

We become our most natural selves on the trail. Our looks gradually change as we adapt to new nutrition and exercise routines and forgo our usual grooming habits. Bodily functions and noises are accepted and discussed. These things I knew from my research.

If others were going to overlook our unattractive aspects on the trail, we would be free to relate to one another in more honest ways than we might have in our coiffed, shaved, neat, and fragrant former lives. We could focus on our inner selves. I was going to save money in the process. By suspending my nail and hair appointments alone, I expected to save over $1,200 over the course of my hike.

Being unadorned promised psychological and financial relief, but it would take me a while to adjust to what amounted to a "come as you are" party. I doubted my trail partner would require such an adjustment. Miles, a natural beauty, had the look of good health; no one would know back surgery and a serious illness were part of her history. Her hair was long enough to pull into a ponytail, so it would stay neat. Her wide smile revealed great teeth, and her skin was beautiful without makeup.

At home I put on makeup every day as part of getting dressed. Foundation, concealer, under-eye brightener, powder, blush, eyebrow corrector and fixative, eye shadow, liner, mascara, and lipstick were my staples. I didn't look like someone who caked it on, but I worked at being attractive. Lately I'd added skin creams and eye bag-reduction ointments. Were Botox and plastic surgery in my future?

For me those were not idle topics. Every day between the makeup and my clothing choices, I was putting on a suit of armor. I *needed* to be presentable to the world. I *needed* to know I wouldn't blow some opportunity because I was caught at my worst. I needed to look my best; it was part of feeling good about myself.

Growing up with an alcoholic mother, I missed the tutoring other girls took for granted. Instead, Mom berated me during her drunken rants. I developed self-esteem issues from hearing my own mother say I was too plain and couldn't get a date. Lacking a positive role model at home, I took my support and advice from teen-age magazines.

Age had not diminished my need to look good. Now that I was older, my skin was betraying me. I didn't have many wrinkles for my age, but a host of brown spots contributed to what the women in TV ads call "uneven skin tones." Over and above the skin issues, for the last ten years I'd thought I was going bald.

In addition to my morning ritual I bought many products designed for nighttime routines, but I abandoned them all; most nights I fell asleep in front of the TV without even brushing my teeth. The products came in sets: Step 1, Step 2, Step 3. I would envision using them, but in reality I would forget I'd bought them and would find them later in a drawer or in the bottom of the bathroom vanity. Once I even bought the same set twice. Somewhere I have nighttime powder that cost $60.

I fully expected to continue my beauty appointments into old age. In fact, I figured I'd need them even more in "the home."

"I don't want to be repulsive," I said to my beauticians. I was lining them up to bring their artistry to me in the old folks' home one day. I remember the time Mom had her nails painted pink at the Alzheimer Center. That appointment transformed her. Our mother beamed as she showed Joe and me her beautiful manicured nails.

I didn't see how any woman conscious of pack weight would take makeup on the trail. Cosmetics fell into the "unnecessary" category.

In one of the books I read, the author made fun of a female hiker who wore lipstick on the trail. I would wear makeup to Georgia, but I would not take any with me.

How would I feel with my beauty treatments stripped away? Could I live with the unenhanced version of me on a daily basis? Would people on the AT care what I looked like? I envied men, who I assumed were immune to the same prejudices and did not have to make the same decisions I did. On the trail their biggest change—besides losing weight—would be letting their hair and beards grow.

It had been twenty-five years since I'd last seen my natural hair color. Now as my two-inch "Jamie Lee Curtis" haircut grew out, it would evolve from artificially light brown to what Joe called "trail mix" and eventually become . . . well, I wasn't sure. I might turn out mousy or I might look gorgeous like "One of the little old ladies who use Silk & Silver," to quote a Clairol product ad from years gone by. The big difference in my case would be the absence of the Silk & Silver product, which was no longer made. My hair would be what it was.

Cheryl Strayed didn't shave her legs on the trail. I didn't need to shave mine; at a certain age we cease to grow leg hair, apparently. Cheryl may not have worried about facial hair either, but I did. When I stopped waxing my chin, I might resemble Grizzly Adams by the time we hit Harpers Ferry. For that reason, I tucked a pair of tweezers in my bag of personal items.

To top off the agony of exposure, I had an outbreak of pimples just before we left. A friend from home had said, "Take a picture of yourself just before you get on the trail." Right. Extra-short haircut, a face devoid of makeup, and now a breakout.

I hoped that in time I could accept my natural self, lose all thought of my own looks, and begin to look outward. The trail community is not vain; couldn't be. As Miles said one frosty morning when my nose was running, "Nobody cares." She meant it in the best way.

Chapter 9

Into the Woods

You're off to great places! Today is your day!
Your mountain is waiting, so . . . get on your way!
—From *Oh, the Places You'll Go!* ©1990, **by Dr. Seuss**

I left home in the dark on March 27, 2015 to pick up Miles at a restaurant parking lot along Interstate 71. I'd packed my car the night before, wrestling the heaviest item—my loaded backpack—over the lip of the trunk and setting my boots and trekking poles next to it to avoid waking the neighbors in the morning.

It was 6:05 a.m. when I pulled out of my street, with hours to go before the temperature would reach its 39-degree max in southern Ohio. At the first major intersection I sat alone waiting for the red light to change. Across from me restaurants and shopping centers lined the road in both directions. On my left past a wooded lot was a church; to my right, the campus of Procter & Gamble's research and development center; but mine was the only car at that hour. As the engine idled in the cold, I thought about the months of planning leading up to that moment. I was finally leaving for my long-awaited hike of the Appalachian Trail!

I had worried about being alone. Now I realized the next 15 minutes would be my last alone time until September. Miles and Mr. M were waiting for me in their SUV with the motor running, in a parking lot lit by street lamps and the warm glow from a restaurant that would soon open for breakfast.

I pulled in and we loaded Miles' gear into my trunk. Mr. M took a picture of the two of us miming "Which way to the AT?" before he left, and then we were off. Eight hours later we arrived in Atlanta, where the temperature was 51 degrees. I left my car with my son, who dropped us off at the lodge at Amicalola Falls State Park for a night of luxury before we hit the trail.

I didn't have to worry about paying yet. Among our many decisions, Miles and I had decided to split certain costs. She would put shared transportation and hotel charges on her credit card, to be divided later by Mr. M. She and I would pay separately when possible for routine purchases along the trail.

Amicalola Falls State Park is well known as the starting point for many northbound AT hikers because, in addition to overnight accommodations, it includes an approach trail to the actual starting point at the top of Springer Mountain. The approach trail begins under an arch behind the park visitor center. I had hiked the first mile of it the previous December when I was in Atlanta for Christmas. As a future thru-hiker, I'd wanted to see the visitor center, the arch, and the approach trail in person. That day I followed the trail up through the woods to a paved parking lot and returned to my car via the 604 stairs that clung to the hill along the falls.

As registered AT thru-hikers, Miles and I declared the date of our departure in advance as part of the voluntary registration system set up that year by the Appalachian Trail Conservancy. We picked up our official green tags bearing our unique hiker numbers at the park visitor center. She was Hiker 849 and I was 850.

I bought a T-shirt in the visitor center shop, drawn to its bright blue-green color. I couldn't take it on the trail, but I could send it home to wear later. On the back was this message: "DISCOVER YOUR WILD SIDE/AMICALOLA FALLS/STATE PARK & LODGE/ OUTDOOR ADVENTURE SINCE 1940." Like the detectives I loved to read about in novels and watch on TV, I didn't believe in coincidences. "DISCOVER YOUR WILD SIDE." Yeah.

The lodge sits on a hill near the top of Amicalola Falls. An impressive structure four stories high, it made an appearance in the movie *A Walk in the Woods* as the place Bill Bryson (Robert Redford) and Stephen Katz (Nick Nolte) stayed before their AT hike. Miles and I didn't know that when we checked in. We were focused on the fact that in the morning *we* would be walking out the front door and into the woods ourselves.

I'd done the mental cataloging: last night in a bed; last "normal" meal; last time in a heated building; last chance to take a shower, put on clean clothes, charge the electronics, or watch TV until time to emerge from the trail and resupply at Neel Gap, some 33 miles to the north.

Instead of watching TV in our room, we fiddled with our packs. We packed and unpacked the food and gear we were taking, an exercise that helped our nerves and afforded us one last chance to lighten our loads before setting out.

The choices one makes when packing for a hike are dizzying. I had a moment of panic in the hotel when I couldn't find one of my small, roll-top dry sacks. After all my planning, packing, and repacking, had I left it at home? Turned out I had combined my emergency bag with my personal and med bag. I was looking for two purple sacks when I had only one.

We brought an empty mailing box with us so we could send items home via the hotel desk. The box would contain anything we didn't want to take on the trail, for example the clothes we had worn to Atlanta. Because we'd obsessed over our pack contents for months, the items we sent home would not make any appreciable difference in the weight of our packs, which in my case was upwards of 30 pounds. Cheryl Strayed had filled her pack at the last minute and then named it Monster when she couldn't lift it off the floor. We set ours on the two side chairs in the room, straps facing outward, so we could hoist them onto our backs more easily when the time came.

My pack was a blue 65-liter Osprey Ariel, a typical backpack for women on the trail. At first I thought I would buy a 75-liter pack; my reasoning was "long hike, big pack." Instead of trying to pare down my load, I wanted to take more. Thank goodness the sales person at REI talked me out of that!

The pack held my tent; sleeping pad, sleeping bag, and liner; food, stove, and utensils; water and water purification system; extra clothing; in-camp shoes; relevant guidebook pages; my Samsung tablet for writing; charging cords for the tablet and my phone; medications and personal items such as toilet tissue; and accessories, some of which (e.g., my headlamp) were necessary and others (e.g., a MicroSpikes traction system to wear on my boots in snowy or icy conditions) were just in case. I also brought an 8-ounce canister of Counter Assault bear spray to wear in a holster on a cloth belt around my waist—and possibly sleep with—but hope never to need.

Spring had officially arrived, but we had to be prepared for winter. At higher elevations, snow was a possibility as late as April in the South. The average daytime temperature in Blairsville, Georgia, where we would stop in a few days, was in the 60s, falling into the 30s at night. Changing temperatures meant a heavier backpack, because we had to carry whatever we weren't wearing.

I slept well in my hotel bed until 3:00 a.m., when I woke with my mind racing between excitement and nervousness. This was what I dreaded, being awake for hours but having to stay quiet. At home I could get up when I wanted; there was no one to disturb. On the trail I'd be packed into shelters with other hikers, but my immediate challenge was to avoid waking Miles during the first night we'd ever spent as roommates. I lay still and suppressed my urge to use the bathroom. Before we'd hiked a single inch, I was living up to my trail name: Early Bird.

A trail name can be chosen by the hiker or assigned by someone else. In the latter case, an observed act or habit is generally the inspiration. I got my trail name sitting in my kitchen. My brother came over one day and we were talking about the AT. I explained trail names to him and said I thought about Early because I'm early for appointments and tend to wake up before most people. I'm usually ready ahead of time, too, but I didn't relish the idea of meeting someone and having to say, "Hi. I'm Ready." Ready for what?

"I want a trail name," I said to Joe, "but I don't want somebody giving me a name because of some stupid mistake I make out there."

He thought for two or three seconds and said, "Early Bird." It was perfect: a good description; not too many syllables; easy to spell and understand.

Miles' young granddaughters helped her choose her trail name, which she liked to say was "better than Dora the Explorer."

If I finish the AT, I will have walked more than four times the distance I drove to get from home to Amicalola Falls. That and other brain teasers kept my mind going in the quiet of our hotel room as I tried not to move in the bed. If I shifted, the sheets would make noise.

I was wide awake. The air in the room seemed charged, as though Miles could hear me think. While I waited for morning, my thoughts rushed ahead to consider where we would be in a few hours.

At 8:00 a.m. the window of our room framed a wooded valley coated with spring drizzle dropping from a blue-gray Georgia sky.

The view was no surprise considering the forecast—100 percent chance of rain—but I could shiver looking at it. The temperature outside was 45 degrees.

I had walked in the rain before and didn't mind it. I had rainwear, and the items in my pack weren't going to get wet. The reason for caution during cool, wet times is hypothermia, a condition in which one's core temperature drops below normal. If a hiker cannot put on dry clothes or climb into a dry sleeping bag, that hiker is in big trouble. In damp weather, wet items are likely to stay that way.

Starting from the inside out, I had lined the main cavity with a plastic trash-compactor bag, Miles' idea. I'd bought dry sacks to hold everything I carried, and I had a pack cover to keep the drizzle out on days like this. Stuffed into its self-pack, the rain cover compressed to the size of a baseball and I kept it in the upper compartment of my pack, known as the brain. That day I was going to need it.

It was our day, the 30th of March, and weather would not put off the inevitable. I dressed in gray hiking pants that later in the year would zip off to Capri length and my new cream-colored Smartwool long-sleeved shirt. Underneath the shirt the dark straps of my sports bra stood out, but it was too late to worry about that. Like beauty routines, fashion would not be a priority on the trail.

On that day, which was both cold and wet, I would wear my orange puffy jacket under my purple rain jacket. My complete outfit also included rain pants, gloves, a wool Buff around my neck, and a knit beanie. In addition to my hiking outfit, I was taking a set of long underwear, known in outdoor-speak as a base layer, and extra panties and socks.

Miles disliked wearing a rain jacket and said she wouldn't put hers on unless we were in a downpour. Part of it was the bother of removing her pack to put the rain jacket on and then later, when she was too hot, having to take her pack off again to remove the jacket. And what do you do with a wet rain jacket? Miles wore a white fleece vest over a red long-sleeved shirt.

We ate from the breakfast buffet and I stole two jellies for my food bag. That would become a pattern. A guitar-playing gentleman who said he wanted to be the next Elvis serenaded us while we ate. From the restaurant windows we could see down the hill to the first trees bordering the lawn. On another day the view would have extended for miles, over valleys to purple mountains in the distance, but that day fog hung between the ridges like window curtains. Everything was wet.

Our destination, the top of Springer Mountain, was 7.7 miles to the north. That night we would sleep in Springer Mountain Shelter. I'd seen the shelter on the internet and was eager to experience it in person, the way I looked forward to seeing lots of the other landmarks I'd read about.

When it was time to go we changed into our boots, strapped on our packs, and grabbed our trekking poles, ready to live in the woods. According to our schedule, it could be four days before we emerged again. I embraced the day, rain and all. Thru-hikers 849 and 850 descended the steps to the lobby of Amicalola Falls Lodge and walked out the door at 8:35 a.m. We crossed the parking lot under cloudy skies, leaving the warmth and light of the lodge behind us. I didn't look back.

Chapter 10

First, There Is a Mountain

Footpath My Ass!
—Title of a 2009 trail memoir by Terry "Bluebird" Croteau

Georgia and Maine are said to be the two most difficult states on the Appalachian Trail. Why? Depending on a hiker's intended direction, one or the other is the usual starting point for those doing the whole trail. The challenging terrain, combined with most hikers' inexperience and lack of adequate physical conditioning, makes either state a rough start.

Whichever state is chosen, the beginning of the AT is on the top of a mountain: Springer Mountain for NOBOs or Mt. Katahdin in Maine for south-bounders. The first task of a thru-hiker is to get to the top of the first mountain. That can be accomplished in several ways. "You can be dropped from a helicopter," as one park ranger said, because any miles hiked before the official starting point do not count.

Miles and I chose to hike the approach trail that starts at Amicalola Falls State Park. After we left the lodge and found the trail, the path rose immediately. Rather than being a gentle introduction, the approach trail mimicked the AT in elevation and difficulty. I was shocked to be huffing and puffing my way upward over exposed roots and rocks, grabbing the occasional tree for support, and needing a crazy number of rest stops.

The Appalachians are mountains. Some people learn that in Geography class. I lived it. Growing up in West Virginia, the only state that lies completely within the Appalachian Mountain region, I was surrounded by mountains until I was 22 years old. With such a background, I should have made the connection easily, but the only way it happened was when my feet connected again and again with the earth.

Up close, mountains are nothing like the simplistic drawings of our childhood: two straight lines meeting in a sharp peak. Neither do they resemble the elevation profiles that run up and down pages of the *A.T. Guide* opposite the listings of landmarks and the mileage of each road, stream, shelter, or town between us and our destination. Up close, mountains can be bumpy, bumpy, bumpy, as I was finding out. It hit me like a V-8 reminder to the side of the head.

By the time Miles and I were making our way up the approach trail, the sun had been up an hour but the sky was overcast. The woods were foggy, limiting our vision. Many trees were bare at that time of year, but patches of green gave promise to the ground.

Miles and I weren't chatty in the woods, just as we hadn't been chatty in the car; and unless we spoke, all was quiet. Those conditions combined to give the trail a spooky atmosphere, and I found myself scanning the woods on both sides of us for animals I hoped would *not* emerge from the mist. I was looking for the real thing, but it appeared I had a talent for seeing creatures in inanimate objects. I was startled to see a black bear in the near distance that later turned out to be the end of a wet log. I saw climbing cubs instead of the burls of trees. I spotted wolves, foxes, monkeys, big cats, and even Dr. Seuss's Grinch in nature's unmoving shapes.

At 9:05 we left the park, passing a sign that designated its northern boundary. We had to cross two mountains and hike up the third that day. On the "ups," or ascents, I was winded in no time, my heart pounding and my legs shaking. The path we followed was dirt, covered in places with layers of dead leaves from many autumns.

We took turns going first. I remember Miles in front. Her boots became my world as I strove to follow her footsteps, literally, over the rough trail. Both of us wore Dirty Girl Gaiters, the hot hiker brand worn to keep debris out of our footwear. Mine were white and yellow with a black bat design; hers were dark blue with colorful butterflies.

My favorite moment watching Miles' steps occurred when she would stop, plant her feet, and take a few minutes' break. I was glad for the breaks—too short at first—but I couldn't imagine Miles, with her prior experience, needing to stop that often. Was she accommodating me? The slow hiker determines the pace, and in our case that was yours truly.

We used roots for stepping stones going up mountainsides. They looped out of the ground everywhere. Before the trail I thought roots would look like snakes, but they don't.

At 12:30 we had gone 3.4 miles in just under 4 hours—less than one mile per hour. That's nothing to brag about, but hikers can expect to do fewer miles their first days on the trail and increase their mileage over time. So, let's turn it around: Miles and I had hiked 3.4 miles! Whoopee!

The rest of our first day was brutal. Those who created the Appalachian Trail and those who maintain it have given hikers many smooth paths: paths that encircle rather than climb straight up; paths that are softened by layers of leaves and pine needles; paths whose switchbacks permit a gentler climb; paths with steps built in by volunteers. But sometimes none of those alterations are in place and a hiker must appreciate and navigate woods in their natural state save for a narrow walking path and a series of white blazes to mark the AT.

We made our way up creek beds, wet or dry. Protruding stones and roots were routine. Beds of big, loose rocks lay on the trail, making me wonder if snakes were lying in wait among them. Crossing a boulder field, I imagined the Incredible Hulk standing high above the trail, tossing down giant boulders before we arrived. The boulders would bounce a few times and break into sharp pieces to test our agility and hiking boots. If he weren't such a nice superhero, the Hulk might have sneered, "Take that, you hikers!"

Sometimes the trail itself is level, and sometimes it slants toward an open edge with a gap far below. When it rains the rocks and roots are temporarily slick, but the ground can remain muddy for days. With a hard rain, springs will gush from the mountaintops to form streams, some to be crossed and others walked as part of the trail. Luckily, my boots were waterproof.

We reached Black Gap Shelter, the only shelter between Amicalola Falls and the top of Springer Mountain, and stopped for a break beside a sign pointing the way to water. By then the sun was out.

"Do you need water?" Miles asked.

How did I know if I needed water? The safe thing to do was to get some.

"I'll wait up here," Miles said.

Water sources located near shelters are generally downhill, the way water runs. I was about to learn that sometimes the water source is quite a distance down a steep grade. I trotted away, still wearing my backpack. The path down to the stream at Black Gap Shelter was long and steep. About two-thirds of the way down it I realized I'd made a mistake by not removing my pack at the top. I took it off and left it on the ground.

I learned from reading *Wild* that water weighs over eight pounds per gallon. I had two bags for collecting "dirty" water, which is water straight out of its source to be filtered before use. Each bag held 32 ounces, the total for both being a half-gallon. Thus, I carried 4 pounds of water—a full bag in each hand—to the place I'd left my pack, put both bags in the pack, and wound up carrying 34 pounds back to the trail.

"When I was hiking out west," Miles told me, "our guide made us carry a gallon of water."

Stocking up on water can be a smart move, but that day it wasn't because I didn't know what I was doing. The decision to refill should be based on the availability of water ahead, the amount you will need until then, and the amount you already have. Consulting my guidebook would have been a great idea. Not only did it list every landmark on the trail; it also included a little water-drop symbol next to each water source: A solid drop meant a reliable source; an outline or partially filled drop meant the source was seasonal or unreliable. But, beyond calculating mileage, I had not forged a working relationship with the *A.T. Guide*.

Once I was back to the trail, I looked over at Black Gap Shelter. It was our bailout point—we had one every day in case we could not make our goal. A father and son were already camped there, relaxing in their hammocks. The shelter looked new. Directly in front of it was a picnic table between two big trees. The sun shining through the surrounding woods was peaceful, and the father and son were friendly, but it was too early for us to bail out. Even the word *bailout* sounded like a failure, and who wants to fail their first day on the AT? Miles and I moved on. We were going to the top of Springer Mountain.

Chapter 11

Springer Mountain

Everything starts at the beginning
—Source unknown

Miles and I reached the top of Springer Mountain just after 4:00 p.m. By then I was exhausted. Other hikers were sitting or standing around, passing the register for new arrivals to sign. The ground was uneven with large layers of rock, and I nearly fell over getting to a spot where I could sit for a few moments.

This was the famed northbound starting point of the AT. We had arrived! The preliminaries were over; from that point every white-blazed mile we hiked would count toward our total. That said, I didn't want to take another step, but after we signed the register we traipsed 0.2 more miles through black mud to the shelter. It was empty despite the other hikers we'd seen at the summit—perhaps because of the early hour.

Most shelters along the AT reflect the same simple design: three sides of unpainted wood, an open front with a support post at the middle, a raised wooden floor, a few hooks or dowels along the walls, and a tin roof. Springer Mountain Shelter, our home for the night, also boasted a small vestibule, or enclosed entry; a partial front wall; and a loft accessed by a ladder—great for avoiding Mr. Bear; but I'd read the loft was a noisy place to sleep. The impact of acorns and other debris falling from the trees could wake a person up in the night. I knew what that was like.

During my women's outing in the Smokies the previous fall, the eight of us shared a shelter with a group of male hikers. The women made a row on the main level and the men slept in the loft above us. I was wide awake and feeling alone as the others grew quiet and fell asleep. The soft snoring above me was a comfort, and I relaxed until a loud crash jolted me off my sleeping pad. It had to be an animal. Could no one else hear the racket? My sleeping companions were still as I inched toward the back wall, hoping to go unnoticed by whatever was invading our space.

Two more loud crashes came from close by, and I knew a killer bear was banging around outside—if it wasn't in the shelter with us. The dark was complete; I couldn't see so much as an outline against the sky.

I had inadvertently left a breath mint in my pocket, so "IT" could be reaching for me any minute. I felt like a sacrifice in a horror movie, cowering against the wall with my heart thumping like a primitive drumbeat.

I eventually slept, and I woke up in the morning whole with my breath mint still in my pocket.

"Did you hear those loud crashes last night?" I asked our guide at breakfast.

"Yes," she said, "I heard the three acorns hitting the roof, one at a time."

With late arrivals a given, Miles and I spread our sleeping gear in a back corner on the main floor of Springer Mountain Shelter to mark our places. We cooked and ate dinner at the picnic table beside the building. Shelters have dedicated spaces for cooking and eating to separate foods and their odors from the sleeping area and reduce chances of our furry friends crawling into bed with us. This shelter had three: the picnic table, a fire ring surrounded by logs, and a shelf attached to an outside wall.

My dinner, though I don't remember the brand or flavor, had one thing in common with every other meal I would fix: It was made by adding water, which I heated in my JetBoil stove. The four pounds of water I had carried from Black Gap saved me a trip to the spring, but I could have waited.

After dinner Miles and I hung our food bags, a safety measure. Black bears along the Appalachian Trail are known to avoid human encounters; however, if one is conditioned to find food in a campsite or shelter, it will return. That was all I needed to hear before heading lickety-split to the bear cables.

Hikers know the saying, "A fed bear is a dead bear." It refers to the fact that, by walking deliberately into a campsite looking for "people food," the animal becomes a danger to itself as well as the campers because it will be reported and then removed or euthanized.

Cables have been strung near many shelters for hanging food out of a bear's reach. A thick wire cable runs horizontally between two trees, 20 feet off the ground. You hook your food bag to a loop that runs from the cable to the ground and pull on the loop until the hook and bag are lifted, and then you secure the loop. Do the reverse to retrieve the food bag. The cables squeak, so the big danger is waking someone up if you retrieve your breakfast too early.

Shelters along the AT have no electricity; thus, most hikers are in their sleeping bags by dark, known on the trail as "hiker midnight." There's nothing else to do unless one builds a campfire to provide light and a reason to stay up. Exhaustion also plays a part. If I needed a reason to retire, two were located below my ankles.

Miles and I slept side by side on the shelter floor with our heads toward the entrance. We were the only ones in that space. A male hiker came in after we were settled and climbed to the loft above us.

It was early spring and cold on the mountaintop. I had packed a sleeping bag liner to slip inside my 32-degree bag. According to the manufacturer, the liner would increase the performance of the sleeping bag—translation: keep me warmer—by up to 20 degrees. The wind blew in, and even with the liner in place I felt it. In addition, my mind was racing. For once it wasn't about bears. The Georgia Appalachian Trail Club, citing a history of "bear incidents," had posted warnings in the area discouraging hikers from tent-camping on the summit of Springer Mountain, but I felt safe in the shelter.

Not every creature needs a bag of food; some take crumbs. At the other end of the size spectrum from black bears are the mice known to invade shelters looking for food, especially when food is scarce outside. Apparently they can't climb a bear cable. Rarely seen in daylight, mice roam the shelters after dark when the hikers have settled down. They've been known to crawl over sleeping bags in their quest, a reason to keep one's head and arms inside.

There were only two of us—three counting the guy in the loft—so what were the odds I would have a mouse encounter that night?

I cinched the hood of my mummy-style bag until the opening was just large enough for me to breathe and peek out, in case one of the little rodents targeted me and tried to get in. I could think of nothing more repulsive. What would I do if a mouse joined me in my sleeping bag? After the screams, I mean. I was zipped in up to the neck. I'd have to loosen the hood in order to get one arm out so that I could lower the zipper—if it didn't stick. If the zipper did stick,

I could imagine feeling the little furry thing in its wild scampering, both of us hysterical and desperate to escape.

My mind was racing right along with the wind that blew across the mountaintop, and I slept poorly my first night on the trail. Maybe it was pure luck that I neither saw nor heard a single mouse that night, or maybe it was the fact that I had removed my eyeglasses and my two hearing aids before lying down and missed the action.

When the sun came up, I had a song in my head. "Morning Girl" from 1969 asked how a girl slept last night. It would play for days.

I got up around 7:00 and had coffee and two cold Pop Tarts. Shortly after 9:00, Miles and I packed up and hiked out. Our destination for the second night was Hawk Mountain Shelter, 7.9 miles north, but first we had to descend Springer Mountain. Its bumpy profile in the *A.T. Guide* was 4.1 miles long. To a hiker struggling over a mountain trail with a pack, every tenth of a mile counts. Mileage in this book reflects that of the 2015 *Guide*.

How long does it take to walk a mile? That depends. What is the hiker's physical condition? What's the terrain? What are the current trail conditions? How about the outside temperature? What is the weather like? Is it day or night? How motivated is the hiker?

Both of us were motivated. One of Miles' tried-and-true sayings was "Let's get 'er done." In the beginning she and I were among the oldest and slowest hikers on the trail. Considering the mountainous terrain, intermittently wet from rainstorms, we aimed for one mile per hour. At first, we rested after every 20 steps. That was our reward. We'd stop in the middle of the trail, stand still for a few moments, take a drink of water or eat a quick snack, and then start again. On the "ups" I struggled to hike 20 steps at a time. The rest periods were too short to savor. Miles introduced me to Ricola herb drops as an aid in climbing the tough grades.

"Cough drops?" I asked, thinking *How about a cable car?*

"My throat gets dry," she said. "I always carry Ricola when I'm hiking. Somehow it helps me get up those mountains." I bummed a few until we resupplied and I could buy my own, unaware it was a peek at things to come.

Chapter 12

Good to Know

**Believe me, you will find more lessons
in the woods than in books.**
—**St. Bernard of Clairvaux**

Miles and I were off Springer Mountain by 10:15. We reached a parking lot at the bottom, where we took our first long break before swinging upward again to climb Hawk Mountain. The trail was gentle; the elevation gain was less than 700 feet—making our hike about one-third the intensity of yesterday's hike up Springer Mountain. It still kicked our butts.

Despite our generally slow progress and frequent stops, when I was in the lead I took off—or tried to. My morning coffee gave me a temporary burst of energy, and for someone planning to hike all day I had no idea how to pace myself. Instead of sprinting, the trick is to start slowly and build to a steady pace that is possible to maintain.

Behind me Miles would say, "Warm-up speed," to slow me down. It had the effect of a hook to the collar.

Among my early lessons, I was learning our paths would not necessarily be the same. Miles was the experienced hiker, sure-footed and capable of covering miles quickly. I had the advantage of height to balance the disadvantage of less experience. Instead of following Miles' every step, my feet were developing their own rhythm, which meant landing someplace else. Life was easier after I realized I didn't need to walk exactly in Miles' footsteps; with my longer legs, I shouldn't try.

We had different ways of hiking past hindrances such as logs across the trail or boulders to be climbed. When height mattered, I was faster. Miles would refer to her shorter legs and would ask me not to look so she could concentrate on her own way to conquer the obstacle. I would turn my back while she made her way across a tricky rock field or slippery creek bed. If I was leading, I wasn't sure whether to wait or go on. I became preoccupied with it, too aware of whether I was doing the right thing.

I knew nothing of the forest, but Miles could identify birds and trees as we hiked. She spotted deer among the trees. Occasionally when I heard a sound off the trail I'd ask her what it was. We were walking a path of decayed leaves when she pointed to a blue patch on the trail and said, "This is where an owl threw up."

"Why is it blue?"

"The color depends on what the owl ate, in this case a blue bird," she said, and I noted the feathers. *All righty.*

Sometimes Miles talked about being on the "lee side" of a mountain. I didn't know what the lee side was, but I knew we were always warmer and out of the wind there.

We were in a bubble of northbound thru-hikers, meaning that many hikers started around the same time. Some hiked solo and others in pairs or small groups. I had pictured a steady stream of people on the trail, like a parade, but the length of the AT allowed all of us to spread out and walk at our own pace if that was what we wanted.

In addition to thru-hikers, section and day hikers were out enjoying the spring weather. I was surprised to see so many people on the trail for a day or a few nights. Being an indoor type, I had no idea of the enthusiasm we would see from locals all along the AT. They were fun to encounter and easy to pick out, especially the day hikers. Their clothes were brighter and cleaner than ours and their packs were smaller, if they carried packs at all. They tended to wear more fragile shoes. Most were cheerful. Some were loud. They smelled good, unlike those of us in the "unwashed" category. A few of the women wore strong perfume, a no-no for anyone in bear country.

Miles must have thought I was more like them—the day hikers. She saw me as privileged, affluent, and living in a white-bread world. "Do you have any black people in your family?" she asked me one day.

"I don't know. I guess I could, but I'm not aware of any," I said. It wasn't her kind of response. Miles liked a simple answer: yes or no.

"Well, I do," she said, ending the exchange.

Much of the Appalachian Trail is only wide enough to accommodate hikers traveling in single file. When people approach from the opposite direction or want to go around, someone must find a wide spot and move out of the way. Miles and I became used to moving aside.

When hikers approached from the other direction, the first one of us to spot them would call "Incoming." The rule in that situation is that whoever is hiking uphill has the right of way over anyone going downhill. Our signal for a hiker approaching from the rear was "One on."

"It's a basketball term," Miles said. No wonder I'd never heard the expression.

We exchanged quick pleasantries with passing hikers, and *pleasant* was the key. "Good morning!" "Beautiful day!" (even if it was raining) and "Great day for a hike!" (ditto) were typical. No one said, "My feet are killing me" or "Damn this mud."

The hiking bubble became most apparent in the evenings when most people stopped and set up camp or claimed spots in a shelter. A few liked to hike at night wearing their headlamps—I met one ambitious man who took to the trail at 3:30 every morning—but after hearing reports of eyes glittering from the undergrowth, I wouldn't have night-hiked for a truckload of my favorite breakfast treat: Honey Buns.

We arrived at Hawk Mountain Shelter at 4:20 on our second day. The shelter is situated on a ridge with a generous amount of flat land in back of it. The shelter was full, so we set up our tents for the first time on the trail.

Mine was a freestanding one-person Marmot EOS, a yard wide and 87 inches long. The height was 37 inches along the highest point of the spine. From there both sides sloped down to the ground. If you've ever lived in a Cape Cod-style house, apply the lack of second-story headroom to a nylon tent. It was difficult for me to execute any movement inside my tent other than lying down. I had bought it for the weight, 2 pounds 13 ounces. I'd practiced putting it up and had slept in it a few times. Once I zipped the vestibule and tent door closed, I couldn't see out except for a strip at the back that revealed a few inches of ground behind the tent. If I heard noises, I wasn't sure who or what had made them.

On Hawk Mountain so many tents were set up in the woods behind the shelter that I would have had difficulty finding mine if it hadn't been bright orange. I could walk right to it after using the privy or going to the nearby stream for water.

With so many other hikers camping nearby, I wasn't afraid of lying in my orange tent in the dark in the Georgia woods, guessing what was going on outside. After seven hours of hiking, I was beginning to appreciate being prone.

Chapter 13

Meltdown

Oh, boo hoo, boo hoo!
—Blondie, from the comic strip created by Chic Young

If two or three tears can constitute a meltdown, I had one on Gooch Mountain our fourth morning on the trail.

Miles and I had left Hawk Mountain Shelter the previous day. We'd eaten breakfast there while other hikers milled around, ate, or packed up. The scene had the busyness of an ant farm. Behind us, tents came down. Hikers returned to the trail. Across from me a gray-haired woman cooked her meal on the picnic table. A hiker named Paisley fixed instant oatmeal in a quart-size, freezer-weight baggie, an idea I would use for the rest of my hike to avoid cleaning a bowl—as soon as I had some freezer baggies, that is.

Soon after we set out for Gooch Mountain Shelter, we came upon a black snake with narrow blue stripes stretched out on a rock. Our footsteps didn't disturb it, so as we passed by I had a good look my first snake on the AT.

The shelter was a 7.7-mile hike, and when we got there it was crowded, so we again pitched our tents. This time level spots were not to be had. We set up camp on a hillside with the ground at a 45-degree angle. When that happens, everything in your tent—including you—slides into the wall at the lowest point. I had an inflatable sleeping pad that slid along the tent floor and a nylon sleeping bag that slid down the sleeping pad. What you do in a case like that is to grab the sides of the sleeping pad, wiggle yourself back into place, and repeat until you're too sleepy to care.

Like most shelters along the AT, the one at Gooch Mountain had a privy, or outdoor toilet. It was located along a path that ran below our tent sites, a cross between convenient and smelly in relation to where we camped. In the absence of plumbing, a typical privy on the trail contains a composting toilet. Next to the toilet is a bucket of leaves to be thrown on top of the waste. The toilet is enclosed, though the degree of enclosure varies, and most privies are unattractively decorated with signs of previous use. I used the soles of my shoes to raise or lower the lid and did not touch the seat. A privy still beats the alternative. I had a trowel for going in the woods—a process that requires digging a hole and burying solid waste—but I didn't want to use it.

One carries toilet paper and hand sanitizer to visit the privy. I'd run out of paper the day before. Miles was glad to let me borrow some, but I was embarrassed to have planned so poorly. We had miscalculated the number of days we'd be on the trail before emerging from the woods at Neel Gap. The Mountain Crossings complex there would be our first stop back in civilization since starting the trail and our first opportunity to buy anything.

We thought it would take us four days to hike to Mountain Crossings. Here we were on the fourth morning, almost 16 miles out. At that point, hiking a 16-mile day was unlikely for us; more like half of that. We would be spending another night on the trail. When you plan at home, your daily mileage is guesswork. I hadn't packed for guesswork.

Toilet paper was the least of my worries. While scrounging through my pack for breakfast items, I realized I was running out of food! I had packed three dinners for what was now a four-night stretch. I'd packed four breakfasts and needed five. I'd miscalculated the lunches too, thinking we'd arrive at Neel Gap by lunchtime on the fourth day, which was today. *Oops.*

In addition to being optimistic, I had considered Miles' prior back surgery in my planning. She wanted to keep her pack light and didn't want to carry more than three or four days' food at once. I packed accordingly, missing the point that if I ran out of food on the trail there would be no place to resupply. I could tell by the contents of my food bag that this was going to happen. Would I be like Bear Grylls, looking for grubs in rotten logs to sustain me?

Blondie in the funny papers would have been crying, "Oh, boo hoo, boo hoo" by then. I seldom cried, but I felt terrible. My lack of remaining meals would become evident when it was time to eat again. I had to give Miles the news.

"I feel like a D-minus as a trail partner," I said as I explained my predicament.

With all her experience, Miles knew to prepare for contingencies, and her food supply reflected it. She also knew she was hiking with a rookie. She had enough in reserve to grubstake me, and that's when I had my mini-meltdown. I wasn't crying because I wouldn't be starving to death in the woods after all; I was crying because she had been nice to me when I'd screwed up.

"Spend money" was Miles' advice that morning. "Spend money when we get to Neel Gap, and don't buy outfits. Buy food!"

The Appalachian Trail passes right through Mountain Crossings, the famous outfitter located at Neel Gap near Blairsville, Georgia. I knew that Mountain Crossings included a hiker hostel and a store stocked with food and gear. I loved backpacking gear and clothing, but I'd already bought mine. Except for food and paper supplies, I didn't plan to buy anything I would then have to carry.

With Mountain Crossings still in the future, our goal when we left Gooch Mountain was to reach Lance Creek Campsite, 8.5 miles away. The weather was raw that day; it was doubtful we would see the sun. Instead, we'd be hiking in fog and drizzle.

We had met two young women on the trail whom we called K and C. They had no trail names yet, and each had a first name that could begin with either letter. I was not sure who was K and who was C, but we kept running into them. The morning we left Gooch Mountain Shelter, I heard K and C talking to Miles.

"We're going to get off at Woody Gap," they said. "There's a hostel nearby where we can take showers and spend the night indoors. We can call a shuttle to take us." A hostel is an inexpensive lodging place. Space is shared with others, but a hostel is a giant step up from a shelter and a bit short of a hotel. Hostels often provide shuttle services, whether free or on a fee basis.

Miles said, "That sounds great."

It sounded great to me, too. *Hostel* and *shuttle* were magic words after my meltdown on the side of the hill. If we stopped at a hostel for the night instead of going to a campground, I might get something to eat—either a meal or a chance to resupply and return some of Miles' food. Stopping would also mean a five-mile day, a compelling thought in the current weather conditions.

As we left Gooch Mountain, my mind kept returning to thoughts of hot water cascading over me, clean clothes, and a bed. I was looking forward to Woody Gap with every step.

Chapter 14

Woody Gap

Tut-tut, looks like rain.
—Winnie the Pooh

Miles started calling me E.B., and other hikers followed suit. She would introduce herself and explain her trail name either with the Dora story or by saying, "Miles, as in distance." I began introducing myself as E.B.—I liked it and knew a name often found its shortest form—but then I would add that it stood for Early Bird. I did the same when I wrote in the shelter registers, being unwilling to give up the longer version.

With my meltdown behind me, Miles and I continued north on the trail. We were in northern Georgia, five miles from Woody Gap.

A gap on the Appalachian Trail is a low point between mountains. Sometimes a gap is merely a flat area to hike across before heading up the next incline and sometimes a gap is the location of a trailhead with a paved road, a parking lot, and buildings. That was the case with Woody Gap.

By the time we got there, I was chilled through and through. The area was lost in white fog and wet with rain. We'd had a preview on the hike there. It reminded me of our morning on the approach trail out of Amicalola Falls, but fog is different in the woods: dissipated. The open area of Woody Gap was pure white, white and thick. When we came off the trail to level ground, I started to walk around the edge of a lake to avoid falling in. That was before I got close enough to see that it wasn't a lake at all; it was a blacktopped parking lot. Georgia Route 60 passes through Woody Gap, and I assumed that would be the route the shuttle would take. K and C, being younger and faster, had hiked ahead of us and were already gone.

We took off our packs, always a great relief, and stood in the shelter of an information kiosk. A few cars were parked in the lot, but we were the only people around. No wonder; the weather was miserable. Rain dripped all around us as I waited for Miles to call the hostel and get us to dry land. My phone reception was abysmal.

As it turned out, Miles wasn't planning to call anyone. I had jumped to the wrong conclusion after hearing the conversation among the three other women. When I heard Miles say, "That sounds great," I thought we were going to the hostel, too. What she hadn't said to K and C was any version of "Save a spot for us."

I couldn't believe it: For the second time that morning, I felt incredibly stupid. In Miles' mind our goal to reach Lance Creek Campsite that day had not changed. We needed to hike on to maintain the schedule we'd made back home. Hiking on would also put us closer to Neel Gap and food. I could see the reasoning, but it was hard to come around when I'd expected to be whisked away to a warm hostel for the night. Would we instead be taking up our packs and poles to hike two or three more hours over another mountain in a cold rain? When we realized we had different outcomes in mind, we agreed to look for a sign to tell us what to do.

It was lunchtime, so we broke out the food there in the rain. In a little while a van pulled over across the road and stopped. I could see a driver, but no passengers. The vehicle was long with several side windows, and it appeared to be waiting. "That looks like a shuttle," I said. "It could be the sign we're looking for!"

Miles tended to use the imperative with me. "Go see."

I crossed Route 60 through the fog and knocked on the driver-side window of the van. A man looked up and lowered the window. He was on the phone.

"Are you a shuttle driver?" I asked.

"No," he said. "I'm a fisherman. I just pulled over to call my wife."

I walked back to the kiosk, disappointed. In a few minutes another man came on foot to stand under the roof of the kiosk with us. He was waiting for his hiking partner so they could continue north. I had nothing, so he was our sign.

When it rains, you hike. We weren't promised sunny days, and we weren't going to get off trail every time the skies opened up. Still, I hoped the weather would improve before we got to Lance Creek. The description "camp in designated sites" in the *A.T. Guide* said it all: We were going to sleep in our tents that night. We had to; the next shelter was nearly four miles up the trail from Lance Creek, smack in the middle of the bear-canister zone.

In our initial planning we had chosen Lance Creek as a stopping point because it was located south of Jarrard Gap, which marked the beginning of a five-mile stretch of the AT where overnight camping was prohibited to anyone who did not carry their food in a hard-sided bear-proof canister. Miles and I were using Ursacks, approved bear-resistant food bags made of a "bullet-proof" fabric. We had lined them with odor-barrier bags to kill the scent of the food, but that didn't make them hard sided.

Ursacks have the advantage of not needing to be hung at night the way a conventional food bag must be. I had taken mine on a previous backpacking trip and had cabled it to a tree. The next morning the Ursack bore no evidence that it had been touched by any creature. I was happy with it, but a forest ranger within the designated five-mile area might not be.

I had to wonder who would want to camp where bears were an obvious issue, food canister or not. I didn't look forward to hiking there, even in daylight.

As we prepared to continue up the trail in the rain, I thought about my tent. I had a rain fly, so water would presumably cascade off the sides, but I had not put up the tent in the rain or packed it wet the next day except back in Ohio. It looked as though I was about to.

Before we left Woody Gap, we used the women's restroom, a treat because it gave each of us a few moments' respite from the rain and was an improvement over the backwoods privies we had experienced. Afterward a couple appeared out of the fog and offered us trail magic in the parking lot.

Trail magic is any gift left for or given to hikers. The particulars are infinite: Snickers bars, a bottle of water, a cooked meal, a ride to town, a bed for the night. Those who provide trail magic are called trail angels. Trail angels expect nothing in return; often they are "paying it forward," inspired by those who helped them on a hike. It is said that trail magic happens when it is least expected and most needed. The couple we met at Woody Gap gave us a pound of turkey sausage snacks and a big box of chocolate-covered malted milk balls. See what I mean? Food. Miles and I enjoyed those snacks as we hiked on.

Once we reached Lance Creek Campsite, I was glad we were keeping to our schedule, but to escape the chill I would have turned on a dime.

When hiking solo, it makes sense to keep your plans to yourself; with a trail partner, that's a bad idea. I blamed myself for not communicating my assumptions to Miles once I thought our plans had changed from a campsite to a hostel for the night. I could have joined the original conversation about the hostel and put in my two cents then, but I hadn't. Thus, we didn't know we had two outcomes in mind until the differences came to light in Woody Gap.

Chapter 15

If This Is Morning,
Then I'm in a Nightmare

Sunshine is my quest.
—Sir Winston Churchill

The velvety voice of Tommy Edwards singing "Please Mr. Sun" in 1959 ran through my mind as I thought the appearance of the sun would be the best thing to happen in days. At least I was done with "Morning, Girl."

Miles and I arrived at Lance Creek Campsite under a gray sky. We hiked in and pitched our tents end to end on a dirt roadbed above the creek. Other hikers had already made their camps near the opposite bank and in the curve of the road just beyond us. A light rain was falling, and some were sitting under tarps.

Miles and I saw one of our friends cooking supper in her vestibule and decided to do the same, although the practice is not recommended. I cooked mine sitting inside the doorway of my little tent with my legs hanging out the door into the vestibule and my JetBoil between my feet on the muddy ground. I left the vestibule open for ventilation.

In cooking where we did, we were risking the possibility of attracting wild animals right to our tents. I suppose there was the additional risk of fire, but that night I wasn't worried about my tent burning down. After we ate, the sky opened and poured rain as if its sole purpose was to drown us.

In no time the ground was a mud pit, and we still had to hang our food bags. In the absence of cables, one hangs a food bag from a high tree limb. It was the chore I dreaded most. That might be why I didn't have a lot of practice. Tramping around to locate the right tree and rock was a pain, and that evening the rain made it all worse. The perfect tree for hanging food at Lance Creek grew on the opposite bank of the creek from our tents, about halfway down to the water. I didn't want to depend on Miles, so I went first carrying my food bag, 50 feet of bright orange cording, and a small bag to hold a rock. To get to the spot I followed the roadbed around and stepped onto what was now a mudslide.

Hanging food from a tree involves skill and a good throwing arm. I was 0 for 2. The best scenario occurs when the branch is horizontal, and the rope lands several feet from where the branch meets the trunk of the tree. That placement is meant to make things harder for Mr. or Ms. Bear. The process of getting the food bag to its ideal spot can be entertainment for others when the person doing it must try again and again. The first step is lobbing a weighted cord over the branch. I found a good rock on the ground, put it in my little bag, tied the bag to one end of the long cord, and threw.

I hit the branch in two tries. Once the cord was over it, I lowered the weighted end and substituted my food bag for the little bag with the rock. Miles joined me and we clipped her food bag to mine and pulled the other end of the cord to lift the bags. Once they were up, we wrapped the loose end of the rope around a different tree and tied it off, making life complicated for the animals.

Isn't this a fine postscript to Woody Gap, I thought as I ran back to my tent. I always had trouble getting in and out of that tent, sometimes losing my balance crunched low on an exit. My joints and bones were showing their age. That evening I scrambled in the door, momentarily forgetting that my pants and rain jacket could have been wrung out for a day's water supply. Everything I had was soaked, including my backpack, which was still outside. There was no room for it in my little tent and I'd used the vestibule space to prepare my meal, letting rain in. By then the rain cover I'd put on the pack was providing little protection. There was no dry place to put anything, and—because we all were forced into our tents by the weather—nothing to do but lie down and wait for sleep.

Water, water, everywhere and not a drop to drink. That wasn't literally true, but my mouth was so dry I could have swallowed every drop of water I had with me. By then, our fourth evening on the trail, I was craving filtered spring water, especially at night. If I didn't have any I'd bring my water filter and a bag of "dirty" water into my tent and filter it there. Craving water was a new experience; at home I had to force it down and rarely consumed the recommended eight glasses per day. My newly awakened thirst had to be the result of hiking all day, and the taste of the spring water was irresistible. I must have been dehydrated my whole life to want it so badly.

Now that it was raining hard, I hated the thought of sliding down to the creek to replenish my water supply if I ran out, so I balanced my thirst against that and stayed in the tent. Maybe the weather would improve by morning.

I woke in the dark. Normally I loved to wake up alone in my tent. I could lie in my sleeping bag warm and dry and think my thoughts until time to get up. I liked to replay the previous day, which in this case had been a rainy mess.

As morning broke I looked out the slit of space between the ground and the bottom of my tent fly. Except for the layers of nylon beneath me, I was lying in a mud puddle. The outside of the tent was wet, naturally, and any other item that had been wet the evening before, e.g., my boots and rain jacket, was guaranteed to be clammy now. The tent had a "bathtub" floor, which meant the waterproof fabric used for the bottom of the tent curved upward and was sewn to the walls several inches off the ground. That saved me from lying in water.

What do you do when your tent gets wet? Pack it up that way and hope for sunshine later; that way, the next time you pitch the tent or spread it out somewhere it will dry. What do you do when your boots and socks and clothes get wet? Put them on anyway.

Miles said she heard me sipping my water in the night. Was that normal, for her to hear me from her tent, or did she have super-hearing? Was I making an unusual amount of noise? I didn't know, now that my own hearing had deteriorated and I slept with my hearing aids removed and stored in their little envelope stuck in a pocket of my tent.

The roadbed was a continuous puddle, making for a sloppy morning as we packed up. *Please*, I thought, *please*. And that's when "Please Mr. Sun" came to mind, creating my next earworm. This is why I don't need an MP3 player.

The sun came out. That beautiful yellow ball was rising in the sky. I had always loved the sun—loved going to the beach, loved being warm—but that day I loved it more. I loved it in a different way.

It was as though the miracle of nature unfolded on the giant stage before me. The only thing missing was the actual swell of music as I recognized the relationship of sun to rain and rain to spring water. I was beginning to appreciate the environment as never before.

My wet boots and clothing would dry. My soggy pack, made heavier by its time in the rain, would lighten; my tent would eventually cease to drip. If the sun didn't bring those miracles to fruition, a night indoors would. It was a mere 7.4 miles to civilization. At last we were going to reach Neel Gap!

Chapter 16

Neel Gap

**So far this hike is challenging.
I knew it would be, but now it is.**
—From my trail journal, April 2015

What is a thru-hike if not one surprise after another?

The morning of April 3 Miles and I set out for Neel Gap, with Gaddis Mountain and Blood Mountain ahead of us. We were still in Georgia and would be for close to 50 more miles. I'd never heard of Gaddis Mountain, which wasn't much of a mountain with an elevation gain of only 514 feet above our starting point. Blood Mountain was a different matter.

A shelter sits on the top of Blood Mountain; that I knew. I also knew it was located in the five-mile bear activity zone we had entered a couple hours after leaving Lance Creek. "No one stays there" was the unofficial word regarding Blood Mountain Shelter. It seemed ironic to me. I'd seen pictures of the shelter on the internet and knew it had four stone walls and a closing door—sturdy enough, one would think, to keep a bear out. The door was painted blood red.

The mountain itself was a killer, what Miles called a "technical" climb. The top was over 4,000 feet above ground level, but from our starting point at Lance Creek the climb was more like 1,300 feet. However, the way up included cluster after cluster of challenging rocks and boulders—the technical aspect. If I thought getting to Neel Gap that day would be a mere slide into home, I didn't have a clue.

Miles hiked with a knee brace. Every morning as part of getting ready, she wrapped her toes with duct tape so she could hike with blisters on her feet, and most days put on her knee brace. If she didn't put the brace on in the morning, we would stop so that she could pull it over her left knee to hike difficult stretches of the trail.

The climb up Blood Mountain took hours. The pointless ups and downs started at Jarrard Gap and developed into a steep, rocky incline two miles later. Near the top, the trail passed under thick rhododendron and mountain laurel bushes. I would come to see those particular plants as a signal we had reached the top of something, whether it was the true summit or not.

That's the trouble with some of the ups on the AT; it is impossible to tell what's ahead. Sometimes we could look ahead and see the path going straight up. At other times it took us through a series of switchbacks or wound around and around a mountain. If I was in the lead and saw the sky instead of trees up ahead or saw the land taper off to a ridge, I'd call back to Miles, "We're almost to the top." I was fooled many times by false summits before I modified my message to "We're almost to the top of something."

The view from the top of Blood Mountain was worth the climb. I was learning the trail had many rewards, all but one of them—trail magic—earned with hard work. The beauty of a mountaintop view to me, beyond its appearance, was the fact that the only way to see it was to do what we did: climb the mountain.

Other hikers were resting or enjoying the view. We stood in the sunshine, took pictures of each other sitting on the steps of the shelter, and eagerly dialed friends and family on our cell phones. Or maybe that was just me, ecstatic because I finally had reception. My service carrier was reputed to be the worst on the trail, and I was finding it to be true. I called my brother, and when he answered I felt like people must have felt the day the telephone was invented: *Why, it sounds like he's right here!*

"I got your mail," Joe said. "There was a package from your friend Anita in Michigan." I knew what it was.

"She sent me a good luck charm," I said, "but I left home before it came. Can you forward the package?"

We decided Joe would send my package to the lodge at Fontana Village, North Carolina. I knew Miles and I would stop there for a night because we had mailed our second resupply boxes there before we left home.

On the other side of Blood Mountain lay Neel Gap, but first we had to make the 2.4-mile descent. I thought going down a mountain would beat climbing up it, but experience was showing me a descent can be rough in a different way. You naturally go faster but still have the usual obstacles. I remember passing a southbound group as

Miles and I took turns making our way around a clump of boulders. I knew what was ahead for them and was glad to be heading in the opposite direction. They may have had similar thoughts about us.

Descents leading to towns can be surprisingly long, especially when actual distance meets hiker impatience. Long before we reached the bottom of Blood Mountain, we could see Neel Gap below us through the trees. It was a bird's-eye view, small buildings and a stretch of gray two-lane split by yellow ribbons. Because we encountered rocks on the way down, we had to go slowly when all I wanted was to get off that mountain. The thought that pulled me on was that I would soon be clean. Clean! I would have clean clothes and clean hair. A chance at a hairdo. Food and toilet paper!

Being on the "before" side of a shower brought back a memory from my childhood, when I was tomboy and bathing was more duty than pleasure. Friday night was "no bath night" at our house. It was a night of freedom for my brother and me because we had no school or church the next day. We were allowed to skip our usual evening routine, wake up without an alarm, and watch cartoons until noon when programs with real people began. Twelve o'clock took us "Down on the Farm with Bill Click." When Farmer Click came on, we clicked the TV off.

Miles and I arrived at Mountain Crossings, the anchor business, in the afternoon. Also known as Walasi-yi, Mountain Crossings is a famous stop on the trail not just because it offers hot showers, beds, and a store but also because the Appalachian Trail runs through it. Both the trail and the buildings were completed in 1937. The Civilian Conservation Corps built Walasi-yi as a dining/dance hall and inn, two buildings connected by a breezeway over the trail. The lower floor of the inn later became a hostel for hikers.

The hostel was full for the night. That was bad news after we'd been on the trail for five days; I was dirty and stinky and more than disappointed. We were invited to tent behind the property and sign up for the hostel early the next day. We decided that taking a zero—a day with no hiking miles—and spending the following night indoors was a good idea, even though that extra night at Neel Gap was not in our original plan.

"Scout us a camping spot," Miles said.

The tenting space that rose behind Mountain Crossings was like our site on Gooch Mountain, where Miles had vowed she'd never again sleep on a 45-degree angle. I first tried the flatter picnic area but figured it would come with a privacy issue. We were forced to climb the hill, where the wind was whipping our clothes against us. Finding a flat spot was like looking for the Lost Dutchman's Gold Mine. Miles found one and began pitching her tent in the wind. I claimed a mildly slanted area next to a cliff and unpacked the components of my soggy tent. The rain at Lance Creek the night before had meant I packed the tent wet that muddy morning. I now unpacked it in a howling wind, setting rocks on the lighter pieces to hold them down until I was ready for them.

We cooked and ate sitting on a log. Our young friends K and C surprised us by arriving on the hill to fight their tents into place. By the time it was dark we were settled, high enough to hear planes as they passed overhead.

I spent a horrible night wondering if the wind would blow me right off the side of the hill in my tent. As I lay in my sleeping bag listening to the nylon walls being sucked in and out, in and out, I pictured myself tightly packed as though in an orange body bag, sailing out into mid-air to ride the wild current to the ground. The wind was constant. Thunder rolled through the gap and lightning flashes intermittently brightened the inside of my tent. It rained and rained. Were we in a hurricane? In the severity of the storm I kept thinking the words *monsoon* and *typhoon*, which would be better applied to the tropics than to the mountains of Georgia.

Once again as campers we were separated from the elements by mere pieces of cloth, yet I felt cut off from the world. I wished I could at least sit up in my tent. I wished it had a window.

At 4:30 a.m. I got up to pee. It was bitter cold and too early to be awake for the day. I hated the thought of lying awake and freezing in my tent for two more hours, so instead of finding a spot on the mountain I walked to the ladies' room in the main building. The restrooms were open around the clock and were out of the wind. I decided to stay there until daylight. I found a metal folding chair in a shower stall, but I might as well have been sitting on an iceberg. After a few minutes I put it back and paced for a while. It was dead quiet, and I had nothing to do. What lured me back to my coffin of a tent was the thought of mountain water to drink. I filtered some there in the tent in that windstorm.

In the morning Miles and I waited outside for Mountain Crossings to open. The moment it did, we put our names in early for the hostel. We packed up our tents and moved indoors as soon as bunks were available.

The bunk room was one of two main rooms in the hostel. The other was a great room that included a lounging area and kitchen separated by a peninsula. Off the great room was the shared bathroom. Miles took a bottom bunk and I had the top. We found places for our packs in the limited floor space and pushed our poles under the bed, leaving items on our mattresses to indicate the bunks were taken. I was grateful to be off the mountain and inside, looking forward to a zero day even though we had chores.

We spent the day showering, doing laundry, and visiting the store. By far, the highlight for me was getting clean; after five days in the backcountry I viewed my turn in the tiny stall as the best shower ever, and that thought would return every time I stood under hot water with soap.

I felt the same urgency about washing my clothes. In the woods I wore the same outfit every day, no matter what had fouled it the day before. That outfit—the same one I'd put on at Amicalola Falls—identified me from near and far. Sometimes I slept in it. The pants went on wet or dry, stiff with mud, smelling of pee—it didn't matter. There was no second outfit, just my long underwear, which I had to save for sleeping or hypothermia. It was squished in my pack to remain dry and save me in the event I fell crossing a stream and soaked my first set of clothes. I did laundry at Neel Gap in my rain jacket and rain pants.

There was a waiting line. With only one washer and one dryer serving all the hikers, whoever was using them had better be present when the machine(s) stopped. Miles and I didn't have the luxury of separate loads. We stood like squatters outside the tiny laundry room, and when our turn came we jammed our clothes into the washer and quickly chose the settings, grateful to finally be in the game and able to walk away for an hour.

I could hardly wait to peruse the offerings of Mountain Crossings. The store sold gear and clothing as well as edibles. I would take Miles' advice to spend money on food, but I had also decided to look for one large piece of replacement gear.

Chapter 17

Shakedown

Don't buy outfits. Buy food!
—Miles

I knew I wanted a pack shakedown at Mountain Crossings. I had read about them: An expert evaluates the contents to reduce a hiker's backpack weight. Mountain Crossings was known for its shakedowns. Miles and I were like minded on that subject. Both of us took our loaded packs into the store.

Mountain Crossings was a wonderland of food, clothing, and gear. The food had its own section, shelf after shelf of dehydrated meals, breakfast cereal, peanut butter, Ramen noodles, snacks, and other essentials sold in individual servings. Ziploc bags—some great for cooking as well as storage—were sold individually, too. Unlike the grocery store at home where quantity makes sense, small packages are a critical component of a hiker's resupply. We don't want to carry more than we need, and we must avoid waste and leftovers. Once a dinner or a packet of oatmeal is cooked, it must be eaten; otherwise—you know: animals.

I was interested in the gear section of the store because I wanted a new tent. On the mountain I had spent hours in my long, narrow one-person tent *awake* and frustrated by the lack of movement possible. My tent was fine for sleeping, but I realized that wasn't enough for all the hours I would spend in it on the trail. Many nights it was my home away from home. I needed to be able to sit up and write, to change clothes, and to bring my pack inside.

I asked one of the Mountain Crossings clerks to help me, and he suggested a Big Agnes two-person Fly Creek model. He set up the tent on the floor while I watched. I wasn't the only observer.

"We have only one of these left," the clerk said, indicating the other hiker. "If you don't want it, this gentleman does." That settled it for me.

Before I laid my money down, I thought of asking Miles to reassure me that she was in for the duration of the hike, but then I realized this was about me. It was about whether I wanted to invest in a new tent.

How the clerk and I came to discuss my orange puffy jacket escapes me now. Maybe I had it on in the store. Maybe I told him about my night freezing on the mountain.

"Your jacket doesn't contain enough insulation for this weather," he said of the REI Revelcloud I had bought for half price. Ever the enthusiastic gear customer, I asked to see warmer jackets and bought a dark periwinkle goose-down jacket that compressed into its own little bag.

"You cannot get this jacket wet," the clerk said, and a few minutes later he said it again: "You cannot get this jacket wet."

Goose down is a warm and resilient filler but it becomes soggy when wet, loses its insulating properties, and is slow to dry. In other words, my new jacket would be useless if I didn't heed the warning. The instructional tag said to hand wash it in cold water, but how old would I be when it got dry? I kept the orange jacket as well because it could be brought back to life quickly in a Laundromat.

The next order of business was the pack shakedown. Mountain Crossings was an ideal place for a shakedown because by then Miles and I, as well as other northbound thru-hikers, had carried our loaded packs for over 30 miles and would be glad to unload those precious items that had been so important back home but were not so precious now—items that were weighing us down.

Miles went into another room, and the clerk who helped me began my shakedown by putting my full pack on a scale. It weighed 36 pounds, a surprise. I expected the weight to be more like 30. Typically, a pack should weigh one-fourth of the hiker's weight. Using that formula, a 36-pound pack would put me at 144 pounds, which I wasn't. I also wasn't 120, but the pack was definitely too heavy. Miles and I hated to remove our packs while hiking because we struggled to get them back on. We set our packs on rocks or logs in order to elevate them the way we had using the side chairs in our hotel room at Amicalola Falls.

After the weigh-in I took everything out of my pack, emptying each separate bag inside as well as the pockets on the outside. I spread my pack contents around me on the floor. The clerk brought over a box that would be sent to Mr. M with the superfluous items in it. My old tent was first. *Bye-bye.*

Like many other hikers, I had over-packed, unfortunately not with food or toilet paper. I knew I'd brought a few of the classic shakedown rejects with me, e.g., the previously mentioned metal trowel and MicroSpikes. I knew it, but at the time I'd wanted them anyway. I had to learn the hard way to be selective.

The clerk, a backpacking expert, began to toss items into the mailing box. I was sorry to see my bear-proof food bag replaced with a lighter sack—Miles made the same trade—and I silently cringed when he gave my unbreakable mirror a casual backhand flip without a glance my way. I'd bought the mirror when I thought I'd be hiking alone and might need it to locate ticks on my body. It was called a Featherweight Mirror, so how heavy could it be? In the hiking world we think in terms of ounces because they add up, but come on. I considered diving after my mirror, but I trusted the process and let it go.

I saved six pounds of pack weight that day. I then did my food resupply, following Miles' suggestion to spend money in the Mountain Crossings pantry. I had spent some serious money on gear as well, but neither the larger tent nor the warmer jacket was frivolous. "Invest and protect" became my slogan regarding gear that would have to hold up on a long-distance hike.

The next day was Easter Sunday, though my awareness of it was minimal. I had noticed that on the trail all days were alike.

I was awake and dressed at 6:00 a.m., not at all surprised to be the only one. No Easter baskets were in evidence. I retrieved a Bear Claw pastry from my pack and went into the kitchen to make a cup of coffee. Someone was snoring softly on the couch a few yards away. The front door opened, and Baltimore Jack strode in wearing black shorts, a knit shirt, and an orange vest. He was a legend of the trail, having thru-hiked the AT seven times from 1997 to 2003. Red-faced and stocky, Baltimore Jack was a familiar sight in trail towns and outfitters. That morning he went into the bathroom and emerged with his shoulder-length gray hair wet from the shower. He walked past me to enter a door marked for staff only, started the washer, and then left the building. That was my wordless encounter with Baltimore Jack.

Miles and I planned to hike out that morning, climb a few mountains, and spend the next night at Whitley Gap Shelter, 6.7 miles away. The day was crisp and sunny as we set out—or, more accurately, up—passing the site of our dismal camping experience on the hillside. I wore my new goose-down jacket. We walked past new leaves poking out of the earth and climbed past green trees in the valleys toward those at higher altitudes that would bloom later. We high-fived each other and looked down on beautiful vistas under a blue sky, and I was full of well-being. The air was fresh and the woods were quiet, as though all the flora and fauna were sleeping in.

I suddenly knew that if I were alone on the AT, I would be all right. We had been hiking a week and had met some great and helpful people. I had a warm jacket and a roomy tent. I was glad to be hiking with Miles, but I knew for the first time that if I ever had to keep on alone, I could.

Chapter 18

A Place for Everything

A place for everything, everything in its place.
—Benjamin Franklin

A backpack is a complex piece of equipment when you consider its inner cavities, pockets, loops, and network of straps. It must hold everything you need for a hike yet be light enough to carry mile after mile over rough terrain. Loading a pack is both science and art.

"A place for everything" was one of Miles' sayings. She put the same items in the same place in her pack every day; that way, unlike some of us, she could immediately find what she needed.

I was always losing things, or thinking I'd lost them, which induced the same reaction: panic. It sounded like a Facebook post from a senior citizen: "I couldn't find my glasses, and they were on top of my head." Ha, ha, but not really.

One memorable panic happened at Neel Gap. We had claimed our bunks in the hostel and put our packs and trekking poles where they would fit. Floor space was scarce, and there was always the chance of tripping someone or having someone knock over your pack or poles.

I couldn't find my green dry sack with the sleeping bag liner in it. It was supposed to be in my backpack, but when I looked I didn't see it. Had I left it on the floor at Mountain Crossings when I spread the contents of my pack for the shakedown? I went back to look; not there. Had it accidentally been sent home? I looked under Miles' bed and in the hiker box at the hostel. Most hiker hangouts keep a box to collect discards. Too many packages of Ramen noodles? Had Mom sent more than enough band-aids? Didn't like the instant mashed potatoes? Put them in the hiker box. Someone will pick them out and enjoy them. If my bag with the liner inside had gone into the hiker box, it had likely been taken back out; the value was about $75.

Maybe someone had picked up my bag by mistake. I made a slight fuss in the hostel, asking the other hikers to look for a green bag.

I found it later in a section of my pack reserved for my sleeping pad. How did it get *there*?

Mom developed Alzheimer's in her 80s. Even though she and I were together several times a week, I missed her early symptoms. She receded from conversations, couldn't work some of her appliances, and was unable to follow written instructions. One day she called to say her microwave was beeping, and she didn't know how to stop it. She went to a neighbor's apartment to ask for help. The result, besides assistance with the microwave, was the neighbor's pronouncement: "You should not be living alone." After her diagnosis, Mom spent her last months in a lovely home for Alzheimer's patients.

My great-grandmother was sharp until her death at age 96. My grandmother, Mom's mother, exhibited some dementia in her final years. When we went to see her at the Union Mission Home she would tell a story, disengage for a few minutes, and then tell the same story again. Her forgetfulness was understandable at ages 100 to 102. Mom was weeks from turning 90 when she passed away. We had longevity on our side, but when I lost an item, put it back in the wrong place, or had no memory of what I'd done with it, I had to think about the downside of old age, the mental deterioration I had seen in my own family.

I learned to check every pocket, the detachable pouch called the brain, and the main cavity of my backpack before assuming a piece of gear or clothing was lost. The process was tedious, but it helped me to look less foolish when I found the missing item among my own things.

Some items weren't lost within my pack. At Neel Gap I noticed in the bathroom mirror that one of my pierced earrings from home was gone from my ear. I was walking around with only one earring in place, easy to do when you abandon all forms of vanity on the trail and send your mirror home. My focus wasn't looking perfect so much as not wanting the tiny opening in my earlobe to close over the next few months. Before we left Mountain Crossings for good, I found a pair of round cork earrings bearing the "AT" symbol with the two letters stacked. The bar across the A serves as the top of the T. I popped them in and was ready to hike.

I had to feel for my *A.T. Guide* pages many times a day after the experience of losing them on the trail. The *Guide* pages are critical; they list every significant detail of the trail. Every morning I tore the day's page(s) from the section in my pack, folded them in half relevant sides out, and put them in a zipped baggie in my left back pocket. If I forgot to zip the pocket, the baggie could work its way out while I was hiking. If it fell out while I was peeing I could hike on for miles without noticing its absence. If I was lucky, a hiker coming along later would find my pages and bring them to the next stopping point where a happy reunion would take place. But that was chancy.

"Check your pockets," Miles would say. "Keep your zippers zipped and your awnings closed." That last referred to the fabric covering the zippers on certain pockets in my pants.

I kept my phone and wallet in the biggest pocket, the one over my right thigh. Losing my wallet would be a disaster; the phone, less so. It wasn't worth much as a calling device, but it held my trail photos and other information I wanted to keep. If I needed my phone, it should be where it belonged.

Miles advised me to stop putting my wallet and phone in one of my boots for the night, as someone could easily steal them. In shelters (where one's possessions are most vulnerable) I often slept with my boots beside my sleeping pad, but sometimes they were wet and I left them on the ground directly in front of the shelter or in the vestibule of my tent. They did not dry in either place, by the way.

Miles gave me other tips on how to pack my gear. For instance, she suggested that after taking my sleeping pad out of its pocket at night, I should put my stove in the empty pocket to avoid having to dig for it in my pack when I wanted my coffee and breakfast the next morning. It was good advice, and I'm proud to say it was not given to correct a mistake. It was something Miles had learned from experience and was passing on. She was once a rookie, too.

Miles was showing signs of taking care of me. Sometimes I needed help, and sometimes I asked for help, but not always. I needed to learn some lessons for myself, and I didn't want her to feel responsible for me.

Chapter 19
Gimme Shelter

**What do you actually need? Food, clothing and shelter.
Everything else is entertainment.
—Singer/songwriter Aloe Blacc**

I was putting it together, *it* being the rationale behind shelter naming on the Appalachian Trail.

We spent the night of April 5, Easter Sunday, at Whitley Gap Shelter near the midpoint of the Georgia section of the AT, having hiked out of Neel Gap that morning. Whitley Gap Shelter is located on a blue-blazed trail. That means exactly what it sounds like: The blazes painted on the trees are blue instead of white. A blue-blazed trail is a side trail off the AT. Such trails can be alternate or easier paths to a destination or they can lead to water sources or views. Some shelters are located on blue-blazed trails as well, typically a short walk from the main trail.

Whitley Gap Shelter is situated 1.2 miles off the Appalachian Trail—a comparatively long walk—and the hike is downhill. As we made our way down after a 6.7-mile hike over Levelland Mountain (a misnomer) and Cowrock Mountain and up Wildcat Mountain, I began to get the drift. We were going downhill now, but in the morning we would have to hike back *up* that hill to reach the point where we'd left the AT. The off-trail distance wouldn't count toward our AT hike but would add to the miles we had to walk just the same.

Thus far Miles and I had stayed in or near Springer Mountain Shelter, Hawk Mountain Shelter, Gooch Mountain Shelter, and now Whitley Gap Shelter. The first three were on mountains; this last one was the opposite. So, if a shelter has the word "mountain" in the name, its location is likely to be at or near the top of one. You'll be climbing to get there. If the shelter has "gap" in the name, it's likely located in a low area between mountains, but that won't save you. You'll be climbing a mountain when you wake up.

When we reached Whitley Gap Shelter, we were surprised to be the only hikers there. After experiencing the blue-blazed trail, we reasoned that others might be choosing to hike on instead of doing the 2.4 miles in and out. The shelter sat on flat land with woods on three sides and a long, grassy area in front perfect for pitching tents. A picnic table completed the picture. The sun was shining that afternoon and the setting was peaceful, but both of us had a sense of isolation.

We got water from the spring located down a hill behind the shelter. It was flowing from a wide black pipe. We were always glad to see a pipe; they were inserted in natural springs to eliminate the need to dip the water out or place a strategic but flimsy leaf to direct the flow into a container. This was the delicious spring water I loved. Of course, we would need to filter it; that was a given.

We spent the afternoon on separate projects. Miles pitched her tent in the sunshine. As I recall, she did so to wipe it down; a sunny day is perfect for drying or airing out a tent. Both of us intended to sleep in the shelter that night, but I saw an opportunity to put up my new tent for the first time. I'd seen a demonstration at Mountain Crossings, but I needed to practice what had been described in the store as easy. We were still by ourselves, and it didn't appear anyone else would be sharing the shelter with us that night, so I pitched my tent inside it. The choice felt safer to me, but it's considered rude on the trail because of the space a tent consumes. Other hikers can arrive late and have nowhere to sleep.

We'd both set up in the shelter when we saw a hiker we knew named Flashback descending the blue-blazed trail. I was relieved to see another person and glad it was a man who had joined us because I'd been entertaining dark thoughts of Mr. and Ms. Bear. In my mind, a man's size and deep voice would be better than mine for scaring animals away.

Later on a few other hikers came down the trail. We offered to make more space, but Flashback hung his hammock and the others pitched their tents nearby. By then I felt entirely safe from the animal kingdom.

It poured the next day as we hiked back up the trail and continued for 4.8 miles to Low Gap Shelter. As promised by the name, it was located at the bottom of an incline. We arrived in time to have lunch there. The area was a mess. The ground surrounding the shelter was pure mud with deep puddles, and the view from inside was a gray sheet of rain and fog.

We were not alone; hikers temporarily escaping the downpour or wisely anticipating a crowded situation later on sat against the walls patiently talking and joking with one another. Some were claiming their spaces for the night, and we needed to do the same or be forced out into the rain to pitch our tents.

We took our sleeping pads from our packs and sat on them, partly as cushions and partly to mark our spots. It was early afternoon. We sat for hours with our backs against a wall. At one point we were sharing a shelter made for seven people with eight other hikers and two dogs. One man had settled in with many of his possessions unpacked around him. He was already in his sleeping bag, reading a book. One's floor space in a shelter, especially in crowded times, is defined by one's sleeping pad. This hiker had spread out beyond that boundary, yet he repeatedly stood up in the unclaimed middle, giving those of us who were seated long, unobstructed views of his bare legs.

In a shelter we seldom pick our roommates. Miles and I could be lying next to each other, a friend, or a complete stranger, male or female. We might have elbow room, or we might be pad to pad, wondering how we'll get out if we have to pee. The person in the next space might snore, change clothes, toss and turn all night, shine a headlamp, or emit foul smells. Although I may have exhibited some of those nocturnal behaviors, my "thing" was waking up too early.

The magic hour for hikers to begin stirring was 6:30 a.m. I don't know who decided that, but it was a consistent pattern on the trail. The birds chattered earlier and sometimes we heard owls calling to one another, "Who-hoo, who-hoo"; but any hiker getting up before 6:30, for instance the diabetic who had to manage his food and medication, moved silently and carefully to avoid disturbing the others.

I woke up anywhere from 2:00 a.m. to 5:45.

When I woke before my usual time, my bladder was the reason. I dreaded leaving the shelter at night. What was out there? In addition, the floor of a shelter is built about three feet off the ground and sometimes the ground in front of it is uneven. How would I get out of my sleeping bag quietly, put on shoes, and exit the shelter without breaking my neck? Instead of trying to get out, I tried to fall back to sleep.

Waking up at 4:00 or 5:00 a.m. instead of 2:00 was a victory except for one thing: When I woke up, my back hurt. The floor of a shelter is unyielding, even with a sleeping pad between it and you. Desperate to change positions, I would postpone rolling over to avoid waking up my neighbors. Thus, the ensuing hours were painful and 6:30 was a relief.

Miles and I were headed next for Blue Mountain Shelter, 7.3 miles away. We were still hiking in the single digits, meaning that we hiked under ten miles per day. For once, the terrain was not mountainous so much as humpy on the elevation chart. We would pass four gaps and a couple of knobs before we started up Blue Mountain.

We were one day behind schedule, not bad for a couple of older ladies who hadn't found our trail legs yet.

Chapter 20

When It Rains

No pain, no rain, no Maine.
—Appalachian Trail saying

Hikers don't wear their rain pants when it rains. Miles alerted me to that strange fact after she saw how I was dressed for the day at Blue Mountain Shelter.

It was raining, and we were going to be hiking 8.1 miles that day. I didn't mind walking in light rain, but by then I knew the difference between that and hiking through the woods in it soaking wet and chilled to the bone. Nothing made more sense to me than trying to stay dry. Why else would I have brought a pair of rain pants?

News flash: Hikers who carry rain pants—and many don't—wear them for warmth, wind resistance, and protection from bugs; but seldom are rain pants worn because water is falling from the sky. Among those who reject rain pants are hikers who make their own versions; Miles and I saw both men and women make rain skirts from black garbage bags, which are lighter and cheaper.

I had dressed inside my tent—a pleasure now that I had room to slip my black nylon rain pants over my hiking pants. I was wearing my rain jacket on top, which should have been an even more obvious decision than the pants but wasn't. I wore it in spite of the facts. After 15 minutes of hiking I'd be so warm that my sweat would cling to places on the inside of the coat and I'd have a rain jacket that was wet inside and out. I'd have to stop, take off my pack, and remove the raincoat. After two weeks on the trail, that was predictable.

I couldn't see the reasoning regarding the pants and didn't want to change now that we were ready to hike, so against Miles' advice I kept them on. We were hiking partners, but we were not going to be "trail twins." In some ways we were trail opposites.

I was hungry before she was. I was tired before she was. Or maybe she was hungry and tired, too, but kept it to herself. Positivity was important on the trail.

She pushed harder. When we hiked I thought of the next break, hoping she would suggest it. If I said, "I'm ready to stop for lunch," she might agree or she might say, "Let's go another thirty minutes," or "Let's look for a better spot." No doubt I needed to be pulled along—we were a bit behind schedule—but I was rarely the one to initiate it.

We had come 7.3 miles the day before. In the guidebook the way looked relatively flat, with the biggest "ups" being our ascent from the sodden ground at Low Gap Shelter and the hike partway up Blue Mountain. My feet reminded me that the trail is rarely flat. We had passed through four gaps—Poplar Stamp, Cold Springs, Chattahoochee, and Red Clay—and on a long-distance hike you can't pass a gap without climbing a couple mountains. I did love the gaps. My favorite thing occurred when the woods on either side of us flattened to gently rolling terrain, our vista widened, and the path kept to level ground for the foreseeable distance.

The sun was shining on Blue Mountain Shelter when we arrived. The site was flat and occupied by lots of hikers. Miles chose to sleep in the shelter that night, but I pitched my new tent. We ate supper together, and I fixed a package of instant mashed potatoes. I'd bought 10 for $10 at Kroger before leaving home. To add protein, I stirred in a packet of tuna. The result was a huge serving, more than I wanted to eat, but I finished it to eliminate leftovers.

Before we hung the food bags my stomach hurt, and I had lost my taste for mashed potatoes. I had nine more packs in assorted flavors: garlic, garlic and cheese, smoked bacon, chipotle, and "loaded." I felt like Bubba listing the shrimp dishes in *Forrest Gump*. A few of the remaining potato packs were in my food bag and the rest would show up in my drop boxes later, but that night was the first and last time I intended to eat mashed potatoes on the trail.

I had a new sleeping technique. Instead of trying to fall asleep, I lay in my tent savoring my quiet time and appreciating that I was not at that moment climbing a mountain. I would relax and enjoy the fact that my boots were somewhere besides on my feet. Of my daily aches and pains, I would think: *Let them heal*. Along those lines, I might swallow a couple tablets of Ibuprofen before bedtime. My technique worked that night and I was soon asleep.

We hiked out in the morning rain. The trail took us through patches of slippery black mud, and I fell twice that day. One of my falls was a sideways slide toward the edge of the trail. It was quick, and if I had not been able to catch myself I'd have gone over. I was glad I hadn't rolled down the mountainside and could hike on, but my rain pants were a mess. I hadn't factored in a spill when I decided to wear them. The mud would dry, but now the pants had a date with a washing machine.

Here is the big secret about rain pants: As I had discovered at Neel Gap, they are useful in the Laundromat to cover your lower body while you wait for your clothes. Pair them with a rain jacket and nothing underneath for an outfit that allows you to remain decent while washing all the damp, smelly clothes you've been wearing for a week.

Seeing them coated with mud, I understood why Miles had warned me to save my rain pants. We were going into Helen, Georgia, the next day to resupply and wash our clothes. I had nothing to wear on the bottom while I did my laundry.

Chapter 21

Grandma in Hot Pants

People will stare. Make it worth their while.
—Gemologist Harry Winston

We had spent three nights on the trail since leaving Neel Gap. On the fourth morning Miles and I hiked 2.4 miles to Unicoi Gap, where we would find a ride to Helen, Georgia for two near-oes in town. A near-o is a near-zero day because part of it is spent hiking. On the way to Helen we hiked for part of the morning; the next day we would leave town later than usual and hike the rest of the day.

Some gaps in the mountains merely provide temporary relief for hikers' legs. Unicoi Gap is a busy trailhead with generous parking space. Miles and I came off the trail there to cheering from two men, Tom and Solo, who stood next to two cars parked on the gravel. The trunks were open to display an array of trail magic that included drinks, donuts, chips, and candy. I was happy to load my pockets with speckled malted-milk eggs left over from Easter.

It was April 8 and we were two days behind schedule. We originally planned to resupply in Helen on the 7th and return to the trail the same day, arriving that evening at Tray Mountain Shelter. I was beginning to see that such aggressive plans were difficult to achieve. Once in town, a hiker becomes susceptible to the lure of a hot shower, restaurant meals, and a bed for the night.

We were waiting for a shuttle but lucked out when Tom closed up shop and offered us a ride into town. He told us he had been providing trail magic up and down the AT for 40 years. After Unicoi Gap he would move north. He drove us past the attractive Swiss-themed storefronts of Helen to the front door of the Best Western hotel. This was our first time in a hotel since Amicalola Falls and the first break we had taken in a town.

It was sunny and warm out, too warm for rainwear even if my rain pants had been clean. Miles and I took turns walking next door to the Dollar General to buy town clothes. While one shopped, the other sat in the hotel lobby guarding our packs—as if anyone would be tempted to steal two stinky backpacks weighing 30 pounds each.

We were looking for cheap solutions to the question of what to wear in town—that town. We didn't intend to leave Helen with the added weight of more clothes. When my turn came to shop, I headed to the Dollar General sale rack where ladies' shorts were 2 pairs for $8. They were made like running shorts except for the fabric, some kind of synthetic that did not stretch. One pair had a camouflage pattern and the other was done in a black-and-white zebra stripe with bright pink trim. I bought both and decided to wear the zebra-patterned pair in town.

We had arrived too early to check into the hotel but the manager, Carol Powell, offered us the use of a conference room for changing our clothes, sorting our laundry, and safely storing our packs while we had lunch and went to the Laundromat. I went commando under my shorts so I could wash my underwear. After I changed, I realized how short my new shorts were. It had been a long time since I'd shown that much thigh in public outside a swimming pool. Miles was smarter; she chose men's basketball shorts, which were down to her knees.

We bundled up our dirty clothes for the walk to the Laundromat. I was mortified at the thought of wearing my new "hot pants" on the street. I hoped no cars would wreck at the sight of me. The shorts would have been fine 40 or 50 years ago, before my wrinkles set in. Hot pants were a trend in the 1950s when I was young. I had a yellow pair with buckles on the sides, and they were tame compared to the tiny little shorts with the wild zebra print I was now wearing. I hoped that few would see them after I tied the sleeves of my rain jacket around my waist and let the coat hang down in order to walk the streets of Helen, Georgia. Oh, did I say, "walk the streets"?

We were in for a busy day. The sun was a gift as we enjoyed a slow lunch on the deck of a local pub. It was one of the few relaxing things we would do before bedtime.

Next, we found the Laundromat and started the wash. At home I babied my clothes through the laundry, eyeballing each garment for spots and spraying the spots with Shout before putting the clothes into the washer. I let nothing but my worst sweats get completely dry in the dryer, instead removing my pants and shirts one by one and hanging them in the basement to dry overnight.

Miles and I had no time for fussiness. We put everything of ours from bandanas to coats to underwear together, regardless of color or fabric; turned the dial to "Hot"; and washed our filthy load skipping "Delicate" and "Permanent Press" for the Normal setting. Afterward we fed the dryer with quarters until every piece was cooked. I realized then that the hurried way we'd done our laundry at Neel Gap was not an anomaly because of the demand. This would be our process every week. I mentally kissed my expensive outdoor wear good-bye at the washer, expecting the worst, but I was wrong. Nothing was stained, shrunk, or mangled. It was a miracle, and later when I showered and put on those clean clothes in the hotel, the Rapture would come to mind.

I was compulsive with laundry, but Miles didn't want us to take time to fold the clothes. It wasn't life or death, but it was another way we differed. When I could, I folded my pile. I hated to ball everything up in a jacket to carry it to the hotel.

The most complicated chore was ahead of us: We had to shop for food. We would be leaving in the morning to re-enter the AT at Unicoi Gap. In the meantime, we had to determine how many days we'd be hiking before our next resupply. Once we knew how many meals we would need, we could return to the Dollar General and buy the groceries.

The Dollar General: If I could sing that, I would. Before we shopped in Helen, I'd never been in one. We were going there because it was next to the Best Western. In addition to clothing, it sold food. But first, back to the room, which was ready at last.

As we put our things down, I caught my reflection in the mirror. I hadn't seen myself for a few days and was still unaccustomed to my new look: basic forest. Between my lack of makeup and my wild, greasy hair, it was as though I were meeting somebody new. Maybe I was.

Miles and I completed another order of business before tackling our grocery lists: We went online to obtain our thru-hiker permits for Great Smoky Mountains National Park, where we expected to be in 12 days, and asked the hotel to print our receipts. Later we sat down at our table for two in the room with pen, paper, and the next section of the *A.T. Guide* to prepare for our trip to the store. To count the meals we would need on the trail, we had to calculate our daily mileage and determine where we would spend each night until the next resupply. We had done it once, at home, but now that we were hiking and had a dose of reality, another look was in order.

We realized the refueling possibilities were few. We were facing six nights in the woods before our next town stop in Franklin, North Carolina. *Yes!* In a week we were going to be in our second state going northbound on the trail.

"How many meals and snacks do we need?" Miles asked.

The answer was sobering: 6 breakfasts, 6 lunches, 6 dinners, and 12 snacks each. We needed to buy the most food we'd carried yet. Food was weight. It was a different way to look at groceries.

I would learn to see food in terms of calories as well, but not in the way I was used to at home. In order to keep my weight in line I always bought low-fat items at home, passing up the ones I really wanted: the high-calorie snacks. Being on the trail and burning thousands of calories a day had suddenly given us permission to buy and consume junk food.

We could resupply inexpensively at the Dollar General—prices were lower than those in supermarkets—but neither that fact nor the need to take in calories was an incentive to peruse the grocery aisles at the end of a long day. Starving in the woods was. I had run out of food once on the trail and didn't intend to do so again.

At least I could food-shop in my clean hiking clothes and bid *adieu* to my $4 short shorts. They would find a home in the hotel trash can before we left Helen, Georgia.

Chapter 22
Beasts of Burden

**What you can't give away you must carry with you,
it is always heavier than you thought.
—From a poem by Margaret Atwood**

After studying the *A.T. Guide* and determining our food needs, Miles and I headed for the Dollar General in Helen, Georgia. This time we ignored the sale racks of shorts to focus on buying enough groceries for six days and nights in the woods.

When Miles and I shopped for food, each of us paid for some of the items we would split; for example, I might buy a 12-pack of Honey Buns and give Miles 6. She might buy a variety pack of Quaker oatmeal and count out half of the packs for me. We bought snacks galore as well as instant meals, stocking up on such dinner staples as Knorr Pasta Sides and Ramen noodles as well as packets of tuna, Spam, vegetables, Cheez-Its, or anything else we could mix in to add flavor or protein.

Mountain House trail meals were my favorites because they were tasty, self-contained, and packaged in sturdy, disposable bags with wide bottoms. The bags could take the boiling water needed to rehydrate a meal and could stand on their own without collapsing, tearing, or falling over. They were odor proof compared to a plastic storage bag. However, Mountain House meals were not always available where we shopped. And they were heavy. With six days of food in our future, we didn't need heavy.

For lunches we bought tortillas, peanut butter, more tuna, jerky, and crackers. Jelly was not available in small packets in stores, so I continued to steal it from restaurants. Snacks we bought in the Dollar Store included Rice Krispies Treats, Nutter Butter cookies, fruit novelties, Slim Jims, M&M's, and Clif bars. I couldn't be without peanut butter, either Jif To Go or the tiny jars of an off-brand we found for a dollar. Individual packaging was key; we couldn't take an ounce more of anything than we needed.

We bought zippered baggies in various sizes: sandwich, snack, gallon, and half-gallon freezer. They served us when we had to divide food into individual portions ourselves. The largest ones made great trash bags on the trail. Because of the packaging, we had to buy whole boxes of those as well as some snacks. Smart merchants in the trail towns cater to hikers' needs, stocking reasonably priced individual portions on their shelves, but who wants to store-hop? The answer is no one who has been walking eight or nine miles a day.

By the time Miles and I finished our food shopping, it was evening in Helen and we still had to sort our purchases and pack our food bags. The process would take two hours, but it had to be done. The next morning, we were heading back to the trail. We used our beds for sorting and organizing our purchases. When two queen-size beds wouldn't hold all of it, we spread our food on the floor as well. Everywhere we looked we saw food, as though we'd brought the inventory of the Dollar General back to the hotel.

Our ultimate job was to cram 6 breakfasts apiece, 6 lunches, 6 dinners, and 12 snacks into our food bags, which then had to fit into our backpacks. The amount was daunting.

We began placing every item that was not individually wrapped in a plastic zipper bag before the second stage, grouping the items. As we worked, discarded product boxes and yellow plastic Dollar General bags filled and then overflowed the trash cans in the room. We set up the bagging operation on the table, but it soon spilled over to the floor, too, where we could line up and count our various meal components.

Sometimes the long organizing process was enough to turn us against the very food we were going to eat that week. Snacks that had appealed to me an hour before in the store—M&M's, for instance—constituted an overdose of chocolate by the time I copped a few handfuls while dividing the contents into daily portions.

I packed all of my wrapped food in gallon baggies according to whether it would be part of a breakfast, lunch, dinner, or snack. Miles did the same. That made finding and selecting items easier on the trail. After we did the pre-sorting and bagging, we loaded our food bags, making sure we had enough to eat but not too much. We would eat the heaviest items first; that was a given. It would take two or three days to feel the difference in our packs, but by the time we reached Franklin, North Carolina, they would be light—just in time for the next resupply.

I lined my cloth food bag with an odor-proof bag of heavy plastic, limiting its capacity a bit but increasing the chances that animals would not smell the contents. We left what wouldn't fit in the hotel room for the housekeeping staff, along with tons of extra baggies and our loose change.

Since the shakedowns at Neel Gap, we'd been carrying our food in bags made of a lightweight material instead of the heavier animal-resistant Ursacks we originally brought and later sent home. The new ones were identical except Miles' was silver and mine was green. Without getting too mathematical, our food bags were designed to hold 15 liters. That's almost one-fourth the capacity of a 65-liter backpack, so this food would take up a fourth of the space in our packs.

The food bags had roll-top closures, designed for three rolls before the clasp should be engaged. That would keep water out. When I had stuffed my meals and snacks in, the bag was full to the top. No way could I close the odor-proof liner bag, let alone roll the top three times.

The bags were 22 inches tall and a foot wide, cylindrical when full. When I stood up and lifted mine, it took two hands.

"Oh, my god," I said. "This thing has to weigh over ten pounds, possibly twelve or fourteen pounds." Miles was in a similar boat.

How was I going to haul a pack bearing ten pounds of food over the mountains of Georgia? I had yet to add the water and Gatorade I would need to start hiking the next morning. Sure, I'd been carrying food all along, but not a six-day supply. This time I dreaded the ups like never before.

"Remember that hiker we saw coming southbound at Unicoi Gap?" Miles said. "He told us his food supply for the section we're starting tomorrow had made his backpack the heaviest it had ever been."

I wasn't looking forward to putting on my pack the next morning. If a man had complained about his load of food, that was noteworthy. Like his, our packs were going to be the heaviest they had been. Besides that, a hotel employee told Miles and me the section we were about to hike was the hardest in Georgia.

Chapter 23

Changes

It is not the mountain we conquer, but ourselves.
—Sir Edmund Hillary, the first man to summit Mount Everest

The manager of the Best Western gave us a ride back to Unicoi Gap. Our destination for the day was Tray Mountain Shelter, only 5.7 miles ahead, but the initial 1.4 miles were straight up. We climbed Rocky Mountain and then Tray Mountain, which was even taller. On an *A.T. Guide* page profile, they *do* look like the mountains we drew as children.

The weight of my food was pushing my pack straps down into my shoulders. In addition, the black gnats of north Georgia had awakened, hatched, or returned from wherever they'd spent the winter. It's hard to bat flying bugs away with a trekking pole in each hand and dangerous to try, so gnats flew around our faces and dive-bombed Miles and me as we hiked. They aimed for our eyes and buzzed our ears, noses, and mouths. They landed in our hair. I had brought a bug net that went over my head and tied at the neck, and it was time to try it out. At least with the net on I could think about something other than bugs. And bears. And my shoulders.

We had been on the Appalachian Trail less than two weeks. Current challenges aside, I had begun to see good changes in myself and my hiking style.

I was no longer the struggling hiker whose own heartbeat frightened her with its ferocity or the pathetic would-be mountain climber who had to rest every 20 or 40 steps. I was a part of this trail experience, having left my other life behind.

According to the experts at Neel Gap, the changes did not mean I had acquired my trail legs—that would happen after 28 days, they said—but I knew I was improving. In the beginning, my pace—and Miles'—was so slow that we stepped aside to let everyone else pass us on the narrow trail. We made it to our destinations, but not before a group had gathered. Our daily fate must have been a subject of speculation, because as the other hikers began to recognize us it was routine to hear someone call out, "You made it!"

Gradually I gained confidence in my own steps.

I hiked with two adjustable trekking poles. For me, the poles were an aid in keeping my balance. Considering the rocks, roots, slippery leaves, and mud on the trail as well as the visual distractions, I was prone—adjective use intentional—to falling; but as time went by I developed a rhythm between the poles and my feet. It was effortless and automatic, allowing me to focus on something besides the careful placement of my steps. Some days I danced over the trail with my poles slightly raised, skirting the obstacles that normally scared or tripped me. Those were my best days.

When I found my rhythm on the trail, I also found my confidence, and I thought of my grandmother. Like many others in the nursing home, she had a walker. Its metal frame protected her on three sides from falling as she made her way to the kitchen at mealtimes. But Grandmama was too proud to depend on the device. She was tall and her posture, straight. Instead of leaning on the walker, she carried it.

When Miles and I started I dreaded every mountain in our path, still clinging to my surprise at having to go over one after another on the AT. But as my legs grew stronger, I marveled that I was able to cover ground using my trekking poles and the strength in my arms. Going uphill I'd put the poles ahead of me, alternating left and right, and let them bear the weight as my legs caught up. I shifted my weight from side to side, taking small steps. With my "slow and steady" method I could ascend a small mountain or one with a gentle slope without stopping.

"You're a machine!" Miles would say. "You got us up that mountain."

I liked hearing Miles' praise. Compliments are nice, especially when one is accustomed to being coached. I was proud that my technique for climbing mountains had not resulted from anyone's suggestion. It had come together on the trail, it was uniquely mine, and it worked.

I was learning about hiking firsthand. You don't know what is involved in a sport until you practice it. For instance, when does a walk become a hike? Are hiking and walking synonymous? It is said that hiking involves more effort, special footwear, and a different kind of path. While walkers can walk on many surfaces, hikers choose natural trails and walk from lower elevations to higher ones. I can vouch for that.

The ups were harder for Miles than the downs. She could fly downhill and make great time over the long ridges, which were often riddled with rocks, but the ups were her nemesis—with a psychological rather than a physical basis. She claimed she couldn't look ahead because when she saw the trail continuing upward she wanted to stop and rest. So she said, but I never saw Miles falter when she led the way up a mountain.

I wasn't perfect. I tended to follow too closely behind her. "Trailgating" was a characteristic of my compulsive personality manifested on the trail. When Miles needed to navigate a difficult section, she asked me to stay back until she had cleared it. I had to learn to leave more space between us.

I was improving every day, but I still lost my balance. Grazing a root or hitting a loose rock with one foot will do it.

"Never put your foot on a loose rock," Miles told me. "It will move and so will you. Step around it." The AT is sprinkled with loose rocks, and falling is a possibility for the vigilant hiker as well as the distracted one. If I did slip or trip, I became cautious and slowed down until the pattern of my poles and feet once again restored my assurance.

One day Miles said, "You seem calmer." She was comparing my demeanor with that of the nervous-Nellie who left Cincinnati with her at the end of March.

After a few weeks on the trail I *was* calmer. The change Miles saw reflected a slowing of my mind. As long as I could remember, I'd been cursed with thought-racing. In quiet times, my thoughts would heat up. I would create mental scenarios, worry in detail about any subject, and do so with an earworm I couldn't banish playing in the background.

Now my mind settled on one or two themes instead of a barrage. The song was always there, looping in rhythm with my steps, but many of the clashing, worrisome thoughts faded as I focused on the simplicity of walking, climbing, and completing the chores of the day.

As my focus narrowed, my world was expanding on the Appalachian Trail. That slim path through a string of mountains was opening up my life experience. The people we met were an education. At home I might have been watching TV.

"My world was too small before the AT," I said to Miles after we high-fived each other upon reaching yet another mountaintop. We assumed our usual pose, standing sideways on the trail, side by side, feet apart, facing out. Our view through the trees was a rumpled landscape coming alive: a hundred colors under the blue sky.

"Lots of people hike to make some kind of change in their lives," she said.

"I didn't do it for that reason," I said, "but it seems to be happening."

Tray Mountain Shelter was past the peak of the mountain. By the time we reached it, I didn't want to sleep in the shelter with its wide-open front. The bugs had continued to plague us, and I wanted to be in my tent with both openings zipped tight. I loved my new tent. After hiking over two mountains I was beyond tired, and I lay in my sleeping bag with daylight all around me. The wind was soothing, and I could hear planes going by overhead. Before I fell asleep I recognized another change: I was not scared; I was happy. Part of it could have been the crowd of hikers all around me. I felt secure.

It was ironic that my good changes were coming together at the same time I began having trouble—big trouble that would define my worst time on the AT.

Chapter 24
A Pack of Trouble

**If you're going through Hell,
keep going.
—Winston Churchill**

My pack was killing me. Even though I'd followed the sensible hiker advice to eat the heaviest food items first, I hadn't felt an appreciable lightening of my load since Helen, Georgia. Every day my shoulders began to ache within 15 minutes of putting on my pack. The pain was sharp and constant. Mile after mile I wished I could remove my backpack, even for a few minutes. That wish dominated my thoughts as I waited for the next chance, walking with half-shrugs to shift the weight to one side and then the other for mere seconds of relief.

I couldn't tell Miles. We were trying to hike farther every day. Our goal was to bring our daily mileage into double digits—ten or more miles per day—and I needed to keep up. She was such a go-getter; how was I going to introduce an issue that was not only negative, but guaranteed to slow us down? As I hiked in physical agony, our talk on the trail remained positive and I kept my misery to myself; at least, that's how I remember it.

The hard stretch after Helen was leading us to the North Carolina border. After Tray Mountain we spent two more nights in Georgia before entering our second AT state.

Deep Gap Shelter was the arena for my next rookie mistake. The shelter presented a colorful scene when we arrived on April 10. The sun was shining. Hikers pitched their tents nearby or assembled on the wide porch to play cards, change into camp shoes, or unpack their gear. Men gathered firewood for the cool spring night ahead. I was thrilled to take off my pack.

We slept in the shelter. In the morning Miles and I stood on the porch getting ready to leave. Last thing before I put on my pack, I stuffed my full hydration bladder into its pocket, applying pressure to move the soft-sided container as far down the sleeve as it would go. Water exploded into my pack, onto the porch, and onto me.

The delicious spring water we drank on the trail could also work against us. Wet belongings mean a heavy pack—something I didn't need—and a wet hiker can become chilled. Aside from those practical considerations, losing my water supply in front of everyone as we prepared to hike out was embarrassing—slapstick comedy gone wrong. I held the empty bladder and regarded the giant puddle taking shape on the porch.

Had I failed to make sure the cap was on tight, or had my reservoir sprung a leak? I needed more water to find out, so back to the spring I went. Water is essential on the trail; I couldn't leave without it. This time I made sure the cap was tight, dried the outside, and began to examine the seams for leaks.

"Turn it upside down," Miles said. "Shake it hard. Try to make it fail."

I squeezed the bladder with both hands, shifting the water back and forth against the seams. I shook it and held it upside down, finding no leaks but proving my own ineptitude. I had been in a hurry the first time and had not checked the security of the cap.

It would be nice to get beyond this rookie stage.

At midday on April 12 Miles and I cheered as we crossed into North Carolina. We posed for pictures at the tree bearing the wooden "NC/GA" sign. The photographer using our phone cameras to record the moment was a young woman who arrived behind us crying because she and her trail partner had broken up. After our brief meeting at the border we didn't see her again. On the trail, we never knew whether other hikers would become good friends or would disappear for good once they were far ahead of us. Sometimes we had companions for a while, and sometimes it was just Miles and me.

She and I didn't chatter unselfconsciously the way women are known to do. The nature of hiking makes talking difficult, and I liked being quiet; but there was something else. It might have been the difference in our personalities, or perhaps our relationship had been defined for all time at the office.

We stopped for lunch at Bly Gap, where in spite of the sunny spring day the wind whipped past us as we ate sitting on logs near a piped spring. After lunch things got serious; we spent the afternoon climbing to Muskrat Creek Shelter. If I thought the Georgia mountains were tough, tougher ones awaited. The climb was relentless, taking us up the real-life equivalents of the steep, jagged lines on the *A.T. Guide* page. In our first three hours inside the border, we had completed our highest climb yet on the AT, and I felt it.

I was miserable. Between the steep mountain slopes and my ridiculous pack weight, I once again wondered what I was doing there. The trail was a challenge in every way, but I wanted to be able to do the necessary miles without whining. I wanted to be a good trail partner to Miles, who had been hiking with injuries all along.

I began secretly taking three Ibuprofen pills every morning after breakfast just to be able to hike. Before the possible dangers of pain killers were a topic of concern, hikers relied on Vitamin I to ease the aches and pains they learned to expect as part of a long-distance hike.

When my first dose of Ibuprofen started to wear off, I took another pill or two as a booster. I did this all day, every day. I kept the pills in a zipped baggie in the right hip-belt pocket of my pack—a pocket I could reach while hiking. I felt no pain as long as I kept taking the pills. As Miles and I moved into 10- to 12-mile days, I felt confident. I could make it. I would take Ibuprofen during the day and combine it with healing rest at night. I had found the answer, and I didn't have to share my secret.

Chapter 25
North Carolina

How thin the line of safety.
—Thru-hiker and author Gary "Rethinker" Bond

The day after we entered North Carolina, it began to rain. And rain. We trekked 12.5 miles through black mud. I slogged along that sloppy trail under the torturous weight of my devil pack, grateful for the pocket of Vitamin I.

Yes, I like walking in the rain; but by that I mean the kind of "walking in the rain" people put in their personal dating profiles, not this nightmare. The weather was horrible and the path, slippery. Miles and I both fell on the trail. Her fall occurred when she was coming off a footbridge. I remember starting toward her to help her up.

"Don't touch me," she said, and I stopped. "Never move a hiker who falls. I know you meant well, but if there is damage, you could make it worse."

I waited while Miles extracted herself from her pack, undoing the hip belt and easing out of the remaining straps before standing on her own. Her spill resulted in a sprained ankle. It turned purple, but she hiked on. Miles was an inspiration that way, refusing to let any obstacle stop her.

I've forgotten the circumstances of my fall; no doubt I was lost in thought and not watching the placement of my feet, but I was not hurt. My pack, plump with food and water and gear, acted as a cushion.

We arrived at Carter Gap Shelter in the pouring rain and had to pitch our tents. Many other hikers had beaten us there, some in the shelter and others in campsites among the dripping trees. The shelter is located a few miles south of Mooney Gap, which because of its annual precipitation of about 93 inches, is among the wettest locations in the eastern United States.

As I lay in my sleeping bag that evening, drops of water began to fall on me. Why was water dripping from the *inside* of my tent? I knew I'd put the rain fly on over the netting; I could look up and see it. The fly was in place, but I had put the tent together in the rain. Had I somehow attached the rain fly inside out, so that the dry side was now getting wet and the wet side was dripping on me? New water droplets formed above me as I realized my mistake.

The daytime temperature had been 68 degrees. How low would it go overnight? More to the point, how long would it take before I was soaked? My sleeping bag, which I took care to keep dry, was exposed to the dripping water. I began to worry as I realized the possibilities: increasing dampness, chill, and the big one—hypothermia. Could I get hypothermia in my own tent? I felt isolated as my mind concocted frightening scenarios. How could I fall asleep? Could I survive the long night ahead? Would anything be dry by morning?

Physical and mental fatigue don't guarantee a restful night on the trail. You might expect the opposite, but for those who are jumpy and unaccustomed to the ways of nature, sleep is elusive. I had a difficult enough time relaxing amid the night calls and rustlings of woodland creatures without the added worry that I would freeze to death by morning. Finally, lulled by a dose of Ibuprofen, I slept.

I dreamed a white-coated maitre d' led me through a banquet room to an outdoor setup for a wedding. It was daytime. The yard was gently rolling and the grass, bright green. A semicircular table decorated with white netting and flowers had been carried to the lawn. Bridal attendants in long, filmy dresses were seated on both sides, but the chair at the center—the bride's chair—was empty.

"Who's getting married?" I asked. I gathered from the long silence that I had arrived at my own wedding. Surprise!

The attendants stood and sang to me. After the song, they quickly dispersed and I turned to the maitre d'. "Who set this up?" I asked. "Who is paying for this?" More silence. "And who is the groom?"

We were in another country, maybe Italy. Church bells were pealing in the distance, and suddenly an old man was beside me. And when I say old, I mean o-l-d. He wore a dark, loose garment with a hood. His face when he turned to me was homely, spotted and wrinkled, but he ruled a town. He had such power that declining this arranged wedding was not an option for me. I was trapped. Realizing my fate, I said it aloud for the first time: "The godfather is in love with me."

In the morning I was delighted to find myself alive. We woke up to more rain, but at least I wasn't marrying the godfather. I was wet, as I'd feared, and I had begun to stink. This was the tail end of the six-day stint in the woods for which Miles and I had bought all that food in Helen, Georgia. My food bag was lighter now, but my shoulders still hurt. I couldn't understand it.

We had an eight-mile hike ahead of us. If I could bear another day of wet, painful hiking and one more night on the trail, I'd be in a hotel room the following morning. Mr. M had made a reservation for us at the Sapphire Inn in Franklin, our second trail town. A hotel room sounded like Heaven.

Miles and I tramped through rushing water and waded in mud four and five inches deep. We climbed Albert Mountain in the rain, crawling up wet boulders and clinging to small trees to avoid falling among the rocks. When we got to the top, the view was obscured by fog. We had lunch under the fire tower that stands at the summit but did not climb it.

I dreaded having to spend another night in my wet tent dodging the trail version of water torture, so it was fortunate that we snagged the last two spots in Long Branch Shelter for the night. It was a new building with two levels designed to hold 16 people. We arrived about 4:00 p.m. to a busy scene: clotheslines strung across the front and filled with damp garments of all colors, poles propped against the support beams, and hikers settling in or beginning to haul out their cooking stoves around the fire ring and picnic table. I spent a relatively comfortable night within the protective walls of the shelter.

The next morning we packed up and left at 7:30 in order to catch the shuttle into Franklin. We needed to get to Rock Gap, the pickup point for the shuttle, by 9:30. I can't speak for Miles, but I would have clawed my way over the 3.6 mountainous miles on my hands and knees to be clean and dry.

We made it to the pickup point in time and boarded. The bus was packed with hikers hauling wet gear. Miles and I sat side by side with our packs on our laps. As we rode toward Franklin in a cold, hard rain, relief moved me to tears.

Chapter 26
Franklin

Room service? Send up a larger room.
—Groucho Marx in *A Night at the Opera*

Eating a 780-calorie breakfast at McDonald's was as foreign to me as the Appalachian Trail had been, yet there I sat consuming scrambled eggs, hash browns, sausage, orange juice, a big biscuit, and coffee. Miles was doing the same on the opposite side of the booth. We had decided to take a zero our second day in Franklin, North Carolina. We were behind schedule, but most of it was weather related and couldn't be helped. Besides, Miles needed new boots.

Franklin is an Appalachian Gateway Community located 11 miles from the trail. As such, it is hiker friendly. Yesterday the town had welcomed us at our wettest, muddiest, and stinkiest when I could not wait to eliminate those descriptions on a personal level.

We were dropped off at the Sapphire Inn around 10:00 a.m. I would discover it was typical of the low-budget hotels in trail towns—warm, dry, and clean enough for folks who have been walking a path of dirt for weeks. *Décor* seemed too fancy a word for the outdated furnishings, but Miles and I were happy to be there. We unpacked and took turns cleaning our muddy tents in the bathtub. The six large, dripping pieces of cloth—two tents, two footprints (used between the tent floor and the ground), and two rain flies—then had to be hung somewhere to dry. We were on the second level of the hotel, so anything that didn't fit on the towel racks or shower enclosure was draped over the balcony outside to be ruffled by the wind. The Sapphire Inn after an invasion of hikers was a bit like a beach hotel, but instead of bright towels drying after a swim, tent parts flapped on the railings. I watched clouds fill the gray sky, praying for an end to the rain.

The shuttle came back at 4:00 p.m. to take us shopping. In the meantime, we did our laundry and cleaned ourselves up. I felt new again.

The bus let us off at Walmart for groceries and then took us to Three Eagles Outfitters. I needed a new pair of undies and wanted a hiker brand that would dry quickly. I saw no women's underpants in the store.

"We keep them under the counter," a clerk said. She retrieved a package of "one size fits all," explaining, "This is all we have."

They were $12. "I'll take them," I said. And that is how I came to own a pair of panties I nicknamed "the wedgie" and wore only when I was desperate. They were black, cut to hit below the waist, and made of a stretchy fabric. The stretch was for larger women. On me the leg openings were too big, thus creating an instant wedgie that guaranteed a few extra wiggles to "unseat" the offending fabric as I hiked along the trail.

We began our second morning, our zero, at McDonald's. Miles was always telling me to eat. She gave me multi-vitamins and calcium pills, which I hadn't brought from home because of the weight they would add to my pack. She gave me apricots and reminded me to eat bananas for potassium, especially during my Ibuprofen phase.

No one outside Hollywood would have called me fat, but I had yet to adjust my eating habits to those of a thru-hiker. I was used to watching my weight at home, where food had never been fuel to me. It was instead a "frenemy," both friend and enemy as I tried to balance my love of eating with my desire to keep my figure. Between the pre-hike eat-a-thon of meals with well-wishing friends and my inability to resist my food resupply snacks as I packed the boxes, I had nearly outgrown my hiking pants before setting foot on the AT.

Unlike *Wild* author Cheryl Strayed and other long-distance hikers who walked the trails to forget or heal, I was not "walking off" anything but the ten pounds I gained before I started. Now I had to learn to eat *more* because of the calories I was burning off every day. When Miles ordered a huge breakfast, one I couldn't imagine for myself, I ordered it, too.

We returned to the hotel to learn that a hiker named Buckle had been hit by a car crossing a busy intersection down the street. According to reports, the accident was not his fault; he had followed the signs for pedestrians, but the driver had proceeded against the traffic signal. Buckle's injuries were painful but not severe. He would be able to continue his thru-hike. We heard later that he was making good progress, stopping only for water.

Miles and I took the sidewalks to downtown Franklin for her new boots. A local outfitter had earned a reputation for expertise in fitting hikers for footwear. As we walked, I thought about growing up in a small town and later living in the suburbs. I had managed to avoid complicated street crossings most of my life. I could sympathize with Buckle, though our situations were not necessarily the same. I feel awkward at intersections, as though at my age I still didn't know how to cross the street.

Miles turned herself over to one of the shoe experts at the Outdoor 76 store. He showed us a model of the bones of the foot and told Miles why the boots she'd worn from home didn't fit correctly. She spent several hours trying on hiking boots, and I watched for a while and then wandered around the store, but didn't stay for the purchase.

For supper we got Subway to take to the room and split a tall Bud Light. I poured some of my beer down the sink and began packing. We were heading back to the trail in the morning. I remember thinking: *I can take a shower tomorrow before we leave, but it seems so extravagant; I just had one yesterday.*

Chapter 27
Sliding In

Fall seven times, stand up eight.
—Japanese proverb

In two days Miles and I would arrive at the Nantahala Outdoor Center. We had just left Franklin, where we resupplied, and already I was in misery, looking forward to the next stop. How could I have forgotten the feel of my pack straps bearing down on my shoulders from the weight of new food?

Humidity was 100 percent. We hiked eight miles—mostly uphill—in fog, mist, drizzle, and rain to reach Siler Bald Shelter but then couldn't find it. A bald is the treeless top of a mountain; Miles and I hiked the slippery trail to the top looking for either the shelter or a sign to guide us to it. You would think a building would stand out on a bald, but the rain was like a curtain around us. Could we have missed the shelter? We turned and started back down, weary from the day, hiking with care on the muddy path.

To our great relief, we found the side trail and then the shelter. If we hadn't, we would have had to camp.

The stone shelter was packed wall to wall with hikers, but they made room for Miles and me. A large overhang provided standing room, and a cooking shelf had been built at the front, so once we were in, we were in for the night. We watched later arrivals walk through wet grass to pitch their tents in the rain.

Dampness rolled into the shelter through its open front and stayed. I removed the rain cover from my backpack and looked for a place to hang it and my dripping rain jacket. Everyone else arrived with the same need, so finding an empty nail was a challenge and I knew that in the morning I would find my things still damp.

The weather had not improved by morning. Rain and mud abounded, and we had a 12-mile hike ahead of us. Hiking the trail was like a game of hopscotch. I had to straddle the worst of the mud puddles by stepping to the left or right on one foot as the path turned. On the uphills water flowed toward us, seeking its level.

"This reminds me of my grandpa's barnyard," Miles said.

When we arrived at Cold Spring Shelter, located on a mountaintop, I was depleted. My shoulders hurt, and I was too tired to get water or cook. I made a token appearance at the campfire ring but ate a Clif bar instead of a hot meal. All I wanted to do was curl up and go to sleep. Miles said she was worried about me. I didn't unburden myself to her, but it was obvious I had no energy. In addition, I had noticed masses of small red dots on my lower legs. When I took my boots off at night I would see that a red rash had bloomed near the top of each sock.

"It's petechiae," Miles said. I was glad to hear the light concern in her tone, for I didn't need urgency. At least the rash would not be my downfall: "Hiker Felled by Petechiae: An AT hiker known as Early Bird, or E.B., didn't realize what she was seeing when she observed the red spots on both legs at the sock line . . ."

I hadn't heard the term *petechiae*, but I concluded the rash must be caused by the amount of walking we were doing. Once I lay down at night, the condition would begin to reverse itself. Often the redness was gone by morning.

The leg rash wasn't my main problem. I was struggling, lethargic and listless every day. My intake of Vitamin I reduced my shoulder pain, but it wasn't a cure-all. I continued to blow off the daily chores hikers must do: collect and purify water, cook a hot meal, organize one's pack and possessions, hang a food bag, study the *A.T. Guide* and plan for the next day. All I could manage was to crawl into my sleeping bag and try to get warm. I hoped my aches and pains would heal overnight.

How was I going to walk 2,000 miles like this? I could barely manage to carry my pack and keep up with Miles. Our daily mileage goals were sure to increase. I couldn't keep taking Ibuprofen day and night. How could I be sharp on the trail? How could I help Miles if needed? I could barely drag myself from one place to the next.

Miles wasn't blind, but I was keeping the magnitude of my challenges to myself. I had to make good on my intention to complete the AT, and I knew I needed to make a drastic change. But what would it be? I could buy a lighter backpack for two or three hundred dollars—mine weighed almost five pounds empty—and send more gear home. Was that the answer? Whatever I did would have to wait; we were still in the mountains.

Hours after we left Cold Spring Shelter we stopped to take in the view from the gorgeous visitor overlook at Wayah Bald. We stood side by side and asked another hiker to take our picture. When I got a phone signal I posted the photo of our smiling faces to my Facebook page.

"Why do you post only happy pictures to Facebook?" Miles asked. "I'm tempted to stick out my tongue."

"I wouldn't post anything else," I said. "My friends are worried enough without seeing pictures of me sprawled in the dirt or you taping your feet every morning." Her new shoes had not eliminated all of her blisters.

Miles and I had another Facebook issue. Before we left home she asked if I would connect, or friend, with some of her buddies on the site so they could see our progress on the AT. She was not part of the Facebook community, but several friends and relatives were.

"Sure, I'd be glad to," I said. I meant it, but I didn't do it. I remember suggesting we look at Facebook together then and there; what better time? We were sitting near my computer. I remember Miles saying there was no hurry, but Memory is a trickster. Maybe it didn't happen that way at all.

We hadn't talked specifics—I had no list of names—and I let the matter drop. Perhaps to me it was a conversation we had, the way our early talks about the Appalachian Trail had seemed before we decided to hike together. To Miles, my lack of follow-through was a slap in the face, the Facebook invitations a small thing to ask—especially when her husband was supporting me during our hike. It was a sore that would fester.

We tramped though more muddy miles to get to our next stop, Wesser Bald Shelter. We were still in North Carolina, and the downpour continued. I was forming a grumpy impression of our second AT state. Rainwater filled our footprints as it had those of every hiker in front of us. I fell three times, the last being the most dramatic.

Wesser Bald Shelter is located down a hill off the trail. From above we could see the hikers huddled inside, the puddles in front of the shelter, and a hill made slick with wet rocks and black mud. Miles went first. That was a lucky thing for me because after a few steps, my feet flew out from under me. I landed on my backpack and began sliding downhill like a turtle on its shell, my arms and legs in the air.

I yelled, "Miles, help me! I can't stop!"

She moved into my path, anchoring herself in front of a tree, and blocked my descent. After serving as the entertainment for those in the shelter below, I emerged uninjured but a bit banged up from my series of spills. I was dripping wet, my pants muddy from hip to hem.

"You have to get out of those clothes," Miles said. She was right. I got my purple-striped base layer—my only dry outfit—from my pack and stood on the elevated sleeping platform, out of the mud. I had to take everything off. How was I going to change in a crowded shelter?

"Anyone who doesn't want to see a sixty-nine-year-old woman naked should turn away now," I said to the group of casual acquaintances and strangers. As one, they turned to face the rainy view outside, and I was soon in my warm clothes.

I like to have my things nearby, but Miles and I hadn't staked our claims to sleeping space yet. I found a nail in one of the walls and hung my hiking pants, my Smartwool shirt, my wet socks, and even my sports bra and panties on it. I had slim hopes they would dry, but what else could I do?

That night while I was sleeping, mice ate holes in my shirt. At least I wasn't wearing it at the time.

I saw the damage in the morning; one hole in the front of the shirt was as big as my face. Whether the mice swallowed the fabric or shredded it for a nest was irrelevant; my shirt was a useless rag. My pants, hung on the same nail, were intact, as were my undergarments. One sock had a small hole, but nothing to equal the destruction of my hiking shirt. We would be at the NOC the next day, and I would have to replace it.

Would the rain ever stop? Apparently not; at 6:45 a.m. the thunderstorms were loud and fierce. Leaving my sleeping bag was the second-last thing I wanted to do. What I dreaded even more was leaving the shelter to hike in the rain.

I kept my purple striped top on; that was easy—it was dry. The pants, not so much. "It must suck to be you," Miles said as I put one leg and then the other into my cold, wet pants. If the rain ever stopped, they would dry on the trail as we hiked.

There was no question we would hike to the NOC. We were five days behind the schedule we had made, a schedule I now knew was too ambitious in the first place.

At least that night we would be warm and dry. The NOC is a recreational complex. We could do laundry and eat in restaurants. I could visit the outfitter, where I hoped to find the cause and cure for my shoulder pain. I felt like my trials of the past few weeks— the horrible pain; the Ibuprofen days (or daze); the fatigue and the deception—were over.

Chapter 28
Miles to Go

Expect the best, plan for the worst
and prepare to be surprised.
—Author and motivational speaker Denis Waitley

We arrived at the Nantahala Outdoor Center on April 20. I noted the date because in six more days Miles and I should have our trail legs.

"On the twenty-eighth day of your hike, your pack will feel like it's a part of you. You'll have your trail legs. It will all come together." We heard that at Mountain Crossings the first week of our hike, and I was counting on it. I was eager to find out how it would feel to have trail legs; surely they would be an improvement.

We left our things in the hiker hostel and went to supper at the River's End restaurant, where we sat across from each other sipping beers and watching the Nantahala River rush by. Why weren't we talking?

Miles could make a conversation with anybody about anything; I had witnessed it many times. Places, books, nature, pets, world events—all were conversation starters for my hiking partner. It was a spark that eluded the two of us. We joined a table of other hikers and the conversation flowed comfortably around me. I ate my dinner, content to be a rock in the river.

We did our laundry after dark, used our headlamps to get back to our room, and turned in.

Morning dawned bright and clear at the NOC. It would be a good day for hiking. I was rested, clean, and on my way back from the ladies' room when Miles passed me on the stairs and said, "We need to talk."

I got a bad feeling. "We need to talk" meant *Miles* needed to talk. I had felt no such urges and was clueless as to what was coming. It wasn't long after we sat down together that I realized I truly must be clueless, like the stereotype; after all, I was one of those women who had taken to the trail with no hiking experience because of *Wild*.

"I can't trust you," Miles said, referring to my general lack of skills as a trail partner. "We should be able to count on each other, and I can't depend on you.

"You ran out of food. What if I hadn't had extra meals to give you? What if *I* had run out? You couldn't have helped me.

"You missed a white blaze directing us away from the edge of a cliff. I crawled out onto a boulder and could have been killed!

"Your falling scares me. You've been lucky so far, but what if you get seriously hurt?

"You're barely making the miles every day. I thought we would be company for each other in the evenings, but you fall asleep right after supper."

None of it was spoken harshly, and everything she said was true; it was our perceptions that were different. I hadn't realized the partner who bailed me out when I ran out of supplies, the one who slowed her pace to hike with me, the one who helped me when I fell was so disappointed, even angry.

Everything she worried about could happen, but was the picture all bad? What about the time Miles lost her balance on a high rock and I grabbed her arm? She said I saved her life.

Now she said, "I feel like getting on the next bus for home." Miles had invited herself on this hike, and I was glad to have her company. Now she wanted to un-invite herself and leave me alone to walk the remaining miles of the AT through 12 more states.

It was a wake-up call. I had to make some changes, and fast, if I expected to hike out with a trail partner that afternoon. I didn't want to go on alone, but I could; and, even if Miles left, the problems wouldn't go away. I needed to have my pack adjusted to stop the shoulder pain. I had to hike without taking Ibuprofen all day. I could send more items home to reduce the weight. I had to be more accurate in estimating my supplies, and I had to pay more attention to my *A.T. Guide* pages instead of depending on Miles to know the details. Could I do all of that? What was the alternative?

First, I went through my pack and eliminated weight. My Samsung tablet and its charging cord were among the casualties— the items I put in a box to send to Mr. M in Cincinnati. From that point on, I would write on paper.

Next, I told Miles I'd see her later and I took my pack to the outdoor store for a fitting. I learned that the pack, as adjusted in the store where I bought it, was too long in the torso for me. In addition, I was wearing it incorrectly. Those issues, combined with a heavy load, had caused my incessant shoulder pain since Helen, Georgia.

When I purchased my pack back home, the hip belt had been "cooked" to fit me, but I was wearing my pack wrong. "Over the hip bones" does not mean across the hip bones, as I thought; it means above them. The hip belt actually goes at the waist, so that the load rests on the hips and not the shoulders. Eureka!

The NOC expert adjusted the torso, made sure I could put the pack on correctly, and then adjusted the shoulder-height load lifters. I couldn't wait for those to work. Before I left the store, I bought a new shirt to replace the one lying full of holes in the trash can in our room. I might have been clueless in general, but at least I was smarter than shelter mice. The new shirt would *not* become mouse bait.

I returned to our room prepared to find it vacated, but Miles was still there and we left the NOC together. I knew right away my shoulders were not going to ache the way they had before. I could hike longer, and that was fortunate because we had to climb a mountain upon returning to the trail. The climb was long and slow—six hours and as many miles—during which we encountered false summits time after time. A hiker we met from Germany passed us and soon afterward yelled down to tell us she had reached the top. Moments later she yelled again: "Sorrrrry!"

Two nights later we set up at Brown Fork Gap Shelter. Miles decided to stay in the shelter, and I pitched my tent. Even though she had not gone home, I was feeling the effects of our talk about my inadequacies. She came up to me while I was positioning my tarp on the ground.

"I haven't been completely honest with you," she began. If that was the case, what could possibly come next?

"My mother is quite ill," she said. "I'm going home in two days. It has nothing to do with you."

I was silent. *Processing*, as the computers used to say.

"If the worst happens, I am my mother's executor," Miles said, implying a long commitment. "I don't know if or when I will come back to the trail."

I was sorry to hear about her mom, whom I knew.

We would reach Fontana Village, North Carolina—gateway to Great Smoky Mountains National Park—the next afternoon, Thursday. Miles' husband would arrive on Saturday to take her home.

I was going on alone, after all. And it wasn't my fault. When I thought about Miles' words later, I wondered: What was the relationship between that message and our talk at the NOC? What had Miles not been honest about?

The distance to Fontana was 12.6 miles, my longest hike yet in a single day. Both of us were exhausted by afternoon. As we made our way down the mountain toward Fontana Dam, Miles made phone reservations for three nights at the lodge in Fontana Village. She and I would share a room for the first two nights, and on Saturday before Mr. M arrived I would move to a separate room.

When we came off the trail at a marina, Miles called a shuttle to take us to the lodge. We checked in and retrieved our packages from the desk. It was wonderful to clean up and have an extravagant dinner of broiled trout, sweet potato casserole, salad, bread and butter, and a glass of wine in the restaurant. I no longer felt the tension that had plagued me for the last few days, because the end of our time on the trail together was near. Miles must have felt it, too.

The next day we had breakfast in our room: food from our packs. We accomplished our usual chores, going from the Laundromat to the General Store, where Miles bought souvenirs and I resupplied. For lunch we split a Supreme pizza on the porch of the Wildwood Grill, enjoying the fact that our hiker hunger had kicked in. We took a leisurely approach to the day, visiting with hikers we knew. The sun was shining, but someone mentioned a bad forecast.

On Saturday as we waited on the patio for Mr. M, I watched the sky. The next morning they would depart for Ohio and I would enter the Smokies alone and hike straight uphill for 11 miles. I was hoping for good weather.

That afternoon the three of us found where the northbound trail picked up and walked part of it, saving me 1.1 miles in the morning. We passed the Fontana Hilton, so named for being one of the nicest shelters on the AT, and encountered trail magic courtesy of the

Noah's Ark Hiking Ministries, a group of widows. We finished with a trip to the marina, where we ate potato chips and drank Bud Light on the water.

I spent my last evening in the lodge getting ready for my hike. I could have gone home, but once again I chose to stay. I was partly scared and partly relieved. How would I fare on the trail?

Miles and I had started the AT at Amicalola Falls on March 30. Sunday would mark 28 days of hiking, the "magic day," April 26. What was magic about it now?

Since the adjustments at the NOC, my pack felt like a part of me—as predicted. I should have my trail legs next, and with Miles leaving I needed them more than ever. She and I made so many plans. We thought we'd summit Mt. Katahdin together. Now it was just me.

Sunday was the day we were promised everything would come together. Instead, were my plans coming apart?

PART 2
NONE ON

Chapter 29

Watch Me Pull a Rabbit
Out of My Pocket

Weather forecast for tonight: dark.
—**George Carlin**

If "One on" meant a hiker was coming up behind us, then "None on" should mean no one was there. "None on" meant one thing to me as I slid my folded registration paper into the thru-hiker slot at the southern boundary of Great Smoky Mountains National Park: no Miles.

On April 26 she and Mr. M accompanied me across Fontana Dam to the point on the other side where the Appalachian Trail enters the park. He wore my pack until the last minute, letting me enjoy the walk without its weight until time to put it on my own back and resume my hike of the AT. By then the trail did not surprise me by winding uphill for miles. Approaching a town from the trail generally means coming down off a mountain, and leaving that town means the opposite.

The day was overcast when we started out from the lodge. Puddles dotted the ground from the most recent rain, and I had put the rain cover on my pack. By the time I stood for a photo at the southern park boundary, I had shed my rain jacket and the sun was out. After we said our good-byes, Miles and Mr. M headed home to Ohio. I turned and headed up the mountain alone.

Wasn't this what I expected all along? Wasn't it what I prepared for?

Now I could return to my original intent, with all of the awareness it required. I would explore the trail on my own and discover how to navigate it without Miles. She had been the main one to interpret our *A.T. Guide* pages; we rarely sat down together to plan the next day's hike. I suppose it was a symptom of the growing awkwardness between us, but it was wrong. We should have been collaborating.

Some nights I hadn't looked at my pages at all. Miles would lie in her sleeping bag studying the next day's route with her headlamp while I closed my eyes to fall asleep. If I did read a section, I soon forgot the details and would have to read the same material again. As part of my improvement plan after our talk at the NOC, I studied my pages even though Miles was doing the same. It was good training for the days following her departure.

Not only would I be navigating the AT alone now; I would also have an opportunity to discover in more depth how the Appalachian Trail was going to change me. It was all good, wasn't it?

When I planned my solitary hike, before Miles entered the picture, I had limited knowledge of the AT. Now I had hiked 165 miles of it. I knew what living on the trail was like. I knew I had a lot to learn. I knew how easily I could fall and hurt myself. I knew I might be alone at night, my scariest time in the forest. Didn't it take more courage *now* to go on?

Signs of civilization disappeared as I continued up the wooded trail. For weeks I had heard other hikers say they looked forward to "getting through the Smokies," as though the 71 miles of trail in the park were obstacles beyond the usual challenges of the AT. What did it mean? I was aware of the regulations spelled out in thru-hiker permits, for instance that we had to get through the park in eight days or less and were required to sleep in the shelters unless they were full. I didn't understand the hiker negativity and didn't want to look at the next week like that. It was important for me to enjoy my hike and maintain a positive frame of mind, especially now.

I was not yet done with the trail, or it with me, but I felt Miles's absence both behind me and in front of me as I made my way up the mountain. I missed her, but I also felt a new sense of freedom. That feeling reminded me of Easter morning when I was climbing out of Neel Gap and suddenly knew that if I had to, I could hike the AT alone.

But was I really alone?

I felt my right cargo pocket for the assurance that Ms. Rabbit, my new traveling companion, was there. My fingers found her shape through the cloth. No, I hadn't tucked a live animal in my pants pocket; Ms. Rabbit was made of glass. The piece was bright electric blue, circular, about the size of a half dollar but thicker, with the clear profile of a rabbit etched into one side.

Ms. Rabbit was a sweet and generous gift from my friend Anita. She had told me to look for the package before I left home: "I'm sending you a good luck charm to take on your hike. It's a glass rabbit I've had for forty years. Whenever I had to do something new, challenging, or scary in my life, I had it in my pocket. Now I want you to have it for your adventure on the trail."

I knew of Anita's fondness for rabbits, but she didn't know I'd been afraid of them since 1972, when I watched the movie *Night of the Lepus*. It's the story of a rancher in Arizona who hires a scientist to control the rabbit population on his land. The solution goes wrong, producing what the entertainment website IMDB calls "a race of bloodthirsty, wolf-sized, man-, horse-, and cow-eating bunnies." I can still picture their hormone-grown bodies, still hear them pounding across pastures in the moonlight.

Luckily, only large, live rabbits give me the creeps.

I missed Anita's package by days, so my brother forwarded the little box to Fontana Lodge. With Miles' departure imminent, the timing was perfect. I opened the box and held Ms. Rabbit in my hand. The etching added personality to the glass and forged an instant connection between us. From that moment I could see one-way conversations in my future, as talking to inanimate objects was nothing new.

Now, glancing around, I spoke to my new companion for the first time. "Well, Ms. Rabbit, it's you and me."

I decided to take it easy my first day in the Smokies. I no longer had to hike aggressively the way I had with Miles. I wanted to find my pace and appreciate a sunny day in the mountains. I met a few other hikers and stopped to take pictures of the scenery, but I wondered: Could a person have it both ways? How could I take more time and still make adequate progress?

I was starting out one week behind schedule. Nevertheless, I decided to stop after seven miles to camp for the night at Birch Spring Gap. On the way I passed the side trail to Shuckstack Fire Tower. I skipped the tower because I had no one to watch my pack while I climbed to it. Bears are known to swipe abandoned backpacks for the food, so I continued on.

The first overnight target for northbound hikers in the Smokies is Mollies Ridge Shelter, nearly a ten-mile hike from the southern park entrance. On that beautiful day, alone for the first time in weeks, I forgot about the shelter mandate. I was not supposed to camp. The mandate was created to reduce the impact on the environment of many people putting up tents. It also offered protection from the bear population, and I was too afraid of bears to disregard it deliberately.

Great Smoky Mountains National Park boasts 800 black bears, not to mention a population of wild boars. Park rangers carry canisters of bear spray—not to be confused with bear canisters, which hold food—and I'd been advised to do the same if I hiked alone through the park.

Here's the thing about bear spray: It must be used with caution, yet deployed quickly and correctly if a dangerous situation arises. Seconds count and snap decisions become necessary. The painful, peppery solution released and ideally aimed at a charging bear's face can be misdirected by wind or hiker error. In worst-case scenarios it can spray the hiker instead of the bear. It can miss the bear or further provoke the animal by hitting a less vulnerable spot than the face. The spray from the can lasts only a few seconds and is effective within 30 feet. In other words, you must wait until the bear is almost upon you to flip the safety cap and pull the trigger. If the spray doesn't reach the animal, the animal might reach you.

I could think myself into a tailspin on the topic of bears, but all of it was academic. The dark scenarios I imagined were rare, and I hadn't seen any bears. Great Smoky Mountains National Park is spread over 522,447 acres. If you do the math, each of the 800 bears has 650 acres to play around in. If one decided to misbehave, what were the odds it would be in my area that night and would pick me? And—most academic of all—I no longer had bear spray with me.

I'd sent the canister home because of my pack shakedown at Neel Gap, but once I knew I would be hiking solo through the Smokies I asked Miles' husband to bring it to Fontana Village. When I held it again, I remembered the metal canister in its holster bumping against my right hip with every step. I remembered it sliding along the belt that held it. Besides those annoyances, it wasn't any smaller or lighter than it had been back in Georgia. I sent it back to Ohio again and hoped I was not making a mistake.

Many hikers pooh-pooh the idea of carrying bear spray. Most of the folks Miles and I met were eager to see wild animals. They believed a bear would run away when encountering a human. That would be good.

I arrived at the Birch Spring Gap camping area at 2:00 p.m. The campsite is located in a big bowl below the trail. That afternoon it was empty except for a green tent and a blue food bag hung from a cable next to a brown hammock. I seemed to be the only person around, but it was early.

By the time I stepped off the trail, the sun was going in and out. A wind had come up. I saw three logs placed at 90-degree angles around a campfire ring to define an eating area. The fourth side was a stone wall. Initially it seemed like a safe place to camp and I wanted to pitch my tent there, out of the wind, but stone walls draw snakes. Instead I hiked down the hill and found a flat spot near a creek.

I put up my tent in a light rain and then got inside. I was tired, yawning in spite of my great sleep the previous night at Fontana Lodge. I drifted for an hour in my sleeping bag and then got up to cook supper. At 5:00 it was chilly enough for my goose down jacket. I cooked a hiker meal in a foil envelope and ate it sitting on one of the logs up the hill. A group of male hikers came by while I was eating, stopped to talk a few minutes, and then hiked on. After supper I hung my whole pack on a bear cable for the night and returned to my tent, stepping on rocks to cross the creek.

As night fell I was still alone despite the green tent on the hillside and the brown hammock with the blue food bag. I took Ms. Rabbit out of my pants pocket with my phone and wallet and put her in one of the mesh pockets sewn to the inside of my tent. "Good night," I said aloud.

Twelve hours later I felt like I'd been camping at Birch Spring Gap forever. It had been about 15 hours since I'd arrived. A schedule that generous would not work as a long-term plan. I thought of Miles and her determination. Now that I was on my own, would I push myself?

I left my tent and was surprised to see Jot and Huckleberry, a married couple I knew. They had come in to camp after I was down for the night.

After breakfast I packed up. Ms. Rabbit and I left the campground at 8:00 a.m. for the eight-mile hike to Russell Field Shelter. I learned two days later that the Birch Spring camping area was being closed because of bear activity.

Chapter 30
Stay or Go?

Quitting is the easiest thing to do.
—Author Robert Kiyosaki

The sun was shining on April 27 as I hiked toward my second destination in Great Smoky Mountains National Park, Russell Field Shelter. Was it a shelter in a field, or was it named for someone? A person hiking on her own can puzzle over questions like that unless she is distracted.

Beep-beep, beep-beep, beep-beep!

It was a familiar signal that would repeat every few minutes in my ear until I changed my hearing aid batteries. Each battery is good for five or six days. When one goes it's prudent to change both, and there is no reward in trying to ignore the beeping.

"If a tree falls in the forest and I have my hearing aids out, does it still make a noise?" I said to Ms. Rabbit. "Let's stop a minute so I can change these batteries."

I looked for a stable surface. My hearing aids are the size of dimes, only thicker, and cost hundreds of dollars each. I had dropped many a battery and even the hearing aids on the carpets at home, ending up on my hands and knees. All the possibilities grew worse on the AT.

"If I drop one of these things onto this path of sticks and earth and light-brown leaves," I said, "I am screwed. If it bounces? Even worse."

Ms. Rabbit had nothing to say, but I knew. A battery, being silver, might be easy to find on the ground, but the device would blend in. I laid everything on a big rock, opened the little doors on the hearing aids, made the change, and safely returned the devices to my ears.

"All right, good for another six days," I said as I swung my pack onto my shoulders.

Where would I be in six days? Through the Smokies or darn close, if things went as planned.

I was surprised I rarely saw anyone else on the trail. Jot and Huckleberry were somewhere behind me. When I met a gray-haired gentleman coming southbound, I was happy to stop and chat. He was a ridge runner, a person hired to cover certain areas of the park on foot. Ridge runners are said to be the ambassadors of the trail. They share their knowledge of the back country, offer help when needed, check hiker permits, monitor wildlife activity, and perform maintenance at shelters.

"Where are you headed today?" he asked.

"Russell Field Shelter."

"My advice is to hike past Russell Field and go on to Spence Field Shelter," he said. "It will add about three miles to your day, but if you don't do it you will have a difficult hike tomorrow. The terrain becomes rougher and you'll feel those three extra miles."

"Thanks." I didn't look forward to the extra miles, but I knew he was giving me good advice.

I ate lunch alone at Mollie's Ridge Shelter. Hikers who spent the previous night there had already cleared out.

After my previous night camping, I didn't want to get stuck between shelters. I covered the 11 miles and arrived at Spence Field Shelter around 4:00 p.m. My first priority was always the same: I took my pack off and laid it on the dusty floor to reserve my space in the shelter. My second priority was to free my aching feet from my hiking boots. By then the boots had hundreds of miles on them, and I noticed the rubber on the front was coming off. I swapped the boots for my camp sandals, leaving my socks on for warmth.

Spence Field Shelter sits on a mountaintop, and the air was already chilly when I fixed a supper of ramen noodles with veggies. I was the lone female sharing cooking space with six men. All of them were friendly. They gathered wood for a fire and built it inside the shelter, where a stone fireplace dominated one wall. A full tarp covered the front of the shelter to stop the wind and keep the heat in. I was inside and cozy by 5:40 p.m. One or two other women drifted in later. I could hear their voices after I snuggled into my sleeping bag and closed my eyes.

I woke up in the dark, gasping with back pain. I slept on a pad, but darn those hard shelter floors! Darn that pack, and darn the mountains. I turned my headlamp to its red-light setting so I wouldn't disturb anyone and looked at my watch. It was 2:13 a.m.

My friend Betty used to say all our thoughts and fears are magnified at night. I was trying to get comfortable among strangers in the wee hours on top of a mountain in Tennessee—or possibly North Carolina, as the AT follows the border for many miles. The fire had gone out. The men and women around me were all asleep now, and I was feeling lonely—the kind of lonely my friend Ms. Rabbit could not cure.

I let my thoughts go where they would.

Did I want more days like the last two, hiking alone with a glass rabbit for companionship? I loved the green forest floor and the tiny flowers that lined the trail by the thousands now. I loved the sunny days that marked the end of the mud and rain we had in southern North Carolina. I liked the hiking community, but most hikers in the group Miles and I had met were now ahead of me. I was enjoying the beauty of the trail, but was it enough? Was it enough to see a handful of cordial strangers every day?

After ten days of hiking northward on the Pacific Crest Trail, Cheryl Strayed wanted to leave it. Staggering toward Kennedy Meadows in *Wild*, she thought about all the other people she knew—the ones who were not on the PCT but were having fun or relaxing in air-conditioned comfort while she was enduring the intense, miserable heat of the trail. "I was going to quit," she wrote. "*Quit, quit, quit.*" Quit and go to Alaska.

When I pictured the Appalachian Trail from home, I envisioned a steady stream of hikers in colorful outfits, chattering away as they walked a dirt path in the sunshine. I knew the weather could change. I knew the trail would hold many surprises, yet entering that parade alone had seemed easy enough. Now the trail wasn't crowded the way I'd imagined. Two days of solitude in the mountains made me wonder: Did I want to keep hiking for the next few months? I wasn't sure I did.

I was planning to resupply in Gatlinburg, Tennessee in two days, but I didn't have to resupply and continue north on the AT. I could get a ride to the nearest airport, buy a ticket, and fly home. It could happen that quickly. I grew mellow as I realized how simple it would be to leave. No more cold mountaintops. No more wood planks for a bed. No more worrying about bears. No more long days of silence. I could be home.

With those thoughts in mind, I fell asleep.

Chapter 31
Out of the Woods

Getting to the top is optional. Getting down is mandatory.
—Mountaineer Ed Viesturs

Cheryl Strayed didn't quit after allowing herself the fantasy of quitting, and neither did I.

Cheryl wrote of her next day in *Wild*: "I hiked in the heat of that day with a new determination . . . I didn't give quitting another thought."

I knew it! Cheryl and I were leading parallel lives, if that was possible across time. My feelings of homesickness passed the next day, too, and I continued to my next destination, Derrick Knob Shelter.

In daylight, on the move, I could see the long view of my hike and no longer wanted to abandon the trail and fly home. I spent the morning hiking over jagged Thunderhead Mountain, a hard few hours. On the way I passed the scenic view at Rocky Top and wondered if it inspired the 1960s hit song of the same name depicting life in the Tennessee mountains.

During those first days hiking alone, I discovered what kept me going. It was curiosity. What was over the hill I was climbing? What would be around the next curve? Would the path smooth out, head upward, or start down? Could I spot the next white blaze? The possibilities renewed my energy and I was like a compass needle fixed on North.

By then I was talking to Ms. Rabbit on a regular basis. "We ought to be near the top of this mountain," I might say to her, "don't you think?" When I was hungry and tired at the end of the day I'd ask Ms. Rabbit, "Where in the h--- is the shelter? We should be there by now." As "we" hiked, I spoke my random thoughts aloud with a wild sense of freedom. Silliness, frustration, and fear flowed out of me, and it was trail therapy. Ms. Rabbit listened well and would not be serving up advice.

I spent the night in one crowded shelter and set out in the morning for the next one, seven and a half miles away, but not before taping my boots. They were falling apart. Not only were the fronts peeling; the soles were wearing down. I could feel every rock I stepped on. At home I'd wrapped two kinds of tape around my hiking poles: silver duct tape and black Gorilla tape. It was a combination of both that decorated my boots as I hiked over the ridges toward my next stop.

I wondered how Miles' mother was doing. I was out of touch with the world beyond the trail. That was part of the attraction of hiking, but I liked to check in with my family and friends occasionally. A weather forecast or a glance at Facebook would have been nice. As I reached every treeless mountaintop or open field I tried my phone, usually in vain.

"This damn thing couldn't get a signal in an AT&T store," I said to Ms. Rabbit.

I stopped for lunch at a shelter six miles out and was glad to see Jot and Huckleberry join the crowd of hikers relaxing in the sun. During lunch I learned our mild weather was about to change. There was talk of a storm coming later that day. The forecast of rain and thunderstorms was driving hikers out of the woods and into Gatlinburg. I had planned to finish hiking to Double Spring Gap Shelter that afternoon, but now I wondered what to do.

"Do you want to come with us?" Jot said. "We're hiking to Clingman's Dome. From there we'll get a ride into Gatlinburg."

Skipping a consultation with Ms. Rabbit, I decided to do it. The possibility of being stuck in the mountains by myself during a storm was too strong to ignore, and I knew how to secure a ride. After hiking with a company called A Walk in the Woods in 2014, I kept in touch with our guide, Jaimie. The company ran a shuttle service in addition to guided hikes through the Smokies.

I tried to call but had no luck. Jot, so named because she liked to jot things down, said, "Go over and stand on that block of concrete. I got reception there."

I was ready to try anything, including crossing the grass to stand on what looked like the cover of a well. It worked! Though I couldn't speak with anyone at A Walk in the Woods, I gave my name and left a message.

"I'm calling from Silers Bald Shelter on Wednesday, April twenty-ninth," I said. "I'll be hiking to Clingman's Dome today with two other people. There are storm warnings for later this afternoon, and we'll need a shuttle to Gatlinburg. We should arrive at the Clingman's Dome parking lot between five and six o'clock."

I hiked out with Jot and her husband. Huckleberry led as we followed the trail under overcast skies. Despite the weather report, I was happy. I had company for the hike and we were on our way to safety. This new plan would put me in Gatlinburg one day early, but I would not be leaving the AT from the same departure point as planned to get there. After leaving town I'd still be behind schedule, and maybe it was time to say, "So what?"

Clingman's Dome is the highest point in Tennessee on the third highest mountain east of the Mississippi, so it was a no-brainer that we'd be hiking uphill to get there. A mist fell on us as we followed the trail through pine forests laden with loose brown needles, past fallen logs bearing the brightest green moss I had seen. I didn't feel pressured by my companions to hurry, but we all felt the urgency of the approaching storm. We stopped for pee and snack breaks but kept them short.

Hiking out became an endurance test as we climbed Mt. Buckley to get to Clingman's Dome. By then it was raining and we were tired and cold. The average high temperature on Clingman's Dome in April is 49 degrees.

At last we left the trail to walk the foggy half-mile of paved road to the parking lot. The weather had gotten worse and now we were in a downpour. We were on time, and I wondered if our shuttle would be there. Had anyone at A Walk in the Woods heard my phone message? I hoped they had because we were now in a cold, wet whiteout with the worst visibility I'd seen since Miles and I entered Woody Gap back in Georgia. It was late in the day and we were 25 miles from Gatlinburg. The only sane way to get to town was in a vehicle.

"Look," I cried, "a building!" as the one-story visitor center appeared out of the fog. *Please be open*, I thought as we headed for the door. I was desperate for relief from the elements. Once inside, we removed our packs and leaned them against a wall.

"I'll go down to the parking lot and look for the shuttle," I said.

Our hopes for a ride dimmed when I had to tell my friends I did not find anyone waiting for us, and those hopes went out when the two rangers at the visitor center told us the building would be closing shortly. In a few minutes we would have to leave. The area had all but cleared of visitors and cars. What would we do?

Suddenly the door to the visitor center opened and I recognized Jaimie beneath a dripping black umbrella. She had come for us!

"You saved us," I said, lurching toward her for a hug. I hadn't been so glad to see someone in a long time.

The tourist town of Gatlinburg, unlike the mountains that surrounded it, was not lost in a whiteout. No storm raged through the streets, and the air was warmer in the valley. The differences were typical for changes in elevation. Jaimie drove Jot and Huckleberry to their hotel and took me to the Gatlinburg Inn, whose location in the center of the shopping district would make it easy for me to get around. I planned to take a zero the next day, resupply, and return to the trail in two days.

Upon checking in I learned that "Rocky Top" was written in ten minutes by a married songwriting team who stayed in Room 388 of the inn. Their 1967 composition became one of the state songs of Tennessee.

After I checked in I discarded my damp clothing and took a shower, wondering if there was enough hot water in the whole town to warm me up. I did laundry and ate a late supper from my food bag—peanut butter and raisins on a tortilla. I bought a Sprite from the vending machine across the hall. While I ate, I parted my curtains and looked out at the parking lot and the busy street beyond it. I raised my eyes to the mountains, jagged silhouettes against the night sky, and thought: *I was just there.* Gosh, it was nice to be indoors and clean, to have a full tummy and not have to hang a food bag. I crawled into bed and slept.

Chapter 32
April Ice

The best laid schemes o' Mice an' Men,
Gang aft agley,
An' lea'e us nought but grief an' pain,
For promis'd joy!
—From "To a Mouse" by Robert Burns

My room at the Gatlinburg Inn had sliding glass doors to a balcony that faced the main street. In the morning I sat on my bed with the curtains open and looked at the mountains again. I had been to Gatlinburg before and was used to thinking of the town at ground level—a colorful daily carnival of tourists and shops and food—yet after a month of thru-hiking I could not look away from the tall, imposing hills framing the downtown. Clouds hung low over the ridges, and I was glad for my respite from the trail.

I feasted at the free breakfast buffet, taking cereal, orange juice, coffee, eggs, sausage, and a biscuit. Bins of single-serve jelly, honey, and Smuckers peanut butter called to me from the food line. They were perfect for the trail, but how could I smuggle out extras? I had nothing to carry them in. The restaurant was filling up, and wasn't that a minister at the next table? He had the voice for it, holding court with a Bible open in front of him. I would have to think about hoarding condiments in a manner I could live with.

I hung my tent pieces on the balcony railing to dry. Clouds were moving in at 9:15 a.m. I left Ms. Rabbit on the dresser and walked a few blocks to the Gatlinburg branch of the Nantahala Outdoor Center (NOC) to pick up fuel and mountain meals. Jot was there doing the same thing. On the way back to the hotel I detoured into Walgreen's for a sack of junk food. Back at the inn I stopped at the desk, glad to see the friendly older lady I'd met when I checked in.

"I wonder if I could buy a few packets of jelly and peanut butter from your restaurant," I said.

"Honey, you just take what you need. We have plenty."

"Are you sure?"

"Why, yes," she said, and I stopped in the serving area on the way to my room, relieved to find it empty. I felt guilty despite being invited to help myself. I opened my Walgreen's bag and dropped in enough packets of peanut butter and jelly to last until my next stop. It would be counterproductive to take more; pack weight was always a consideration.

At 2:45 I was sitting in a rocker on my balcony eating Cheez-Its while dark clouds crossed the mountaintops. It was mostly sunny in town, but I knew any hikers remaining on the AT could be drenched by rain. Tomorrow I'd be back on the trail. My plan was to get a shuttle to the Clingman's Dome parking lot in the morning. Meanwhile, some porch time was in order.

At home my brother and I like to sit outside in good weather and talk about life while we people-watch or enjoy nature. He has a little porch off his apartment, and I have a deck at the back of my condo. I called Joe on my cell phone and we shared some lighthearted long-distance porch time while cars crawled by and tourists clogged the sidewalks of Gatlinburg. It was good to laugh; I realized I hadn't in a while.

That evening I put my tent in its bag and organized my pack for the next day. When I was done I turned on the TV for the first time since leaving Amicalola Falls and watched it until I fell asleep.

In my scurrying and organizing to get back to the AT, I almost missed the news. Clingman's Dome Road, where I needed to go, was closed due to ice and snow! On the last day of April, a cold front had swept through the mountains and left the road impassable. No doubt the trail was treacherous.

I booked my room for another night. Even though I was no longer splitting hotel bills with Miles, cost was a non-issue compared to the danger I could have faced had I stayed on the trail. Conditions were expected to improve in another 24 hours, so I secured a ride for the next morning through the front desk. The same woman who offered me a free supply of peanut butter and jelly recommended a taxi service that could pick me up at 7:00 a.m.

I thought of a couple lines from a poem by Robert Burns. In modern English they would have read, "Our best-laid plans can go awry."

I woke up at 5:00 on May 2, got out of the taxi with my pack three hours later, hiked back up the paved road past the visitor center, and re-entered the trail. Jot and Huckleberry had managed to day-hike this section before the storm while I sat eating crackers and Fruit Roll-Ups in town, so I was alone except for Ms. Rabbit. I felt my pocket for her familiar shape.

"Let's rock and roll," I said, watching my footing. "Well, not literally."

The woods were hushed, the way you might think after a storm. Snow clung to the pine branches above me.

It wasn't long before I came to a cooler someone had left by the trail. In it was a Tupperware container full of big Snickers bars.

"Trail magic!" I said to Ms. Rabbit. "I can't eat nuts—diverticulosis—but I'm taking one of these." The candy bar was a hiker favorite. I put it in my pack, figuring I could at least hand it off to someone who missed the stash, and continued on.

I had hiked halfway through the Smokies in four days. My hiatus in Gatlinburg did not count toward the eight-day limit for thru-hikers. My plan for my return to the trail was to hike from Clingman's Dome to Icewater Spring Shelter, just over 11 miles of extreme ups and downs. The large trailhead at Newfound Gap would provide a break 8 miles in.

"But what about the larger picture, Ms. Rabbit? What about the next two months?"

I had to assume Miles was out of the picture. According to the schedule she and I made—a schedule that didn't allow for ice storms and other hiccups—I should have exited the Great Smoky Mountains five days ago. But that was only half the trouble.

Miles and I were doing a "flip." If she had stayed on the trail, we would have hiked north to Harpers Ferry by July 2 and taken some time for ourselves before Mr. M picked us up two days later for the drive to Maine. After our time in Maine, he planned to return home. Miles and I were going to hike south until we reached Harpers Ferry again.

"That plan flew out the window a week ago," I said to Ms. Rabbit. "The flip would have been fine if Miles had stayed, but now things have changed. Now I have to think about what works for me."

I remained torn between the schedule and the way I felt. I wanted more time, but I didn't really have it. "Can I even make it to Harpers Ferry by early July?"

The timing was important even without Miles. It is said that if a northbound hiker doesn't reach Harpers Ferry by July 4, that hiker is not likely to make it to Mt. Katahdin by October 15.

"And what if I do reach Harpers Ferry on time? I no longer have a ride to Maine. Do I still want to do a flip? Do I want to get *myself* to Maine and hike south?"

I answered my own question. "No. Definitely not."

Aside from the cost of traveling there, Maine seemed cold, remote, and far from home now that I was alone. I had been sightseeing years before in southern Maine, around Portland, but on the AT Mt. Katahdin lay 285 miles north of the Maine-New Hampshire border. I was headed there regardless, but flipping was suddenly too sudden. I wanted to approach Maine gradually.

I was back to Plan A, the solo plan I had abandoned weeks before my departure for the AT. I was now on a different journey from the one Miles and I had begun.

After some trail magic at the busy Newfound Gap trailhead and parking area, I hiked on to Icewater Spring Shelter. The day was sunny and the trail was loaded with hikers going in both directions. I passed a side trail to Charlie's Bunion, a scenic stone outcropping on an otherwise sheer mountain face. The sign read "CLOSELY CONTROL CHILDREN," and hikers were advised to climb Charlie's Bunion without their backpacks in order to maintain their balance on the rock. That was enough to stop me, even if I hadn't been too tired to hike the additional distance for the view.

My sense of isolation came back that evening as I sat on the step of the shelter to change my shoes. I watched the other hikers, all younger, sitting in groups on the grass or putting up their tents in pairs as the orange sun sank toward the valley behind them. One young woman's voice rose above the others as she spoke her every thought aloud in a constant stream of chatter. I got up and took a path around the building, where I passed a father and his middle-aged son cooking their supper together.

Miles could find common ground with anyone we met, but she was not there and I knew I must expand my social boundaries. I stopped and introduced myself to the two men. We chatted about common hiker topics—weather, nature, and the trail experience.

That night I fell asleep thinking about new boots. My feet were not holding up against the miles of hilly, rocky trail. I wondered why I hadn't looked for new footwear in Gatlinburg, but before I could answer my own question, reasoning slipped away. At least I was not thinking, "Quit, quit, quit" or longing for home.

Chapter 33
Don't Fence Me In

Freedom is nothing but a chance to be better.
—Albert Camus

In the Smoky Mountains the Appalachian Trail hop-scotches between North Carolina and Tennessee. It then follows the border for another 94 miles and crosses into Tennessee for good at a place called Devil's Creek Gap. I looked forward to having two states behind me on my hike, but I would not have both feet in Tennessee for another 122 miles.

Had I become one of those hikers who looked forward to getting through the Smokies? For me the park wasn't an obstacle so much as a milestone.

My plan was to spend three more nights in Great Smoky Mountains National Park. I would hike to Peck's Corner Shelter, sleep there, and go on to Cosby Knob Shelter the next day. Davenport Shelter would be my last overnight stop before I reached the northern boundary of the park. At the boundary I would relinquish the thru-hiker permit I carried, putting it into a metal box near the exit as proof I had completed that section of the AT and was moving on.

After strapping on my pack and bidding *adieu* to Icewater Spring Shelter, I reached into my right front cargo pocket to make sure I'd put Ms. Rabbit there. I was relieved to find her familiar shape resting against my phone. Ms. Rabbit had become important to my thinking—at least when I thought out loud.

"So," I began on the downhill mile toward Charlie's Bunion, "how am I doing, Ms. Rabbit?" I'd been on my own for a week. For hours on end, it was just Ms. Rabbit and me, climbing the hills and walking a path that kept getting narrower with every growth spurt of the surrounding plant life.

"Have my hiking skills improved?" I said. "I think so. I'm still alive—I'll take that as a positive sign. My shelter mates still pass me in the first fifteen minutes of the day, but I haven't fallen lately. I got turned around once on the trail, but I realized my mistake and corrected it."

Becoming disoriented is easy in the woods. Shelters look alike. Woods look alike. Plants look alike. The white blazes along the AT are identical, and it is possible to hike for miles in the wrong direction. A side trail can add to the confusion, especially when you're tired and disoriented at the end of a day. Once you arrive at a shelter, you might see a path to the privy, another one to the water source, and the path back to the AT—the one you came in on.

I figured out that if I turned right to take the side trail to a shelter from the AT, I should turn right to return to the trail and continue north. If I turned left to go to the shelter, I should turn left to get back on the trail. Simple.

One morning I emerged from a shelter and started up the trail as usual. I hiked a few minutes and noticed the scenery looked familiar. *I have been here before*, I thought.

I looked around. I was standing in a field of wildflowers, as disoriented as Alice in Wonderland. The trail looked the same in both directions. I went back, read the posted signs, and once again set out as before, knowing I was right. The feeling of familiarity passed once I spotted a few landmarks that were new.

"I wonder what Miles would say now about my abilities," I said, placing my feet sideways to slow my descent through a patch of dry sand and scree. I pictured her ahead, cautioning me to stay back. I had slipped so many times she expected me to fall, and what if I fell into her, injuring both of us and leaving no one to get help?

"Was I really that bad?" I asked Ms. Rabbit. "Never mind. You weren't there, but I don't think so. True, I made a bunch of rookie mistakes that first month, but I was learning. I do want to be better, but what is 'better'?

"The object isn't to become another Miles," I said to Ms. Rabbit and the wind and the trees, "and I don't want to worry about measuring up. I'll work on my trail habits, but now I need to let her go and become a better *me*."

I reached Peck's Corner Shelter at 2:15 p.m. after thinking I would never get there. The hike was just under seven and a half miles. It should have been a cinch with no high mountains to climb, but the ridges I encountered instead were named "The Sawteeth" for a reason. By the time I put my sandals on and sat in the sun with the other occupant of the shelter—a man who was reading—I was worn out.

I half-watched for the talker from last night, dreading to see her come down the trail between the foot-high shoots of yellow grass. I was spared when she hiked on.

The evening was uneventful, and I left Peck's Corner Shelter shortly after 8:00 the next morning, stopping for lunch on my way to Cosby Knob. I loved lunch, not only for the break from hiking but also for the food I packed. My usual fare was peanut butter and jelly rolled in a tortilla, Cheez-Its, a Fruit Roll-Up or packet of cookies, and water or Gatorade to drink. Today it was water. My one bottle of Gatorade was so delicious it hadn't lasted long.

Two young men I thought of as "the dudes" made an appearance and then lingered inside. I had met them the previous night. As nice as they were, they didn't seem cut out for hiking. Their equipment was heavy—huge rolled sleeping bags hung off the outsides of their packs—and their slip-on sneakers were wrong for the trail.

"Why are they staying inside the shelter so long?" I murmured to Ms. Rabbit around my tortilla. "How long does it take to pack up?" Usually hikers wanted to make progress before 12:15 p.m. It took me a few minutes to see the smoke drifting out past the tarp and realize they were not packing their things at all; they were most likely getting high.

Clouds were gathering in the sky, so I put the rain cover on my pack. I had hiked five miles before my lunch break, leaving another seven-plus to be covered in the afternoon.

Rocks, rocks, and more rocks bruised my feet on my way to Cosby Knob Shelter. It was a long afternoon. "Where the hell is that shelter?" I said to Ms. Rabbit at least twice. After hiking 13 miles I arrived exhausted—nothing new there—but glad to catch up with Jot, Huckleberry, and The Hiker. Miles and I had met him at the Laundromat in Fontana Village.

Signs in the shelter warned of bear activity. Only two of us obeyed the direction to hang our backpacks from the bear cables outside. Apparently bears didn't hesitate to come into a shelter and grab packs off nails or pegs. I experienced nothing unusual during the night but heard in the morning that a bear had stolen a woman's tent while she was hanging her food bag on one of the cables.

I was on the trail early with "only" seven miles to Davenport Gap Shelter, the last shelter in the Smokies. The word *Gap* was apropos after a three-mile descent of 2,400 feet from the summit of Mt. Kammerer. I followed another hiker in, arriving at the shelter at lunchtime. She went by her given name but would later take the trail name True Story, a direct quote from the frequent claims she made in conversation.

I disliked Davenport Gap Shelter the minute I saw it. The dinky grounds were hilly and bare. The shelter bore a prominent warning sign about bears, and a chain-link fence with a door had been constructed across the front, top to bottom. After a minute I got it: The bears weren't caged, so the *hikers* had to be. Did I want to spend the night in a cage with my food to avoid mishaps with bears? When my companion hiked out after lunch, I knew the answer: not for a second.

In the movie *You've Got Mail*, when Meg Ryan's character breaks up with a boyfriend her soon-to-be-ex asks, "Is there someone else?"

"No," she says, "not someone else . . . a dream of someone else."

I felt that way about bears. I wasn't chased by them—I hadn't even seen one—but I felt chased by the *possibility* of bears. I hiked on.

Chapter 34
Whoops!

Two roads diverged in a wood and I—
I took the one less traveled by . . .
—From "The Road Not Taken" by Robert Frost, 1920

I left the Smokies, crossed the bridge over the Pigeon River in bright sunlight, and walked under the noisy I-40 overpass on my way to Standing Bear Farm in Hartford, Tennessee. There I would spend my first night north of the park.

In the distance I saw the gravel road that led up to the hostel. The sun was relentless as I climbed beside the guardrail, seeking every tiny spot of shade from the trees growing on the fringe. The interstate was far below me now. My back was wetter by the second under my pack, and I was feeling foolish. Every time I rounded a curve, the scenery was the same—more road. The hostel was nowhere in sight.

Thank goodness for cell phones—even mine. I got out my *A.T. Guide* pages and found the number for Standing Bear Hostel. A woman answered.

"It sounds like you've come too far," she said. "There's a set of steps leading up the mountain from the gravel road. You should have seen them on your left. Take those steps and be careful; they're steep."

"So, I need to turn around and go back down the hill?" I changed course near a wide, shady spot beside the road, glad I now knew what to do.

I was dusty, tired, and way too warm. After expecting to park myself at Davenport Gap Shelter, I had hiked another three and a half miles, emerging from the woods to feel like I was on a scavenger hunt in Hell.

I backtracked and found the steps I'd missed, but no hostel awaited at the top. I hiked on, looking for it through the trees. I was back on the Appalachian Trail, and the AT would take me over a mountain and along a creek before I spotted buildings.

"Oh, Ms. Rabbit," I groaned, "I'm a sweaty, stinky mess. Will we ever get there?" I loved that Ms. Rabbit let me complain, at the top of my lungs if I wanted.

Complaining didn't mean I was going to quit or even take a break. It was an opportunity to release my feelings. Miles liked everything upbeat—a "buck up" approach that didn't come naturally to me. I had bucked up plenty of times in my life, but not by ignoring my circumstances. I needed to let off steam occasionally.

"How much farther can it be?" I cried. "My feet are numb!" Maybe I was negative, but in that wild moment the negative felt like a positive because I was expressing it freely.

I hadn't lost my curiosity about what was around the next bend, and I kept hiking over that unexpected mountain, but by then I wanted nothing more than to arrive. Once I got to that desperate point on any day, I would begin seeing things. A gray rock cliff in the distance would look like the side of a shelter; a bright, flowering bush among the greenery of the woods would stand out and resemble a parked vehicle.

After I descended the mountain I wound my way through woods on flat ground and came to a road. It was the same gravel road I had traveled before! I looked off to my right and saw the grove of trees where I had turned around.

In going up the steps and hiking over the mountain I was following the AT, which was the right thing to do. I might have missed the stairs the first time, but I didn't miss the irony. If I had continued up the road in that dusty, hellish heat I would have been here an hour ago. The hostel was in sight.

Standing Bear Farm is a collection of unpainted structures connected by gravel pathways. After my long day, I was thrilled to step onto the property. A bearded man in a flannel shirt, jeans, and boots introduced himself.

"I'm Lumpy," he said. "I'll give you the guided tour." We walked past the office, a primitive laundry, a kitchen, various housing options, and a resupply store.

I claimed a queen-size bed in the building called The Cabin. It was a cozy setup. Across the room was another bed where a married couple would settle in and their sweet dog would find a spot on the floor. The Hiker took the loft above me, climbing past my bed on a ladder.

After a shower I headed for the kitchen, where the woman who shared my brief stop at Davenport Gap Shelter was taking a pizza out of the oven. She offered me a slice.

"Have some. I made it myself," she said.

The pizza was amazing, as was the can of Budweiser I drank with it. A group of us sat around the table, and the "cook" let me rave about the pizza for a while before admitting she had not made it from scratch. The future True Story was earning her trail name, and I didn't mind that the laugh was on me.

I was clean that night, but my clothes were not. I couldn't bring myself to scrub them on a washboard, put each piece through a wringer attached to a galvanized tub, and expect them to air dry by morning. Besides, the primitive equipment reminded me of the time one of my grandmother's hands became caught in the wringer of her washer. Ouch!

In three days, still crossing state lines, I would hit the next trail town: Hot Springs, North Carolina. Hot Springs was known as a hiker-friendly town. Surely I could find automatic washers and dryers there.

I charged my phone and was able to post a few pictures to Facebook before I fell asleep. In the morning I cooked my usual breakfast of coffee and oatmeal using my Jetboil on the front porch and topped things off with a Honey Bun.

Lumpy wished me luck as I took up my poles to hike the gravel road back to the northbound trailhead. I followed the AT up the steep incline of Snowbird Mountain for the next four-plus miles to the grassy bald on top. After that and a few bumps along the ridge, it was downhill to Groundhog Creek Shelter, my home for the night.

Chapter 35
Strike Up the Band

Nothing is as simple as we hope it will be.
—Jim Horning, American computer scientist

The floor of Groundhog Creek Shelter sloped uphill on one side. The flatter side was taken, evidenced by two sleeping bags spread in the space, so I laid mine on its inflatable pad close to the middle. It was 3:30 p.m. and I'd hiked just under seven miles, earning the right to plop down at the picnic table in the sunshine.

My companions were two men doing a section hike. The older one had hiked the entire Appalachian Trail that way, and his friend would finish this section and the AT when they reached Hot Springs. They had been hiking the trail together for 15 years.

"We'll be leaving early in the morning," one said. "We don't cook breakfast. We like to get started as early as possible."

The other added, "We'll be gone before you're awake."

Did they realize they were talking to *Early Bird*? If they could pack up and slip silently back to the trail before I woke up, it would be a first.

A couple came in and pitched their tent away from the common area. A young woman arrived alone and joined us at the table after laying her things where the floor began to slope. She was chubby. If she rolled or slid in the night, I would know it.

The shelter wasn't crowded that night the way shelters can be when people are bumper-to-bumper. Some hikers chose to cover another six-plus miles and camp on the scenic bald at Max Patch with its 360-degree mountaintop view. Camping on the bald was prohibited, but hikers hoping to see beautiful sunsets and sunrises took their chances.

Two more men arrived at the shelter before bedtime, taking spaces that were left on either side of the floor. One served as a buffer between the chubby girl and me. If she slid, she would bump into him, so I could have relaxed if he hadn't sounded like a bear in his sleep. My eyes flew open every time he huffed and snarled in a strange version of snoring. Finally, I slept and woke hours later in the dark, aware of the two older hikers planning to sneak out early.

At 6:00 a.m. the first one got up to pee with his headlamp on the brightest setting. I felt the light in my face and watched it move around the inside of the shelter and over the prone bodies while he climbed out of his sleeping bag and left the shelter.

After two more well-lighted trips they began to pack up. To their credit, they didn't exchange a word in the 45 minutes it took them to organize their gear, but they could have staged a musical with less commotion.

These two thought they were slipping out unnoticed? Nice guys, but they had been hiking the trail long enough to know better. In another setting, their headlamps could save ships. I would say something if I caught up to them later, but for the moment I wanted to escape their escape. I turned over and covered my head, determined to block out the light and noise. Behind me their bags rattled and pads scraped. Boards creaked and boots clunked. Zippers zipped.

Zippers—specifically, mine—were a pet peeve of Miles'. She maintained she could sleep near me even though I woke up in the early morning hours, except when I had to work a zipper on my sleeping bag or tent. I tried to be quiet—I did—but in my defense, how does one go to the bathroom zipped in a sleeping bag? If we were tenting, I also had to unzip the tent door and vestibule to get outside. I didn't dare leave an inch of the door unzipped while I was inside the tent, and bugs were the reason.

Putting up a tent at the end of a day is like waving a little welcome sign for every flying, hopping, or crawling creature in the vicinity. I developed a routine to reduce the chances of sharing my sleeping space with spiders, ants, and gnats. I would spread out the flattened tent with the door closed, add the poles to give it shape, and complete the staking process. I then unloaded my pack outside and inspected each piece of gear for bugs before quickly unzipping the door partway to shove the item in and zip the door closed again, repeating the process until every item I needed was in the tent.

The walls of my tent were solid near the bottom and made of netting on the sides and top to let in air. The bottom was snake-proof, or so I hoped. Gnats and spiders could get under the rain fly, which I flung over the top and secured last, but they could not get through the fine netting. Lying inside the tent, I could see them moving above me but knew they couldn't come any closer.

As I lay wrapped in my sleeping bag at Groundhog Creek Shelter in the pre-dawn hours listening to the sounds of practiced preparation, I could sympathize with Miles trying to snatch a few more winks before giving in to my morning noise.

At 6:45 the two masters of stealth hit the trail. An hour later I was on my way, running my plans past Ms. Rabbit as I tackled the first mountain of the day.

"We have two thirteen-mile days ahead of us if I'm to reach Hot Springs by the end of Friday," I said. I planned to take a zero in Hot Springs on Saturday. It was my next resupply point, and I was desperate to do laundry. In addition, I could look for new boots.

"Today we'll go over Max Patch, take a long downhill swoop, and then go up to the top of Walnut Mountain. It looks like the shelter is right on the peak." It sounded easy, but it wouldn't be: 6.4 miles to the mountaintop at Max Patch and another 6.7 miles after that. It was May, warm in the south, but I was ready. I breathed the mild mountain air, glad to be alert.

"I'm fully awake, Ms. Rabbit. No more Ibuprofen to get me through the days! It's a relief. My pack fits, and I'm awesome on the ups."

I liked the steep ascents better than the "downs." My rhythm kicked in as I warmed up to each climb. My arms and legs moved in a graceful and deliberate way, my poles clicked in time, and my 69-year-old body was as integrated as a symphony. My feet were tender, but my struggles with shoulder pain were behind me now.

The absence of trees on the approach to Max Patch did not make the mountain less steep than wooded ones. I could see the brown path winding upward and other hikers strung along its length. At the top I took pictures of the gorgeous hills all around and then removed my boots and socks. I sat on my pack, let the grass tickle my feet, and contemplated the state of my world.

"To recap," I said to Ms. Rabbit, talking softly now, "you and I are scrapping the flip-flop hike. If Miles comes back, will we revert to the flip?"

I didn't want to. Changing course again would be a pain, and the flip was complicated. Miles and I had planned to interrupt our southbound hike for two weeks to return to Ohio so that she could take a planned vacation with her husband. During that time I would get a ride to Georgia to pick up my car.

"Isn't hiking supposed to be a life of simplicity?" I asked Ms. Rabbit.

"If she comes back," I said, "where will I be?" I needed to stick to my new/old plan. I had to arrive at Harpers Ferry in two months, meaning I needed to get through Tennessee, Virginia, and a few miles of trail in West Virginia by July 4. Could I do it?

"The obvious answer is to make up the miles lost in April." It made me tired. I enjoyed hiking at my own pace, which was more leisurely than Miles', but I had realized my two goals—taking my time and making up miles—were mutually exclusive. I had an aggressive few weeks ahead.

"Look at these boots," I said. "The tape is already curling. I definitely need to visit an outdoor store in Hot Springs. Get ready to say good-bye to two hundred dollars."

And then it hit me.

"Oh, my God, Ms. Rabbit." If the flip was a pain, at least the logistics had been worked out. My plan to continue hiking north was complicated in a different way: My *A.T. Guide* pages for everything north of Harpers Ferry were on my desk at home!

"Sure, I can follow the white blazes, but the *Guide* has all the information about water sources, shelters, distances, towns, hostels . . . everything! I'll have to figure this out. For now, we'll keep going."

I chugged some water and looked around. Other hikers had stopped for lunch on the bald. They sat alone or talked quietly in pairs or groups. Some stood and others enjoyed the soft, green grass. I took Ms. Rabbit out of my pocket.

"Aside from the organizational questions, what would it mean to me if Miles came back?" I said. "How would we hike together? How could I reconcile my own style with hers? 'Hike your own hike' isn't just an expression. I might not love being alone out here, but I need to find out what I do love.

"Do I want her to come back? That's a hard one, Ms. Rabbit."

On the way to Walnut Mountain I came upon three other hikers stopped at a cool stream and decided to do the same. We rested in the shade of a tree and had snacks. I liked the way they were easy with each other.

The sun was out when I hiked on, but before I reached the shelter the weather changed. Black clouds blew sideways above me as I raced across the last bald before the thunderstorm broke. Walnut Mountain Shelter was full, so I rushed to set up my tent. The rain came and I zipped myself inside with my food bag. I wanted nothing more than to eat for a while. I didn't want to worry about anything. I was tired, especially my feet. The 13 miles had felt like 23.

In a while the storm passed and the sun came out long enough to dry my tent. I got water, hung my food bag, and reached for my trail pages. They were gone. No doubt my pages were lying on the trail somewhere. A hiker coming behind me might find them and return them to me—it had happened before—but losing *Guide* pages was a serious problem; every page covered approximately 20 miles of trail. I *had* to be more careful.

I copied notes for the next 13 miles from another hiker's *Guide* and then got ready for bed, putting away my wallet and phone, hearing aids, glasses, and Ms. Rabbit before I climbed into my sleeping bag. It was my favorite part of the evening: time to appreciate where I was and relish a few moments of pure bliss because I had nowhere to go but to sleep.

Chapter 36
Hot Springs

Surprise, surprise, surprise!
—Gomer Pyle, TV character

I woke up at 5:00 a.m. in my tent on the top of Walnut Mountain and got out to pee, first unzipping the door just far enough to grab my sandals from the vestibule. Once they were on my feet I unzipped the door again and squeezed through it. I hated leaving my tent in the dark, not only because the possibility of wildlife was scary, but also because the acrobatics of getting out of the low doorway without falling over presented another kind of challenge for me.

It was May 8. The full moon behind the black outlines of trees was like a picture, but the ground still bore the gloom of night. As I stepped away from my tent I was glad for the reflective strips that would lead me back to it after I answered nature's call.

Back in the tent, I took a pre-moistened, unscented Wilderness Wipe from my pack and cleaned up. I had seldom felt so stinky and disgusting from head to toe. Today I wanted to get an early start. I had 13 miles to cover, worn-out boots, and a keen desire to get a hot shower and spend the night in a real bed.

I ate breakfast, packed up, and got on the trail by 7:30. I had a pleasant little downhill before hiking up the formidable Bluff Mountain. By the time I climbed it and descended the other side, I was halfway to Hot Springs.

It was fortunate the trail was well marked with blazes and foot traffic picked up as it always did when we neared a town. I lost my copy of the route again. Hadn't I just vowed to be more careful? This time it was the trail notes I'd copied the previous evening. My *Guide* pages for the same section were somewhere on the other side of Walnut Mountain.

My feet were tired and bruised. I was hot. When I was a few miles out from Hot Springs, I began to wonder if I could make it to town. I knew a shelter was coming up soon. It seemed ridiculous to consider staying there for the night instead of continuing, because I was so close. If I could just hang on, I would be clean in a few hours. I could wear my sandals for a day. In three miles I would have access to a soft bed and groceries, restaurants and laundry facilities. Beer, pizza. A shoe store.

It was a tug of war: the temptations of the civilized world vs. the three miles required to get there. When I came to the side trail for the shelter, I took it. A break might make the difference.

The sun was shining. It made the forest look friendly, the way I liked it. As I approached Deer Park Mountain Shelter, I was not surprised to find it empty; most hikers would disregard a shelter so close to a trail town with its hostels and watering holes, especially so early in the day. I took off my pack, leaned it against the picnic table along with my poles, and sat down on one of the benches. Someone had left a bag of candy on the table and now it was melting in the heat.

I removed my boots and socks. Ah! The feeling of air on my feet was fantastic.

The picnic table was new, but the shelter wasn't. Its corrugated tin roof sagged in the middle, and the log construction wouldn't have stood up to a level. Wasn't there a nursery rhyme about a crooked man who lived in a crooked house? Just inside, sticks that hung from strings would allow hikers to store their packs off the ground.

The setting was peaceful at that time of afternoon. The acreage in front of the shelter was generous, with flat spaces for tents. The nearby hill was covered with soft, brown pine needles, and I could see through the trees. Nothing could sneak up on me here.

I sat alone with my feet resting in my sandals and had a snack. It revived me, but did I want to get back on the AT? The alternative was to unpack my gear, enjoy a tranquil afternoon, and start fresh tomorrow.

"What should I do, Ms. Rabbit?" I asked aloud. "My feet feel better now, but how long will that last? This is a beautiful place, but when night comes I won't feel the same way about it. The shelter has nothing beyond the basics to recommend it. If I do stay and I'm alone, I'll be afraid."

In that instant I recognized my turning point. "Thanks, Ms. Rabbit," I said, grabbing my socks and boots. "That turned out to be an easy one."

When I saw three women and a white dog taking a break along the trail, I recognized them from Standing Bear Hostel. I had been trying my phone in order to make a reservation in Hot Springs for the night, but I had no service. One of the women was using her phone, so when she was done I asked if I could borrow it. I called Elmer's Sunnybank Hostel, a place I'd read about. It was full, but I made a reservation for the next night and decided to try Laughing Heart Hostel, which was just off the trail. I wouldn't have to walk far to get there.

I was almost to the bottom of the hill leading into Hot Springs when a woman called to me from below. She was standing in front of a kiosk full of messages.

"E.B., there's a note here for you," she said.

What? Who would leave me a note?

I pulled the paper down, unfolded it, and read: "I am in Laughing Heart Hostel. May 8 Friday. Don't leave without me!" It was from Miles.

PART 3
THE RETURN

Chapter 37
Together Again

Forward is the direction of real life.
—Cheryl Strayed in a comment on Facebook

I read the note and then reread it. It was not written in Miles'
careful cursive but flung onto the page in large, blue printed letters
with a Sharpie and punctuated with exclamation points. It was a
simple message. My hiking partner was staying at Laughing Heart
Hostel, a short distance from where I was standing, and she was
ready to continue our hike.

"What?" I said to Ms. Rabbit. "*What?*"

Even when I knew I had a note waiting at the bottom of the hill,
I didn't imagine it was from Miles. Over the last two weeks I had
thought about her in the past tense.

Since we parted at Fontana Dam, I had been mapping my own
path for more than 100 miles of the AT. Except for Ms. Rabbit, I had
returned to my solo hiker status, one I expected to embrace for the
remainder of the Appalachian Trail. I had reverted in theory from
our "flip" to my original plan, a northbound hike to Maine. Now
a moment I thought was far in the future—if it existed at all—was
upon me. In minutes, Miles and I would be reunited.

How quickly could I process this information?

Miles' mother must have rallied from her illness—good news—
and Miles was enthusiastic about returning to the trail. Through her
note she was reaching out to me as though we had no tension in our
history. As though she hadn't told me three weeks earlier how badly
I was letting her down.

What had changed? I had been working to improve on the trail,
but we hadn't been together in weeks. She didn't know any more
about me today than she had at Fontana Dam. Maybe her time at
home blurred her memory. Maybe she was hoping for the best. So
was I, but now *I* had trust issues.

I have admitted to being sensitive and analytical when it comes
to human behavior. The note in my hand held layers of meaning.

The last sentence, "Don't leave without me!" surprised me the most. It was a friendly plea from the woman who not long ago was done with me as a trail partner. I got that she missed the AT, but had she really missed me?

Miles was experienced and resourceful. She didn't need me. Further, I wasn't interested in being criticized. The trail was hard enough. It required our focus and best efforts every day.

"I guess Plan B is going to unravel now," I said to Ms. Rabbit. "Or is it Plan C? I'm praying for flexibility along with my shower and shampoo."

I had been hiking all day, and I felt it. My clothes were disgusting. I needed to be clean, and I was so tired I had considered sleeping in a shelter three hours ago. I put on my game face and headed for the hostel, calling "Miles!" once I was on the property.

Inside I put my things down on one of the bunks and went back out, where I found Miles sitting at a table with two other hikers enjoying a cold beer. One—let's call her Rose—had just had a haircut on the premises.

"We're getting Mohawks!" Miles said. Though she may have considered shaving her head on that hot North Carolina afternoon, Miles kept her hair. All was jolly as the hostel owner set a beer in front of me and we caught up.

Miles was in good spirits, and I fit into the camaraderie like a long-lost missing piece. I could ruminate on my trust issues later.

Her mother was indeed better, and once that was established Miles wanted to be back on the trail. Her home in Ohio backs up to three acres of woods, woods that called to her like their cousins lining the AT.

"I kept opening all the curtains in the house," she said. "I felt closed in.

"After visiting Mom I unloaded my pack and cleaned my tent outside. I played with the dogs in the yard. I wanted to be outdoors. Mr. M noticed my restlessness, and one day he said, 'You want to go back, don't you?'

"Didn't you know I was coming?" she said. "I e-mailed you three times."

"With this phone? No, I didn't get any of your messages. I found out you were in Hot Springs when I got off the trail and read your note."

The four of us ate out and I did laundry. I snagged a single room for the night, and the next day I moved to Elmer's, where I had a reservation. Rose and Miles went along, as Rose hoped to stay there too. We were going to share a room.

Elmer's Sunnybank Inn is a big old house with lots of history. For example, Earl Shaffer—the first person to thru-hike the Appalachian Trail—stayed there, presumably during his 1948 hike. Elmer Hall bought the place in 1978 and began a tradition of housing and feeding guests, primarily hikers. The house is crammed with furniture and musical instruments, but that day it was nearly deserted.

We followed a staffer up the stairs to our room, which included two beds and a door opening onto a balcony.

"I can't stay here," Rose said. "It's too crowded. There's too much going on; it's like a carnival."

The guide and Miles and I looked at Rose, because no one was in the room but the four of us.

"I knew it as soon as we started up the steps," Rose said, referring to the presence of beings we could not see.

I was moved to Room 5, a single, as Rose made a quick exit. Her parting words were, "Let me know your dreams."

Miles and I went shopping downtown and I got new boots. Hot Springs wasn't Franklin. There were no shoe experts to spend two or three hours showing us models of feet and fitting me with the best possible hiking boots. I tried on the three available pairs in my size and asked the clerk to comment on the fit. Aren't employees supposed to be schooled in feeling toes and judging width? This one did little to inform the buying process, so I took my chances with a low-cut pair of Oboz, a brand I didn't know. I hoped I'd made a good choice. A shoe store is a poor substitute for the trail when one is testing hiking footwear.

I also found a merino wool T-shirt on sale, a pair of shorts, and a lightweight day pack. Miles had discovered the day packs and bought one when she was home. Made of nylon, they were too small and light for the trail but were perfect hands-free town bags. Otherwise, we had only our pockets or our heavy backpacks as containers.

We resupplied and now I had a heavy food bag. Otherwise, it was a good day. We would hike out in the morning.

I was signed up for a gourmet dinner prepared by our host at Elmer's, but with only four of the required six guests registering, the dinner was cancelled. At 8:00 p.m. I walked through the house, which was quieter than a lonely mile on the AT. Was I the only overnight guest? Even Elmer had disappeared. I took a shower and headed for Laughing Heart Hostel, where I hung out a while with Rose, Miles, and True Story. In the morning Miles and I would be hiking together again.

"I'll pick you up at Elmer's at nine o'clock," she said. That would be after my gourmet breakfast.

I returned to Room 5 at Elmer's, where I spent the remainder of the evening with the only other occupant: Ms. Rabbit.

"I don't feel a thing in this room," I said.

It was quiet without TV or the internet. I sat down and looked through the books and brochures on the desk, but by then local history couldn't hold my interest. It wasn't long before I stretched out across the bed and fell asleep in my clothes.

I didn't remember a single dream.

Chapter 38
A Breaking-in Period

"Rabbit," said Pooh to himself. "I *like* talking to Rabbit.
He talks about sensible things . . ."
—From A.A. Milne's *The House at Pooh Corner*

Miles and I left Hot Springs on May 10, Mother's Day, with 11
miles to hike. Our destination was Spring Mountain Shelter.
The elevation profile in the *A.T. Guide, Northbound* showed the
four mountain peaks we would scale that day, each higher than the
one before it. That would be the trail debut of my new low-cut hiking
boots. And why were low-cuts called boots and not shoes?

The Oboz brand was said to have the stiffest soles in the business—
good protection on the rock-lined Appalachian Trail. That was the
"sole" fact I heard about them from other hikers. Right now mine
were stiff all over. I'd soon know if they were going to work. I hoped
so; I'd sent my old pair to our home support, Mr. M. A person hiking
can't carry an extra pair of boots.

The day was sunny and hot. I liked to brag that I didn't sweat,
but that day proved me wrong. We had good water supplies, so when
we came to a stream or spring we didn't just fill our containers. We
soaked our bandanas, wiped ourselves down with cool mountain
water, and then tied the wet bandanas around our necks. They dried
quickly in the sun, making it a rinse-and-repeat kind of day until we
reached the shelter at 7:00 p.m.

Miles' e-mails came through when I had phone service again.
The first, sent the day before she arrived in Hot Springs, contained
the tentative question, "Would you mind some company on the
trail?" The second message, "Heading Out," announced she would
be arriving via shuttle and hoped to re-enter the trail close to where
I was. Message No. 3 was titled "Urgent!!!!" It said, "I am in Hot
Springs!!!!"

Miles had written another note by hand the day she arrived:
"At Laughing Heart—Where is EB (Early Bird)? "Miles is in HOT
SPRINGS!! Thurs. May 7th (Need to meet up!)"

Her repeated invitations told me Miles was sincere in wanting to find me and hike together again. She could have stopped after the first one, or the second or third, using my lack of response as a convenient excuse to go on without me, but she didn't.

The reason she wanted us to hike on together still eluded me, so I asked her.

"I know you missed the trail," I said, "but what I don't understand is why you want to hike *with me*. We've met lots of others. If I'm such a bad hiker, why come back to the same arrangement?

"You've changed," she said, pointing out that after our talk about my shortcomings I had immediately fixed my pack issues at the NOC. She noted I had become more vigilant in studying my *A.T. Guide* pages, improving my awareness of the trail and my ability to look out for her. Obviously, I had made it from Fontana Dam to Hot Springs on my own, so I couldn't be a complete failure.

I thought Miles' reasons were less about me and more about finishing her hike. She loved being on the trail and had set a goal to complete all 2,189.2 miles.

My feet hurt at the end of that first day, but no worse than they had in my high boots. I hoped I wouldn't get blisters from the new ones. How would I walk if I did? Miles could hike with blisters for many miles, but I didn't fancy doing the same thing. A night of rest would be like medicine for my feet.

I was the first one up. I retrieved our food bags from the bear cable, set Miles' outside her tent, and took mine to a fallen log, where I unpacked my breakfast items. I kept my food in gallon zipper bags, one for each type of meal plus one for my coffee supplies and another labeled "Food Trash" for the used papers and packages I would carry until we reached a trash container. Food trash was kept separate from "trail trash," which meant everything else.

I set up my JetBoil and put enough water in it for coffee and instant oatmeal and got out my spork and collapsible mug. I liked breakfast, but I *loved* being able to savor my coffee. It was one of the benefits of being an early riser.

Packs tend to be heaviest after a resupply, and it's always the food bag. Mine should have felt lighter after I'd consumed two meals.

"Wow!" I said when we loaded up to hike. "This pack feels like somebody climbed into it last night and is still there." Miles smiled at my joke, an encouraging sign since she was quickly supplanting Ms. Rabbit—who liked everything I said.

I continued to carry my little blue good-luck charm, but now I rarely needed her for conversation. I had moved her from my pants pocket to my pack when Miles returned to the trail.

The eight-mile route to Little Laurel Shelter was a jagged path of peaks dipping to gaps and ravines and ending with a climb of almost 1,300 feet. The shelter was only halfway up the last mountain, which meant the other half of the climb would greet us in the morning.

We arrived at 6:35 p.m. and hurried to pitch our tents under a dark, threatening sky. Then, at Miles' suggestion, we ran for the shelter with our food bags swinging. We could cook supper under roof and escape the violence of the coming storm, temporarily sharing space with four girls from Florida, a father and his son, The Hiker, and True Story. We had just made it inside when the first loud crack shook the forest. Behind it came an outburst of thunder, lightning, and chilly, drenching rain. Our friend Rose hiked in after the worst of it. She had been caught in the storm and was wet, but safe.

After dinner the sun emerged and we returned to our tents. Before turning in I studied my feet. I had three pieces of duct tape on them to forestall blisters, thanks to the new footwear. I was also developing a painful bruise under my right ankle from that shoe bumping up against the underside of it on uneven sections of the trail. My foot would hit the ground on an angle, forcing the outer edge of the shoe against my ankle bone. Every repetition increased the pain until I had to shift my weight deliberately as I walked. In addition, I now noticed my toes were pinched in the shoes. On the downhills they were pushed into the front and sides.

That jamming of toes is how hikers lose toenails. Who could forget Cheryl's/Reese Witherspoon's bloodcurdling scream in the opening scene of the movie *Wild*, when she pulled a loose toenail free?

"Is that all?"

That would be Ms. Rabbit's snide comment on my whining if she could talk. Who needed a mirror when she reflected all the good and bad parts of myself back at me? The important point was: She couldn't talk. It was my own inner voice I was hearing.

Tomorrow we planned to hike a difficult 14 miles. I lay down thinking I needed to get my old boots back, but that wouldn't happen out here. I prayed for my aches and pains to heal overnight and gave them a head start with a Tylenol before bedtime. Maybe the new shoes would be fine with a bit more breaking in.

I had the same hope for Miles and me.

We were not discussing our hike the way we had at home. I figured it was because we wouldn't agree on the next day's destination. Summer was coming. The woods had filled in with green leaves. The path narrowed where the grass grew high. The days were getting long, and that meant more time to hike each day. Stopping was a goal for me, but Miles hated to waste the light. She would look up at the late afternoon or evening sky and calculate how many more hours of daylight we had to reach some point beyond our original goal, how many miles we could cover if we kept at it.

Our 14-mile day began with an uphill followed by 12 miles of uneven ridgeline before the trail descended into Flint Gap and rose again for another three-quarters of a mile before reaching Flint Mountain Shelter. This detail was brought to you by the *A.T. Guide, Northbound*. When we stopped for lunch I looked at my pages. The high points of the hike, elevation wise, had "Big" in their names: Big Firescald Knob; Big Butt Mountain. I found a different high point in the mileage column: In the last six weeks I had hiked 300 miles of the Appalachian Trail.

That night my feet thanked me for lying down. I took two Tylenols and soon fell into a deep sleep full of dreams. Our next day's hike would be a blessing at only 8.8 miles.

Trail Days was on my mind. The most famous hiker gathering on the AT would take place over the coming weekend in Damascus, Virginia, and I wanted to go. The annual event attracts past, present, and future hikers, but I knew I would not be interested in the future; this was my one chance to experience it. It would take us off the trail for a few days.

Participating in Trail Days wasn't important to Miles the way it was to me. She and I had talked about it in our planning sessions at home, when we thought some friends from Ohio might meet us there, but that plan hadn't worked out. If not for me, she would have let the idea drop.

Miles had the stronger personality. I was the quiet one, the one more likely to give in; but that time I persisted and she agreed to go.

Talking Miles into it wasn't my only challenge. When I first scheduled Trail Days into my plans back home, I expected to be closer to Damascus by now. We were 175 miles away. If we went, we couldn't walk there. People hitchhiked all the time, but Miles had assured Mr. M she wouldn't be one of them. I didn't care to stick my thumb out either, so the alternative was an expensive shuttle ride.

By then we were regularly running into Rose and True Story, who were hiking separately. True Story wanted to attend Trail Days, and she agreed to split the cost of a shuttle to Damascus with us. Miles called her friend Tom, who owned a shuttle service with his wife. He had driven Miles from the airport to Hot Springs.

We had a ride to Damascus. It was going to happen!

Miles, True Story, and I camped near Hogback Ridge Shelter the night before we left. We were still in North Carolina, Damascus being the first town over the Virginia state line. The next morning we had to hike two-plus miles to Sam's Gap, a trailhead near the border, to meet the shuttle at 8:30. As the person most likely to wake up first, I was the "alarm" for the two of them.

"Wake us up at five o'clock," Miles said. I set my phone alarm in case my usual sleep pattern failed me.

It was dark at 5:00 a.m. Miles's tent and mine were in close quarters with others. I thought about the two noisy guys from Groundhog Creek Shelter. Now it was my turn. Could I dress, eat, use the privy, pack up quietly using my headlamp for light, and get the other two up? I wasn't worried about Miles oversleeping—she didn't need an alarm. Miles would hear me moving around, but True Story had chosen a tent site at the bottom of a hill. In order to wake her up I had to find the path and then find her.

We started on time and soon spread out over the distance as True Story outpaced us and Miles fell behind when she made a stop. She caught up but I was still in the middle, booking along until we had Sam's Gap in sight, and then I fell and hit my head.

Doggone it! The best soles in the business weren't keeping me upright. I hated falling. I hated the embarrassment and the feeling I was letting Miles and myself down.

When my brother and I were kids, our parents let us eat dinner in front of the television. Before we got TV trays, which were invented around 1952, Joe and I set our full plates and glasses in front of us on the floor. Every night like clockwork, Joe's glass got turned over and a mad rush ensued to get a dishtowel and mop up the milk before it soaked the carpet.

I thought my falls must be like that to Miles: predictable, a cause for eye-rolling, and good for a moment of panic. When my first instinct was not to assess the damage but to spring up and assure her I was all right, I realized I was paying too much attention to what my partner thought.

In the car she introduced us all and then spent the ride catching up with Tom. True Story joined the discussion from time to time, and I looked out the window. I sometimes felt stupid when I contributed so little to a conversation, but that day I was happy to watch the scenery from the interstate, marveling at the speed of mountains, little towns, and isolated houses flying by. In doing so I realized I had no idea what Damascus looked like. I wasn't sure what we would find there. I'd read about Trail Days, but I hadn't researched it the way Miles would have.

Sheer, cold panic washed over me in the car. I had insisted on this side trip, an investment of money—which we had, and time—which we didn't. Now my burst of assertiveness was triggering an equal and opposite reaction: regret mixed with an overblown sense of responsibility for what lay ahead. What if Trail Days was a waste of our money and time? What if Miles didn't like it?

What if, what if, what if? Get a grip! Ms. Rabbit again. Maybe I should find a place for her on one of my shoulders.

It was our fifth day out of Hot Springs, and I was praying Miles would remain engaged with our driver and would not ask me questions about Trail Days I couldn't answer. For pure humiliation, ignorance was as bad as falling.

Miles and I were wired differently. She was the extrovert and was more assertive. For me, assertiveness had a high price. On the trail I didn't mind leading the way up a mountain, but in other ways I was a better follower. Our differences didn't make either of us right or wrong, but would they make us good trail partners?

Conflicting thoughts swirled in my head as we rode toward Damascus. One second I was glad to be on my way to Trail Days, and the next I felt like jumping out of the car.

Chapter 39
Trail Days

If you never did, you should.
These things are fun and fun is good!
—Dr. Seuss

Damascus, Virginia, bills itself as "The Friendliest Town on the Trail." Home to about 1,000 residents, Damascus is a designated trail community. The AT, the Virginia Creeper Trail for bicyclers, and the Virginia Birding and Wildlife Trail are among several that intersect there. During the annual Appalachian Trail Days festival, shortened here to "Trail Days," the townspeople welcome thousands of hikers and other visitors.

Trail Days includes food, events, vendor booths, and entertainment from one end of town to the other. The downtown, consisting of one main street and several blocks of side streets, offers restaurants, outdoor stores, churches, a clinic, a post office, a Dollar General, and other businesses.

Contrary to my wild imaginings, Miles approached the weekend with as much enthusiasm as anyone there. We arrived quietly to a quiet town. Preparations were in progress and some businesses, for instance the first restaurant we tried, were closed. We got breakfast at a combination store, gas station, and restaurant called Cowboys.

It had become our habit to "chow down," now that hiker hunger had kicked in and we needed to put thousands of calories into our bodies to make up for what we burned each day. Typically our breakfasts consisted of juice, coffee, eggs, and/or something substantial that I would never touch at home: pancakes, hash browns, biscuits, and even gravy.

A sports field became tent city for the festival. Suspecting a party atmosphere, Miles and I passed on that location and left our packs on the property at The Place, a hostel run by the Methodist Church. A man called Marine One assured us we'd have bunks in the hostel as opposed to places on the lawn to tent, but officially we couldn't get inside, pay, or claim our beds until 3:00 p.m.

"Crazy Larry will do your laundry for five dollars," Marine One said.

Crazy Larry ran a hostel on another street. If we could get our laundry done, we could check off that chore for the weekend. The price had gone up to $8, still a bargain. True Story and I dropped off the dirty clothes and picked them up two hours later, clean.

In the afternoon Miles and I moved into The Place, taking Bunks 21 and 22. The hostel, which operated on donations, was a tight ship: signs indicated no alcohol, no bad language, no boots inside, and no washing clothes in the kitchen sink. We almost didn't get in, not because of any bad behavior on our part but because Marine One wasn't the person doing the admitting. Miles insisted we had been promised beds, and we got them.

The bunks were wood; I had the top. No bedding was provided. We slept on our mattress pads and sleeping bags, glad to have our corner of a room in the hostel. Our stuff was safe there and the place was clean and well run. There was one shower for everyone in the house. Our roommates were four men.

Miles and I could walk one block and be downtown. When we went to dinner, Damascus was bustling. The streets and stores were filling up with hikers and private yards were dotted with tents. When we stepped inside Bobo McFarland's and looked for an empty booth, two diners jumped up and ran to us. It was K and C, our young friends from the early days of our hike! The four of us explored Trail Days together.

"You're our trail moms," they said.

Saturday was another beautiful day in Damascus. Miles and I had breakfast at Cowboys. I wore my new low-cut boots, hoping to find a store that carried the Oboz brand so I could get a second opinion: Were my shoes a mistake? If so, what could I do? I knew I could not return shoes I'd bought in Hot Springs, but I did purchase insoles at an outfitter to raise my feet in the shoes and relieve the brutal ankle-bumping I experienced on the trail.

A sock salesman was in the store for a Trail Days promotion. He gave Miles and me free socks! We weren't familiar with the brand, but hiking socks cost $15 to $25 a pair. These were not just free; they were advertised to be *blister free*. I wasn't plagued with blisters, but I could be. These lined socks promised to be awesome.

We ate a free lunch, courtesy of one of the hiking organizations: peanut butter sandwiches, Fritos, and a drink. We spent the afternoon with K and C wandering around town and through the packed vendor area in the town park, wearing our new socks. We passed the booth of David "AWOL" Miller, author of the *A.T. Guide*. Maybe he had some trail pages that came with grommets and safety pins. Just kidding.

We passed ministries offering free coffee, food, and services to hikers including showers, haircuts, sewing repairs, and veterinary examinations for trail dogs. We watched a hot-dog-eating contest.

We saw familiar faces throughout the day: Baltimore Jack, Tom from Laughing Heart Hostel, and the Tom who provided trail magic and gave us a ride to Helen, Georgia, back in April. The four of us— Miles, K and C, and yours truly—ate dinner at a restaurant called the Old Mill. Afterward Miles and I resupplied at the Dollar General. We would be returning to the trail the next day.

In the evening Miles and I attended a talk by then AT speed-record holder Jennifer Pharr Davis at the Damascus Methodist Church. Pharr Davis is an engaging speaker and her husband, Brew, entertained us with songs, but all through the presentation I kept smelling feet. They were mine!

When Miles took her boots off later, the same thing happened. It was the free socks! Unlike the wool hiking socks we were used to, these were made of synthetics: polyester, nylon, and Lycra. They might prevent blisters, but after a few hours of duty they sure smelled sour! Miles sent hers home; poor Mr. M, opening that package. I kept mine for a few weeks hoping the benefits would offset my tight shoes, but I tossed them when the smell continued.

We had breakfast at Cowboy's on Sunday morning and then packed up. I was leaving Trail Days with a good feeling. My worst fears had not come true. Miles and I spent time with friends, ate well, shopped, and enjoyed the comparative comforts of a hostel. We lost three days of time on the trail, but hiking isn't just about hiking.

Tom picked us up in the shuttle at 1:00 in front of the Methodist Church and drove us back to Sam's Gap. It rained on the way, so I savored every moment in the car before we got out, took turns peeing, and found the northbound trail. We would hit Damascus again in two weeks—on foot.

Chapter 40
After Damascus

Just because you are right, does not mean I am wrong.
You just haven't seen life from my side.
—Poster from Amazing Things

The week following Trail Days took us from our shuttle drop-off at Sam's Gap, North Carolina, into the northeast corner of Tennessee. It was 2:45 p.m. by the time Miles and I were back on the AT after Trail Days. "Shuttle Tom" had told us in the car to look for a campsite about two miles in. Our *A.T. Guide* page showed a campsite at Low Gap, 3.7 miles in. Most likely we had two references to the same campsite, but that was irrelevant because we looked left and right for miles and saw no campsites at all.

We started up a mountain. At a certain point in a climb, you leave the dense woods and see a lot of sky. If the path twists between large rocks and doglegs around one spindly tree after another, as it did that day, you find yourself grabbing onto the trunks to pull yourself up. That's when you know you are not going to find a level area on which to put up a tent. Instead of setting up camp, you continue hiking.

The trail rose in a never-ending spiral toward the rocky peak. I felt like I was in the 1993 movie *Groundhog Day*, in which events repeated. We seemed to be passing the same crooked brown tree again and again.

By the time we stopped for the night we had hiked nearly eight miles in more of the "Bigs": We crossed Big Bald and followed the ridge past Big Stamp, the latter being a saddle—another term for a gap. When we realized we were almost to Bald Mountain Shelter, we kept going and arrived to find a Boy Scout encampment.

The Scouts had pitched their tents in front of the shelter, so it was empty. After we settled in I realized my *Guide* pages were missing. Again. I backtracked for a few minutes, thinking the paper would shine like a beacon against the black dirt and mud along the ridge, but I didn't recover my pages until another hiker brought them to me. He had found them farther back on the trail long after I'd hiked on.

Picking up others' trash or forgotten items can be risky. I could identify with losing objects on the trail and being grateful for their return, but I didn't always want to touch objects we found on the trail. Hikers are justified in avoiding germs or declining to carry extra weight. The solution is to leave the item in a prominent place. Once Miles and I found a shoe and hung it on a branch at eye level. Another time we found a pair of sunglasses and did the same thing. Once we saw a set of tent poles and left them beside the trail. Someone would miss those in a few hours.

We left Bald Mountain Shelter and hiked nearly 19 miles to Erwin, Tennessee. On the way we passed Devil's Gap and no longer were skirting the North Carolina border.

Though it was not a day of high mountains, our feet felt the miles. We spent the night of May 17 at the famous Uncle Johnny's Nolichucky Hostel, located a mere 68 feet from the Appalachian Trail and about the same distance from the Nolichucky River, which flows through Erwin. We could see the river all the way from the top of Temple Hill, growing larger as we descended toward town.

Uncle Johnny's is a group of weathered buildings that include cabins, showers, a store, and laundry facilities. We took bunks in a cabin, which was a detached single room about eight feet by ten with its own door and small front porch. We visited the store, ordered pizza for supper, and washed our stinky clothes. I was surprised when Uncle Johnny closed up shop at 8:00 p.m. and left the premises.

The next morning Miles and I took the free shuttle to the Huddle House and ate a huge breakfast before fattening our wallets at an ATM. We re-entered the trail with an easy agenda: four miles to Curley Maple Shelter. It was enough after our 18.8 miles the day before. Miles had a blister as well as a sore ankle. My shoes felt all right with the new insoles, but I still liked to take them off.

We arrived at 3:00 p.m. It had been a pretty hike, though the last mile was up a mountain. I supposed I should stop being surprised by mountains.

"I think I'll sleep in the shelter tonight," I said.

"Why do you say you *think* you will? Why not just say, 'I'm going to sleep in the shelter'?"

I didn't see an appreciable difference.

"A lawyer friend of ours says *think* is the weakest word in the English language," Miles said. "By eliminating words like *think* and *guess*, you can communicate more directly."

We did have a communication problem, and it played out from long, awkward silences to occasional outright conflict. By then Ms. Rabbit was reduced to a pocket trinket. I missed the comfort of easy conversation. I missed the freedom to speak my mind.

To me the issue with Miles was our aforementioned wiring differences—our minds didn't work the same way—but she saw something else and aimed her rehabilitative efforts at a new target: my communication skills.

Miles could immediately see a direct answer to a question; I had to think through it before answering, and sometimes I would do so aloud. It drove her crazy. She would ask me a question and then couldn't understand why I could not instantly choose: Did I want to stop or hike on? Sleep in my tent or in the shelter? Do laundry tonight or tomorrow? Eat now or later? Each instance required only a one-word answer, if you thought like Miles did. I, on the other hand, seemed incapable of making those snap decisions.

"Yes or no?" she would say. "Stay or go?" And when I hesitated or began to process the alternatives out loud: "It's not a complicated question. YES or NO?" She wanted one word, and one word only. When I sought to explain, she would put up both hands, palms out, and say, "I'm done."

My style reflected my aversion to confrontation. When I tried to avoid an argument, I could be wishy-washy. I could obscure my own point, burying it in language. She said I was being evasive; I thought I was being tactful. Both of us were right, but I didn't know it that day or even that summer. I was finding out instead that, though I liked watching makeovers on TV, I didn't like being the subject of one. I had no intention of changing my speech patterns to please someone else. Why should I?

I rolled out my sleeping pad in the shelter, hung my food bag there to claim a hook, and ate a late lunch. My feet and I enjoyed a peaceful afternoon.

In the three days since Tom dropped us off at Sam's Gap, Miles and I had covered almost 30 miles. We had both feet in Tennessee, but we were more than 100 miles south of our original goal. According to the schedule we made at home, we should have been 15 miles from the Virginia border.

Chapter 41
Do Unaka?

Miles and I hiked 13 miles to our next stop, the first 6 of them uphill, cracking our daily average of 10 miles. Whether we could maintain it over a longer distance would become important later.

We encountered two instances of trail magic on the way. The first had me questioning whether Miles' powers included extrasensory perception.

"You need potassium," she said shortly before we emerged from the woods directly across a two-lane road from a white pickup truck where B.T. (Brother Tom) was offering coffee, water, lemonade, fruit, banana bread, and brownies to hikers. I split a banana with Miles and had a brownie for dessert.

Halfway through our hike we found more trail magic at a clearing called Beauty Spot. We were about to hike over the bald when we spotted two vans in a gravel parking area. Their occupants were unloading coolers, baskets, and other containers. We wandered over to find the trail group Riff Raff setting up to serve hot dogs, coleslaw, chips, and drinks. After we ate we came away with Riff Raff wrist bands. I wore mine for weeks afterward.

The sun illuminated the Roan-Unaka (the latter pronounced with a long *a* in the middle) Mountain Range as we hiked through woods thick with ferns and a spruce forest with a covering of needles on the ground. I led most of the day, loving all 5,184 feet of Unaka Mountain. The downhill was steep and the footing hazardous, but I remained upright. My feet got tired, but my legs were awesome. My endurance was improving all the time.

We stopped for the night at Cherry Gap Shelter, a primitive building where a group of male hikers had already set up. We pitched our tents, and I made a trip to the water source. When I returned Miles was practicing throwing a bear line over a tree limb. I was the one who needed practice, but I managed to assist most nights instead of throwing the line. I contributed a little bag so we could zip the rock inside and wouldn't have to tie the cord around it. Each evening I searched the ground for a rock that was heavy enough, yet would fit inside the bag. I looked for the right tree. In the mornings I got our food bags down to make up for rarely hanging them at night.

At Cherry Gap Shelter I met a self-described "aspiring" writer who had married a Romanian woman and moved to Bucharest. His story was immensely interesting to me as I had toured parts of Romania in 2005 and had published a book based on my experiences there.

It was May 19. At our current average rate of ten miles per day, we were ten days behind schedule. Mr. M had assured his wife he would find us wherever we were on July 3, the meeting day originally scheduled for Harpers Ferry.

According to our northbound calendar, we would be spending the next night at Clyde Smith Shelter, nine miles north. I can't recall why we took a winding, rutted gravel road instead to a hostel two miles short of the shelter. We hiked past a long fence lined with tarps or possibly a giant roll of opaque plastic to arrive at Greasy Creek Friendly.

Miles and I looked across high grass at an unpainted house sitting on a slight rise. The words *tumbledown shack* came to my mind. We then looked at each other as if to ask, too late, if stopping here was a good idea.

The lined fence abutting the property was the work of a neighbor known to hikers for his animosity toward the hostel. It was said he did everything in his power to discourage visitors to Greasy Creek Friendly. Was he looking at us from behind the tarp right now?

We walked to the side door, where our hostess instructed us to remove our packs and lean our poles against the house. She showed us the adjoining bunkhouse and then allowed us in the main building. The entry was a small room that held a supply of food on shelves, an ice cream freezer, and spaces for boots and clothing. All of the living area was on one floor, the main attraction being a long dining table in the middle. The kitchen was on one end of it and the living room on the other.

There were rules—bathroom rules, kitchen rules—rules enumerated on papers spread out on the table. Miles and I arrived in the afternoon, hungry. It was there that I ate the best cheeseburger I have ever tasted. Was it because we had been eating trail food and anything would be an improvement? I say no; it was the cheeseburger.

The Facebook request Miles had made of me back home came up again during a quiet moment between lunch and dinner. Because she had no Facebook account, she wanted us to sit down together so that I could connect with her friends and they could then follow my hiking posts. It sounded simple, as it had before we left Ohio, but it didn't happen.

At Greasy Creek Friendly I discovered my phone was dead. Soon it was sitting on the table in a bowl of uncooked rice for the night. In the best-case scenario the rice would wick extra moisture from the device and restore it to life.

Miles was beyond frustrated. "We're supporting you in so many ways," she said, referring to the packages sent and received by Mr. M as well as hotel reservations, trail research, and record keeping on both their parts. "We're driving you to Maine! And you haven't done the one thing I asked."

I had entered some of her friends' names at points along the trail when my phone was working, though it would have made more sense for Miles to join Facebook and manage her own contacts. She would tell me a name and I would type the name in the Facebook search bar. If the person had a Facebook account, I sent a friend request.

I'd noticed a pattern in the photos of us I posted when I did have phone service. One after another showed me with an expression of pain or confusion on my face. I thought I was smiling in those pictures, but I wasn't.

More hikers arrived, including a couple hiking with his elderly dad and two young women we'd met earlier on the trail. Miles and I rode with our hostess to pick up carry-out pizza from a store so tiny the only eating area was on the deck. We brought our warm pies back to the hostel, riding through the town of Buladean on the way. It was named for Beulah Dean, daughter of the community's first postmaster. We may have left the trail, but we were still in the country.

In the evening we did our laundry. Later, when I couldn't find Ms. Rabbit, I thought I'd accidentally put her through the wash. I went back and looked in both machines and on every nearby surface with no luck.

We sacked out in the bunkhouse and woke up to rain. After breakfast we waited for the downpour to abate, finally leaving Greasy Creek Friendly at 11:20 a.m. We hiked uphill for two miles and stopped for lunch at Clyde Smith Shelter, where we had originally expected to be waking up.

We were still in the Roan-Unaka Mountain Range and had reached the formidable Roan Mountain, where the Appalachian Trail stretched along the crest of its five peaks for 14 miles. The biggest "up" was in front of us as we packed up after lunch. The steep trail led to our destination, Roan High Knob Shelter, eight miles away. The shelter, the highest on the entire AT, was known for two things: the view and the cold.

Chapter 42
Ash Gap

*Even God cannot make two mountains
without a valley in between.*
—Gaelic proverb

It was another instance of not quite making it to our destination. Miles and I left Clyde Smith Shelter after lunch and hiked six more miles. The last three were spent ascending Roan Mountain at about a 45-degree angle between the sky and level ground. Because of the terrain and because we left Greasy Creek Friendly so late in the day, our total distance was eight miles instead of the ten we planned.

We crossed a knob and headed downhill, hiking the short distance to Ash Gap. According to our *Guide* pages, we could camp there. The trail flattened. We chose a campsite and put up our tents. We found a suitable tree and I hung a line for our food bags while Miles watched from the doorway of her tent. It was my turn for sure. I was proud and relieved when that orange cord slid over the chosen limb on the second try.

Miles went for water and I waited at the top. The *Guide* showed the water source as being one tenth of a mile away, but she was gone so long I wondered if she would ever return.

At an elevation of more than 5,000 feet, the weather changed before my eyes. I was sitting on a log waiting for Miles when a chilly fog blew toward our camp, obscuring land and sky in its path. As I watched it move in and shrink the space around me, I recalled the 1957 movie *The Incredible Shrinking Man*, in which the main character was at sea, enjoying the sun on the deck of his cabin cruiser, when a mist passed over him and changed his life forever. Before long he was six inches tall and living in a dollhouse.

While Miles was gone I got out my JetBoil and food. I was cooking dinner when Rose walked off the trail and pitched her tent a short distance away. Her arrival was good news; the more, the merrier—especially on that cold, foggy mountain.

I had my head down cooking and didn't pay attention as Rose set up her tent. When Miles came up the hill at last, she saw Rose's tent sitting next to the tree where we would hang our food bags that evening. *Oops!* If we put aside the fact that Rose's tent was made of fabric and supported by a few thin poles, a bear could have stood on it to reach our food.

Miles didn't chide Rose for failing to notice my orange bear line hanging next to her tent site. Instead, they scolded me for failing to warn Rose off the spot where she could have become bear bait for the night.

We laughed it off. I took my licks and Rose moved her tent, but in moments like that I felt like an outsider.

We finished supper and the food bags went up. The temperature dropped, sending us into our tents by 9:00 p.m. Even in my sleeping bag I was too cold to fall asleep quickly. It was Thursday, May 21. Tomorrow the Memorial Day weekend would begin. At home the swimming pools would open. People would be arranging patio furniture and putting on shorts. Warm thoughts brought little comfort on a night so cold it penetrated every layer of cloth around me.

In the morning drops of water clung to the outside of my tent. I was glad when the sun rose and began drying the fabric.

At 6:52 Miles was outside her tent. She told Rose and me she was going to climb back in; it was too cold to hike. I got up wanting coffee and fixed my usual breakfast, then crawled back into my tent. We would hole up for the next four and one-half hours, not leaving Ash Gap until 11:30.

I'd been having trouble hearing and wondered if my hearing aids were failing. During one of my active phone sessions I sent a message to my audiologist, who suggested I change the wax guards on the hearing aids. I couldn't sleep the morning away, so I got the kit from my pack. Wax guards are tiny things, like little letter *o*'s. I used the special tool to extract each one and replace it. The process, though delicate, took only a few minutes, and it worked.

When we hit the trail, following the ridges of Roan Mountain, the sun was shining. We had a good day with one exception: rocks going on for miles. We parted company with Rose at a picnic area with a public restroom. She wanted to do her laundry in the sink.

Miles and I intended to visit Roan High Knob Shelter to see what we had missed by stopping short of it the night before. However, we missed the shelter, passing it by. According to the *Guide*, it was located a tenth of a mile off the trail, but neither of us spotted a marker.

We ate lunch sitting on a grassy hill overlooking the parking lot at Carver's Gap before climbing the remaining peaks of Roan Mountain. A few miles later we were descending the mountain for good. At the bottom sat the red converted barn known as Overmountain Shelter. Set in a gorgeous valley, its message to me was, "You are finally over the mountain!"

We had gone nine miles since packing up at Ash Gap. My feet were tired and sore from the rocks. Miles and I climbed the ladder to the roomy loft and put up our tents side by side on the wood planks. We did it for warmth.

I didn't cook that night. Instead, I walked outside to find a woman sitting on a blanket dispensing trail magic. I ate a banana and two cookies before going back to my tent. It was early, but I was ready to fold. Reaching Mountain Harbour Hostel the next day would be a treat. I looked forward to a bed, a shower, clean clothes, and a resupply package from Mr. M.

Chapter 43
Turtle

The dynamics are changing.
—Miles

I liked it when we hiked with someone else. Miles would do the heavy lifting of conversation and I could think my own thoughts and join in if I felt like it, letting the new person be the focus.

We had left Rose to her laundry the day before. For the nine miles from Overmountain Shelter to Mountain Harbour Hostel, it was the two of us. Miles and I hiked over balds and meadows, enjoying 360-degree views from high places. Hump Mountain was the highest; before that, Little Hump Mountain. We stopped for lunch on top of Hump Mountain and then spent the second half of our hike going downhill. On the *Guide* page the downhill route could have been the mirror image of our climb up Roan Mountain two days earlier. The slope angles and mileage were almost identical.

Once we were off the mountain we had to walk a two-lane road to get to the hostel. We were almost there when I slipped off the edge of the pavement and fell underneath the guard rail. Something, perhaps the rough surface of my backpack, stopped my slide; if not for that, I would have landed in a deep gully and could have required a rescue. Miles thought I was a goner when she saw me slide under the railing, but I escaped with scratches down the outside of my lower right leg.

I felt better after my leg was bandaged and I was clean. Miles and I picked up our drop boxes at the office. When we opened them, I was surprised to find a note from her in mine, along with a bag of her homemade snacks. She'd added them to my drop box during her time at home.

Both of us now had more supplies than we could consume or carry. Though the exchange didn't lighten our loads, Miles gave me a bunch of vitamins she didn't need and I offered her my sack of Ibuprofen; I had plenty. Why I sent myself an abundance of bug wipes, I couldn't say, but they weren't the only items to go straight to the hiker box below our sleeping loft.

We did our laundry, and as I was climbing the ladder to the loft with a bundle of clothes I noticed a woman sitting alone on a couch in the main room. We smiled at each other. She must have come in when I was elsewhere.

Miles and I were signed up for the highly recommended gourmet breakfast on Sunday morning. For our $12 we were invited into the owners' residence—also a b&b—on the hill above the hostel, where breakfast was served buffet-style at 8:00 a.m. sharp.

When we arrived, the dining-room table and several smaller tables in the kitchen were set. Conversations were in progress. Before breakfast we helped ourselves to coffee and juice; at the appointed hour we joined the self-service line for the meats, sweets, and casseroles laid out on a kitchen island the size of a twin bed. The meal was delicious, and we were all clean to receive it.

Every seat was taken. Rose, who caught up with us at the hostel and spent the night in her tent, joined another table while Miles and I sat down with two hikers we had not met. One of them was the woman I'd seen on the couch. Her trail name was Turtle. She was in her fifties and was hiking alone.

We liked Turtle, and she liked us. Around 11:00 Miles, Rose, Turtle, and I left Mountain Harbour and returned to the AT as a foursome. The weather was great that day. The scenery was varied, and our mood was light. We stopped for lunch at Jones Falls, a short hike off the AT, and after we ate we took off our boots and socks to cool our feet in the water.

I led the pace most of the way as we passed the next shelter and hiked another eight miles to a campsite downhill from the trail. The site was crowded with men. Miles took an available spot near their tents. Rose found a site that suited her, and Turtle and I pitched our tents next to each other up near the trail. After dinner we located a high limb for the food bags, and one of the men threw the line.

My feet were tired, as usual, but the rest of me was okay. *More than okay*, I thought as I lay in my tent winding down for the day. I loved that time of evening, but it was a slippery time for my thoughts. I remembered something Miles told me—that my mind seemed less cluttered in the woods. *But how did she know?* I wondered as I felt myself sliding into sleep.

The next day Turtle, Miles, and I hiked to Black Bear Hostel near Hampton, Tennessee. Rose was somewhere behind us, hiking her own hike.

Back home Miles and I had penciled in a stay at Kincora Hiking Hostel. It was nearby and was run by the famous trail advocate Bob Peoples, whose name was immortalized on shelter walls; but that was before we knew the hostel was a haven for cats. Miles liked cats and had a few of her own, but I kept picturing furniture covered in cat hair. That may not have been what turned us toward Black Bear Hostel, but going there was a good decision.

The hostel was clean and well run. It included food for resupply, drinks, laundry, a bath house, and a picnic area. Miles, Turtle, and I had a cabin to ourselves. Inside were two sets of bunk beds and a small table, electric lights, and a plug to charge our phones. The front porch with its pair of wood benches gave us space for sitting. There I encountered trail magic times two.

Another group of hikers cooked their supper that night in the picnic area. We were watching with envy from our porch when one of them brought each of us a plate of steak, potatoes, and onions! I got out my Swiss Army knife to cut my steak and dropped it in the process. Mine was the smallest model, small enough to fit through the cracks between the floorboards of the porch. I couldn't have done that deliberately if I'd been trying for a carnival prize. We tried several methods to retrieve the knife, but there was no way to recover it. I was shocked when one of the steak-cooking hikers gave his own knife to me.

Turtle lost her watch between the boards of that porch. One day when Black Bear Hostel is torn down, someone will find a treasure trove under the porches.

We woke to a drenching rain. I looked out the back window of our cabin at a person lying on the wet ground, huddled in a bivy sack—a tight shelter for the person in it. We were dry and my feet felt better than they had the day before; however, we were not about to set out in the rain. When the weather cleared Miles, Turtle, and I slack-packed for the first time.

That morning we left our heavy packs in our room and wore day packs to hold food, water, and emergency essentials for the one hike.

We took the shuttle to a point on the AT nine miles ahead and hiked back in order to end up at Black Bear Hostel for another night.

The three of us had fun together. Our light packs made the day a joy. We had a new habit of checking our phones during breaks, and when they worked our lunch and break sessions were extended. We called it the cyber café.

In between phone sessions Miles and Turtle talked about classical literature, current events, and other topics I tended to avoid. I heard Miles drop the name Angela Merkel into conversations and was embarrassed because I didn't know who Angela Merkel was. Did I live under a rock in real life, not to know the Chancellor of Germany for the last ten years?

Turtle was a delight, intelligent and personable. She was a nimble hiker as well. The three of us took turns leading. I thought I lost my *Guide* pages again, but they were in another pocket. Miles reminded me to keep my pockets zipped.

"Empty your pockets" would have been helpful back at Greasy Creek Friendly. Because I didn't, a few of my pages went through the wash there and were shredded to bits. Another hiker took photos of her pages with my phone so that I would have them on the trail.

After our hike a couple staying at Black Bear offered to wash our clothes. Turtle and I gave the guy the socks off our feet. I had more socks, but I expected the clean ones to show up; items have a way of coming back to us on the trail. I hoped that was true of Ms. Rabbit, because I couldn't find her. I left a note on the counter in the office, complete with a sketch of my missing good-luck piece.

Rose joined us for our second night in the cabin, taking the fourth bunk. She planned to hike a different section the next morning, but Miles, Turtle, and I would strap on our regular backpacks and continue north together. Destination: Vandeventer Shelter.

Chapter 44
The Sisterhood of the Fair Ladies

How wild it was, to let it be.
—Cheryl Strayed in *Brave Enough*, © 2015

It was May 27, midweek; Memorial Day had come and gone. Miles, Turtle, and I were hiking nine-plus miles to Vandeventer Shelter, which is located on a ridge high above Watauga Lake in northeastern Tennessee. By the end of the week we would be in Virginia.

The three of us had taken the shuttle from Black Bear Resort to the previous day's starting point. From there the AT took us through a large area around Watauga Lake known for bear activity. The shelter there was closed for the entire year because of it. I was watchful as we made our way along the trail, but I saw nothing but woods and, as we climbed, the lake far below us.

We had fallen into a comfortable pattern, making good mileage while enjoying the journey. Sometimes we hiked in silence and sometimes we chatted back and forth. We hiked single file, taking turns in the lead. We held our cyber café sessions on fallen logs and high rocks. *Truce* is a strong word, but our time with Turtle was a period of calm for Miles and me and a period of cohesion for the three of us.

Turtle was the glue. She was introverted, yet friendly; assertive, but non-threatening. She was not easily ruffled. Her personality was a perfect fit for the space between Miles and me. It was an antidote to the tension that had shadowed us like an animal.

Turtle called herself a brave introvert because she had taught herself to function in a social world when she often felt like withdrawing. One day when the three of us were hiking she said, "E.B., you might like the book *Quiet*. It's about introverts."

I knew I fit the description, which I thought was "quiet and shy"—maybe in my case, not so brave. But how could someone research and write a book about that?

"Thanks," I said." I'll have to check it out when I get home."

Instead of being more like Miles as I had suspected, Turtle was more like me. I hoped she would continue hiking the trail with us. On the AT one never knew. "Hike your own hike" was a strong message to every hiker. Now and then Turtle would want to hike alone. She was fast, and she would get ahead of Miles and me and then wait for us along the trail or meet us later at a shelter. Her absences were of a shorter duration than Rose's, but I felt them more.

The area around Vandeventer Shelter was crowded. Tents were everywhere. The shelter backed up to a bird's-eye view of Watauga Lake and the surrounding countryside. That was the second benefit. The first was its location past the "bear ban" area. I was relieved, as always, to escape that threat.

The shelter itself was nothing spectacular. It was old and slept only six hikers. The walls were covered with graffiti, some of it about Kincora Hiking Hostel owner Bob Peoples. One entry read, "On the third day, God said, 'Let there be Bob Peoples.'" We settled in and then sat in back of the shelter on Turtle's sleeping pad to eat our dinners.

I had a hard time sleeping that night. Drainage down my throat kept me awake. In addition, my ears seemed to be stopped up. When I changed the volume on my hearing aids, I could barely hear the beeps from the right one. When Turtle and Miles chatted on the trail, I couldn't distinguish what they were saying unless I was in the middle. Was it the hearing aids, or was I getting sick?

Turtle was having problems of her own. She was experiencing bodily soreness and weakness, causing her to need more rest than usual. The symptoms would come and go. When they were present, we took more breaks and our stopping points reflected a majority vote. "Stay or go?" Turtle and I voted to stay.

After Vandeventer Shelter our next hike was a challenging 14.5 miles to Double Springs Shelter. It was a gradual upward hike along a ridge, rougher and more difficult in real life than it looked on the *Guide* page. We stopped for lunch at Iron Mountain Shelter, where I put a note in the register about Ms. Rabbit, who was still missing. We ate with a hiker named Caesar who dubbed the three of us the Sisterhood of the Fair Ladies. I liked that we were seen that way.

The afternoon brought thunderstorms. The sky was gray, and rain poured on us. The trail turned into one long puddle. I had my rain jacket on but still felt soaked. A bright spot occurred when a southbound hiker told us we'd find trail magic ahead. It was true; someone had placed an orange box full of snacks that stood out against the wet ground beside the trail. We sat on a log and ate. I remember the trees, their trunks dark from the rain.

We hiked over a bald in that storm, exposed to the elements. If I'd been alone, I wouldn't have done it. A hiker caught on a mountaintop in lightning is in a bad spot, and trail wisdom is not encouraging: let go of any metal objects, e.g., trekking poles; avoid seeking shelter from rocks or trees; crouch down and balance on the balls of your feet to reduce the area of your body that touches the ground; and separate yourself from others so that if one of you is struck, the rest may avoid the same fate.

When we reached Double Springs Shelter, it was full of hikers trying to get dry. Finding a permanent (i.e., overnight) spot in a shelter in bad weather is tough. You have to wait it out. Some of those gathered at Double Springs planned to hike on. Some decided to eat first and then hike on. Others would stay the night. We got in for the night because a male hiker moved out and put up his tent to give us room. Trail magic comes in all shapes.

I didn't cook that evening, but my dinner was delicious: a peanut butter and jelly sandwich and M&M's.

Our status as Sisters on the trail was never plainer than the night Miles, Turtle, and I spent at Abingdon Shelter. We hiked nine miles to get there, walking through another thunderstorm. Turtle was in the lead. The shelter is located at the top of a mountain, so we slapped through mud, straddled puddles, and climbed the slick trail, arriving wet around 3:00 p.m.

We were the first hikers to arrive at the shelter. Most of the people we met were doing another ten miles, eager to get into the next town, Damascus. We took advantage of the abundant real estate to spread out our things, reorganize our packs, claim our sleeping spots, and change into dry clothes. We gaily strung three clotheslines for our wet clothing. It was a modest version of a cliché: the movie scene in which women's stockings and undergarments take over a bathroom.

No one hiking by on the trail would miss the fact that women were staying at Abingdon Shelter.

My suspicions about getting sick were stronger that night. I was congested and had a sore throat. The drainage I'd first experienced at Vandeventer Shelter was continuing. I knew there was a clinic in Damascus. I'd passed it during Trail Days, but we would arrive on Saturday afternoon. Would I have to wait until Monday to see a doctor? It would change our schedule; we hadn't planned to spend the whole weekend in town. How would my Sisters feel about that? I had a feeling Turtle wouldn't mind. She was slowing down.

I felt the contents of my personal dry sack—the one for medications, hairbrush, tissues, and related items—to find the Ibuprofen. I found my pills and a bonus: Ms. Rabbit was buried under my supplies at the bottom of the bag!

In the morning I was out of food. We had acquired another guest, a woman named Sunshine. Before we set out for Damascus, she gave me two Pop Tarts. Miles gave me a tortilla: shades of Gooch Mountain our fourth day on the trail—minus the meltdown.

Had I learned anything? Sometimes I wondered.

Miles invited Sunshine into the Sisterhood. It was a nice overture that didn't matter in the end. Sunshine was a much faster hiker than we were. We followed her down the long hill into Damascus and wouldn't see her again. That was the way of the trail.

The ten miles into town seemed endless to me. Would we ever get out of the woods? We reached the Tennessee/Virginia border six and a half miles in and were excited to eat our picnic lunch in Virginia. Miles, Turtle, and I posed for pictures around the sign marking the entrance to our fourth state on the AT.

Virginia contains one fourth of the Appalachian Trail. Hikers make jokes about "the Virginia blues," a reference to the time it takes to get through the state. After hiking 385 miles through the previous two states and zigzagging between them, I had the Tennessee-North Carolina blues.

Damascus was a welcome sight. We could resupply and I could visit the clinic—in addition to the obvious: sleep in a bed, take a hot shower, and wash my clothes. The Sisterhood was moving indoors, and none too soon.

Chapter 45
Signs of Sinus

Today I feel like putting an OUT OF ORDER sign
on my head and going back to bed.
—Comic strip character Aunty Acid, created by Ged Backland

Crap.

As we settled into Woodchuck Hostel in Damascus, I was sure I had a sinus infection. If I was right, nothing in my med bag would touch it. In addition to a sore throat and drainage, I was continuing to have trouble hearing. With my ears stopped up, I was in my own world.

Hiking on in this condition would be miserable. I knew from experience I would not feel better without a prescription, and luckily I would have one if I could hang on for two more days. I eyed my twin bed with longing, and I imagined Turtle felt the same way about hers.

We had three of the four beds in an upstairs room of the hostel. A male hiker we rarely saw had taken the other bed; mixing the sexes in sleeping quarters was the norm on the trail. Except for the rumpled linens, food wrappers on a bedside table, and his presence under the covers at night, we had the room to ourselves.

We agreed to stay in Damascus until Monday. I would visit the clinic early. I hoped Turtle would do the same, but she and Miles were planning to pack up while I was gone so we could hike out of town once I had my medicine.

Miles doubted my self-diagnosis. "It's allergies," she said.

"Let's change bodies" might have been my snappy comeback if I'd felt better. "See what you think it is, then." But I said nothing.

Allergy symptoms, like cold symptoms, can be similar to those of a sinus infection. That's why I insisted on seeing a doctor. Years ago when I was working, I mistook my first sinus infection for a cold. Initially I went to work feeling bad. After all, was I a wimp who could be sidelined by a cold? One day I mentioned to a co-worker how terrible I felt, and she suggested a cure: "Mince a clove of garlic in a glass of water and drink it." Ah, that was why I smelled garlic when I walked past her desk. Nevertheless, I was desperate. As soon as I got home I prepared the garlic and water. I drank the mixture down and then shivered with revulsion. It was horrible! I got into bed and stayed there the next day. I took drugstore remedies, but my condition did not improve. Nothing worked until I went to the doctor and discovered the true nature of my illness. Once the sinus infection was diagnosed and I began taking my prescription medicine, I got better.

Woodchuck's was a short walk from downtown Damascus. Turtle, Miles, and I cleaned up and walked into town. We ate fish and chips for supper at Bobo McFarland's.

"Let's buy three men's white cotton undershirts at the Dollar General," Miles said. "We can wear them while we do our laundry. Let's also buy a package of three pairs of women's panties and each take one. We can leave them when we return to the trail." She was thinking of pack weight. I was thinking: *Yay! Underpants.* As for the shirts, they were not undershirts to us; merely part of our town wardrobe, to be worn with our usual undergarments.

I carried a device on the trail that allowed me to urinate standing like a man without having to lower my pants. Because I had that device, a pStyle, I did not need a privy every time I had to pee; instead, I would find a tree and stand behind it. The night we spent in Abingdon Shelter—when we hung our things on three clotheslines to dry from the rain—I walked away to pee before bedtime but didn't get the pStyle correctly into place. Instead of channeling the liquid out the front, it overflowed. I was wearing my rain pants while my others dried, and I accidentally soaked my underwear and both legs of the rain pants.

There were no secrets in a one-room shelter. I quickly zipped the affected garments in a gallon baggie and changed into my last hope, my town shorts. I used a bath wipe from my pack—unscented—to make myself presentable to everyone but the bears. My fondest wish that night was to get to Damascus and a washing machine.

So, we were going to buy cheap clothing and discard it. We would indeed look like Sisters after we put on identical white shirts. I didn't mind. I needed something to wear. Everything I owned was dirty.

I slept poorly our first night in Woodchuck Hostel despite the comfort of my bed. I'd bought some over-the-counter sinus pills at the drugstore hoping they would relieve my symptoms. I should have known better. Not only did they fail to work; I also had trouble falling asleep and then dreamed a weird dream.

On Sunday I was the first one at breakfast shortly after 6:00 a.m. I helped myself to coffee, cold cereal with milk, and waffles with strawberries and Cool Whip. I didn't feel any better; in fact, I had to leave the breakfast table because my nose was so stopped up.

After breakfast I found myself in a familiar dilemma. It was not yet 7:30 and many guests were still asleep. What would I do until the stores opened at noon? I changed my hearing aid batteries and wax guards, hoping to improve the quality of sound reaching my ears.

Once Turtle and Miles were up, we did our laundry and Woodchuck drove us to the grocery store. By 10:30 we were chilling out at the hostel. We went into town and ate lunch at Bobo's. Afterward Miles and I shopped. I was looking for a new rain jacket. Mine was ineffective—easily soaked and slow to dry—as demonstrated during the recent thunderstorms on the trail. Turtle returned to the room and napped.

I coughed and sniffed through another night and was thrilled when Monday came. My trip to the clinic was a success, if you can say that about a sinus infection and possible bronchitis. I went to the drugstore, got my medicine, and took the first dose back at the hostel. It was satisfying to announce my diagnosis to Turtle and especially to Miles. *Told you so.*

The three of us left for the trail at 11:00 a.m. Between soreness and fatigue, Turtle's body was rebelling. Miles' feet and knees bothered her, and I was days from being cured. We hiked out of Damascus, went 1.9 miles up a mountain, and took a near-o, pitching our tents at the first campsite we saw.

It began to rain at 1:00 p.m. We stayed in our tents all afternoon. I drifted, dozed, and let my medicine work. At 6:30 we emerged to eat and hang our food bags. Now that we had taken an afternoon to rest and recuperate, we decided to leave by 8:00 the next morning in order to make it to Saunders Shelter, eight miles away. With that challenge ahead, I returned to my tent for the night.

We were a fragile Sisterhood, two of us weakened by our symptoms. Miles told me later she would have preferred to hike on.

Chapter 46
Virginia Rain

The nicest thing about the rain is that it always stops. Eventually.
—A.A. Milne, writing as Eeyore

Marion, Virginia, was our next town. We expected to reach it in four days.

Miles, Turtle, and I left our camp above Damascus at 8:10 a.m. on Tuesday, hiked to the turnoff for Saunders Shelter, and went on. Our near-o day must have worked for us to pass our destination. By the time we came to a campsite, we had hiked ten miles. Turtle and I were beat.

The alternative to camping was hiking another four miles to the next shelter. The forecast once again was rain in the afternoon, so we put up our tents—by now impossible to dry—on a site between the trail and a pond near Beartree Gap. Who named those places? We scrambled into our tents moments before the watering began. I was grateful to be stopped, set up for the night and protected from the rain, but it was another short day on the trail.

On Wednesday I woke at 5:45 a.m. I cleaned up and changed my underwear in my tent. A live bug dropped out of my clothes. On top of that, I was now wearing the wedgie, my least favorite article of clothing. In a while I would have to get water. I couldn't hike or cook without it, and I'd made do after we arrived in order to skip a wet trip to the stream. I was starting to feel better, but I lacked my usual energy.

We hiked up White Top Mountain that day. It was one of those endless ups, but the sun was out and my mood improved with the weather. Turtle hiked alone for part of the day. We saw her several times, and she camped with us that night. Miles and I reached the campsite at 4:20 p.m. My feet were glad to be off the trail, and maybe the tents would have a shot at drying.

It was a pretty evening. I ate my supper—Mountain House Beef Stroganoff—and we hung the bear bags before turning in. Tomorrow we would hike through Grayson Highlands State Park. Grayson Highlands is a highlight of the AT, not only for the beauty of the landscape, but also for the wild ponies that live there.

I woke up to water dripping off my tent. The sun came out later, but all day the sky looked like we were a minute away from a storm. Dark clouds hovered as we made our way over the rough balds of Grayson Highlands, marveling at bushes full of pink rhododendron blooms. Ponies grazed as we walked by.

The rocky terrain made hiking difficult for me. I was slow, afraid to take my eyes off my feet. Turtle led as we navigated tons of rocks of every size from pebbles to boulders. Her feet flew from one rock field to the next, never missing. It was as though she had been transformed from the person we saw in Damascus, the one who wanted nothing but bed rest. It was a good sign. I hoped her mysterious illness was gone.

We ate lunch at Thomas Knob Shelter, near the highest peak in Virginia. A couple who also stopped there to eat put a bag of Fritos on the picnic table and opened it. We were salivating from the smell. In that moment I understood what motivated a bear to climb trees or enter a campsite to follow the scent of food. The couple offered us some of the salty snacks. I could have eaten the whole bag and could tell Miles felt the same way, but we restrained ourselves to a few chips each.

The three of us hiked another five miles downhill to Wise Shelter, which was near the north end of the park, and slept inside that night. The shelter had nothing to recommend it except three walls and a roof, but it was a palace compared to a wet tent. It was our first time in a solid structure since Damascus.

On Friday morning I took the last of my sinus medicine. I had been feeling better every day.

That same morning I realized I was low on food, and we were 30 miles from Marion. I did not miscalculate; because Turtle and I had hiked sick, the three of us made more stops than we planned. I figured Miles must be getting antsier by the second. She was driven to make progress on the trail.

"CFM," she would say. "Continuous forward motion."

We hiked ten miles and stopped for the night at Hurricane Mountain Shelter. It was only 3:00; lots of daylight left. The sun was shining when we arrived, but the sky was soon giving us another message: rain.

Turtle settled in to write in her journal. Miles hung a clothesline under the overhang to dry her tent, and I did the same after putting my damp sleeping pad in place on the floor. A trail runner called Storyteller came and cleaned up the trash around the shelter. Built in 2004, it was one of the newest shelters I'd seen on the trail. Storyteller was one of the few trail runners I'd seen in 500 miles. Because he was there, I went to the privy to change into my rain pants. I also put on a jacket.

It started raining just as I returned from changing clothes. That was the fourth time I'd made it into a shelter or tent just before a rain. Storyteller entertained us with local lore and then hung our food bag for us, as there were no easy trees. I was ready to crawl into my sleeping bag at 7:00.

A middle-aged man we called Blue Suit joined us in the shelter. He didn't look like a hiker; what hiker wears blue coveralls and street shoes? Turtle and Miles were friendly to him, but I pretended to be asleep. He brought back all the uneasy feelings I'd ever had. If Blue Suit didn't give us an occasion to use *vomit*, our secret signal word for creepy people, I didn't know who would.

I fell asleep for real, and in the morning we were all fine. Blue Suit left the shelter before we did. He was smoking a cigar when he hiked out.

Chapter 47
The End of the Up

The top of one mountain is always the bottom of another.
—Spiritual teacher Marianne Williamson

The distance from Hurricane Mountain Shelter to the town of Marion was 20 miles, more than Turtle, Miles, and I covered in a typical day. We planned to camp overnight at a spot Storyteller told us about and hike into town the next day. The sun was shining when we set out, and our first day should have been easy. It would have been, but Turtle had a headache and I fell.

We weren't vying for the AT speed record, but my sinus infection had cleared up by then and I felt better than I had in a week. Turtle, after demonstrating her hiking strength in Grayson Highlands, was having symptoms again. The net result was a slowing down.

Miles couldn't abide the slow pace, so she hiked ahead. Turtle and I stayed together. I was in front, feeling spry, when I came to a big rock in my path. It was over a foot high, so I should have walked around it. I didn't. I planted one foot on top of the rock and thrust my body upward.

Big mistake.

With my center of gravity thrown off, I wobbled on one foot, lost my balance, and fell over the edge of the trail. I felt like I'd been catapulted off the side of the mountain. If I hadn't come to rest against a log a few feet down the hill, who knows when I would have stopped tumbling. I scraped my back when I landed, but the log saved me from a worse fall.

Turtle pulled me up to the trail and put a bandage on my back. I was glad Miles had not been there to see my accident. "Never step on a rock" was one of her laws of hiking. That feat would be impossible if taken literally, considering the rocky terrain we covered on our journey, but Miles was referring to single stones that lay in the dirt but might not be anchored. I now knew better than to step on *any* rock when I could walk around it.

We caught up with Miles when she stopped to talk to a ranger beside the trail. When we resumed hiking, she led the way. Turtle and I endured the inevitable speeding up. Nine miles in we passed Timpi Shelter and kept going.

We were hiking up a steep incline when we came to a trail intersection with a signpost. The sign said, "Raccoon Branch Campground." Miles arrived ahead of me, so she read it first.

"I wonder if the raccoons are having fun running the campground," she said.

"What?" I hadn't seen the sign yet. Coupled with my spotty hearing, Miles's statement didn't make sense to me. I was asking her to repeat it as I caught up, but she thought I didn't get the joke.

"Oh, forget it," she said. "It was just an attempt at humor."

The trail runner at Hurricane Mountain Shelter told us we would find a beautiful campsite "at the end of the up," which meant at the top of a mountain. We crossed two mountains rife with humps but did not find such a place. We did find trail magic; a cooler sitting beside the trail provided me with oatmeal, Ramen noodles, and snacks for my food bag. It was another instance of trail magic appearing when I needed it most.

Miles was still in the lead, and she was like a robot. After we had followed her for ten miles I told Turtle, "I'm not hiking up one more mountain."

We had given up on "the campsite at the end of the up" because— ha, ha—the ups never ended. Our goal by then was a gravel road, and we finally came to it. Turtle and I sat down on the ground, refusing to continue. We were wiped out.

"Look at it this way," Miles said. "We're four miles from Marion, an easy hike in the morning." She climbed the slight hill above us to look for a campsite. By then she knew her companions were done. We set up camp among some trees near the trail, cooked, ate, hung our bear bags, and got into our tents. I slept hard.

In the morning I was the last one to pack up. Miles and Turtle watched me until I had everything ready to go. There's a creepy feeling. To top it off, I tripped on a branch leaving the campsite and fell. The ground was covered with sticks and leaves. I brushed myself off, embarrassed until Miles lost her balance too. She managed to avoid a total fall, and on we went.

We hiked to Mt. Rogers Visitor Center expecting to catch a shuttle into Marion and were surprised to find out the shuttle did not run on weekends. The *Guide* hadn't mentioned that fact. We got a ride with a middle-school teacher who had just dropped her brother off there to begin his hike. We checked into the EconoLodge in Marion for one measly night and settled into our room on the second floor. It was a standard room with two queen beds. In the absence of straws, we drew coffee packs to see who got to sleep alone. Turtle won.

We ate lunch at a Mexican restaurant, where I bumped my bottle of Corona with my elbow and turned it over while trying to make room on the table.

"Spilled your beer again, did you?" Miles said, rendering me five years old except for the nature of my drink.

When we returned to the room, Turtle closed the drapes and lay down. All of us needed clean clothes, so Miles and I gathered our laundry and Turtle's and walked a mile down the street to the Laundromat. It's ironic but true that after signing on for a 2,189-mile thru-hike I resented having to walk while in town. The day was bright and hot. I was sweating in my one clean outfit: rain clothes.

After the laundry was done I couldn't wait another second to change. I went into the Laundromat bathroom and put on my clean town shorts and a T-shirt.

In the room Miles and Turtle sat with their heads together over the *Guide*, talking about the trail. It was what I hoped Miles and I would do, but it seldom happened. Later the three of us went out to resupply, stopping first at McDonald's for burgers.

I hated to resupply late in the day. The walking was bad, but the thinking was torture. Turtle must have agreed; in the middle of our trip to the grocery store she abandoned her basket and left for the hotel, saying she was overwhelmed. She decided to take another day in Marion. Miles and I planned to get the 9:00 a.m. shuttle back to the visitor center and continue hiking.

"I don't know what to say to Turtle," Miles said when we were alone. She was referring to the fact we were leaving our friend behind.

I was losing my sometime ally and the glue in our threesome, but the truth was the truth. Miles and I had goals to meet, and Turtle wasn't in shape to keep up. She felt terrible but had not sought medical help. "It's simple," I said. "We have to go."

In the morning the three of us had breakfast off the tiny hotel lobby. The manager watched us while we chose our food from the buffet and ate. Several times he crossed the little breakfast area pretending he was paying no attention to us.

"Hikers steal food," Miles said when he returned to his desk. "He expects us to do the same." By then I had lots of food, thanks to Drop Box No. 4 which Mr. M had sent to the hotel. I took two jellies for the road anyway.

We said good-bye to Turtle. Miles and I carried our packs and poles outside, where the shuttle picked us up at 8:45.

Chapter 48
Cobwebs for Breakfast

What have I gotten myself into?
—Cheryl Strayed in *Wild*

It is said that the first hiker of the day—or the tallest hiker—will inadvertently clear the cobwebs spun overnight on the limbs of trees across the trail.

On June 8 Miles and I rode the shuttle to Mt. Rogers Visitor Center after leaving Turtle in Marion. It was a pretty morning, but the driver said thunderstorms were expected later. At least we were starting with everything dry.

We weighed our packs in the visitor center. Mine weighed 35 pounds on a people scale, 6 pounds off my new goal of "under 30." If my pack was heavier than expected, I wasn't. I weighed 132 pounds with my boots on and items in my pockets. Miles weighed the same.

Before we hit the trail, we experienced a mini-reunion. Hikers we knew—Scribbles, Giddy, Jumanji, Crusty Beard, and Superfeet—but didn't expect to see again were waiting for rides. We'd lost track of them after they passed us on the trail and could be anywhere from a few miles ahead to back home. Every time we saw our friends again it was a great surprise.

We should have been nearing Buchanan, Virginia that day according to our planning calendar. Instead, we hadn't yet reached Atkins, 200 miles south. We had abandoned hope of reaching Harpers Ferry by July 3 and were now aiming for Waynesboro, Virginia.

The new plan was for Miles and me to exit the trail at Rockfish Gap, where my trail angel friend Judy would pick us up and drive us to her house in Waynesboro. Mr. M would meet us there July 3 for the car trip north to Maine. Waynesboro was 326 miles away. At our current rate of ten miles per day, it would take us 32 days to get there if we took no zeroes.

It didn't compute.

First of all, would we really hike 32 days straight without a break? I didn't see how; we never had. By that plan we would have to resupply and do our laundry on the fly: *CFM, continuous forward motion.* Second, even if we made our way north like bats fleeing the mouth of Hell, we didn't have 32 days. We had 25.

We could not be late. Our reservation to enter Maine's Baxter State Park and climb Mt. Katahdin was for July 7.

"I want to talk to you," Miles said when we had shed our packs in a clearing to take a break.

The ground was bare, dark, and flat. It offered seating in the form of a few large rocks and logs. We sat down facing each other.

"We were going to meet Mr. M in Harpers Ferry, and now it's Waynesboro," she said. "If we continue doing ten miles a day, we won't make it to Waynesboro in time. I know Mr. M is willing to come for us wherever we are on July third, but I don't want him to have to drive through half of Virginia to find us. I don't want to disappoint him."

When we fell behind schedule, Mr. M told us repeatedly to have fun and do our best, but not to worry, he would find us; but I could see Miles' point.

"I don't want to disappoint him either," I said. Miles' husband had done a lot for me on this hike.

"Here is what I think we should do," Miles said. "Let's aim for twelve to fourteen miles per day. If we do that, we can make it.

"We'll get up earlier every morning, and we won't cook breakfast. We can eat a Clif bar to save time." It was a suggestion spoken by a person without a coffee habit. I had a coffee habit. *Best part of waking up*, as the Folgers people liked to say.

"Not even my morning coffee?"

"There's a water shortage here," she said. "If we don't cook breakfast, we'll save water and we can be on the trail by seven o'clock. By starting early, we'll also take advantage of cooler temperatures."

This must be what is known in novels as the Dark Night of the Soul, the point when little hope remains. I had the same goal as Miles—to get to our pickup point—but I thought it might kill me.

Aside from the coffee issue, my feet had not adjusted to the new boots I bought in Hot Springs. The Superfeet insoles I bought in

Damascus had improved the fit, and at a rate of ten miles per day I was comfortable enough until about eight miles in. Would I be hobbling into camp every day now that we were adding two to four miles?

"I'll try it," I said, "but you're asking a lot." And then, to myself: *Today is the first day of the rest of your hike.* Continuous forward motion, put into practice.

That afternoon, when we had hiked 11.5 miles, we followed the trail through a grassy field to a two-lane road near Atkins, Virginia. Across that road sat the Chill Out Inn (not the real name).

"Do you want to stop here for the night?" Miles asked.

I said it without a bit of coaching: "NO! Do you?"

"I'm tempted."

I was surprised, because Miles didn't miss much. "Don't you remember what the trail runner Storyteller told us about that place?" I said. "He called it the worst hotel ever. It was so bad he wouldn't take a shower there after being in the woods for days. He said the bed was so filthy he slept on top of the covers in his sleeping bag."

Instead of signing the register of doom for a night in the Chill Out Inn, we decided to hike on; but first, a break. We bought Gatorade and ice cream at an Exxon station and sat outside. Miles noted the notable: It was fun. We hiked on through fields of thigh-high clover, hay, and Queen Anne's lace. Livestock were grazing, dark against acres of golden wheat. They paid us no mind as we passed by.

I was getting tired. After two more miles we came to Davis Campsite and stopped. As usual, we pitched our tents moments before a thunderstorm began. I heard a loud crack of thunder shortly after getting inside. We had no idea another hiker had stopped nearby to stand under a tree. Later he told us lightning had struck close to us. "My hair stood on end," he said. I'm glad you're safe."

I ate a cold supper in my tent and then offered to hang Miles' food bag with mine. It was still raining. The length of cord got soaked and wouldn't slide over the wet tree limb with the weight of the two food bags on the other end. I could not pull them more than four feet off the ground, so we kept our food in our tent vestibules that night. Neither of us was bothered by animals, perhaps because of the nasty weather.

I found a big blister on the outside of my left heel, and it was only our first day of increased mileage. We would get up in the morning and try our cold-breakfast routine. I missed my coffee already. And the oatmeal and the Slim Jim and the Honey Bun.

I like Clif bars. I do. I ate them as snacks for months before my hike, buying 10 for $10 at Kroger. I paced myself to avoid overindulging and becoming sick of every flavor before I hit the AT. The recipes were dense, filling to a point, but the product size had shrunk over time. That was my complaint: The wrappers would indicate larger bars inside, but the packaging had not caught up with the economies applied to the food. A Clif bar sliding around in a too-big wrapper: That was my breakfast. Until . . .

"Something's on my face," I said to Miles. I ran my left hand over my cheeks, mouth, and chin—a tricky move when that hand is strapped to a trekking pole.

I stopped and turned. "Do you see anything?" She didn't. The filaments were so fine they were invisible in the early morning light.

We had left camp at 7:00 as planned and I was leading the way up Little Brushy Mountain when I walked straight into the first cobweb. *Bon appétit* was not the first phrase that came to mind.

Chapter 49
Mind Control

If you want to forget all your other troubles,
wear too-tight shoes.
—*The Houghton Line,* 1965

When our cold-breakfast plan didn't take hold, I was ecstatic. We stayed with our other goal, the one that demanded we cover 12 to 14 miles of trail per day. Some hikers would call 12 to 14 miles a short day; 15 to 20 miles would be more like it for many of our northbound contemporaries after the 545-mile warm-up from Georgia. Our plan was a stretch for me, but I embraced it and did my best.

Miles could out-hike me, no question about it. I was capable but inconsistent on the trail; some days I could fly, but I didn't always want to. As we increased our mileage, my feet suffered. Oh, I don't imagine the woman with 18 blisters back at Mountain Crossings would have called it suffering; Miles didn't. Besides being stoic about her own medical issues, she had a point. As injuries went, I had none: no sprained ankles, no blown-out knees, no history of back problems, and no serious damage from falling. Nothing to cry about.

I was still miserable from the ankles down. Was it the walking or my shoes? Likely, both. In the early afternoons, after eight or ten miles on the trail, the bottoms of my feet would be numb and I would limp to compensate for my shoes bumping my ankles. I suspected I had chosen the wrong pair, or at least the wrong size.

As summer settled in and the days grew longer, it made sense that we should be able to cover more ground, even when starting later, but that did not translate into desire for me. I fantasized about reaching our destination and shedding my boots for my camp sandals. I could barely wiggle my toes in the hiking shoes, and I longed to feel the air on my feet. When it felt the heaviest, I dreamed of taking off the blue albatross that was my pack. I would picture it on the floor of the shelter instead of on my back. If Miles had similar goals, she rarely spoke them aloud.

We had a good hike from Davis Campsite to Knot Maul Branch Shelter. After spending the previous evening camped in a thunderstorm and then packing up wet tents, we hiked in sunshine. We crossed fences on stiles, taking turns climbing the ladder-like structures, and stopped for lunch in a farmer's field. The owner had mowed a path through waist-high grass and made a flat spot at the edge of the woods. We arrived to find hikers eating or reading under the trees while their tents, ground cloths, and sleeping bags dried in the sun. Miles and I unpacked ours and spread them on top of the grass along the path before we ate. The nylon pieces rose and fell with the breeze.

I spent the night in my tent and Miles stayed in the shelter. It wasn't animosity so much as a lack of anything to draw us close.

The next day we hiked 15 miles, including Chestnut Ridge, the biggest climb we'd done since leaving Tennessee. On the way we met a southbound hiker who had just seen a bear a half-mile from where we were standing.

"It was the biggest bear I've ever seen," he said, "right on the trail." Our path led where his had been. I dreaded the next few minutes.

"Let's review what to do," Miles said. "We'll keep walking, but we need to scan the area as we hike. Which side do you want?"

"I'll take the right," I said, hoping never to see what I was imagining: a dark, rippling mass of fur moving parallel to us in the bushes. *What would I do?*

We were walking through woods and fields. A bear would be easy to spot in a clearing—not that I wanted to—but once we were surrounded by foliage, the job would be more challenging.

"I've got the left side," she said. "Scan with your eyes, but don't be obvious. Don't turn around." I wanted to turn around in the worst way.

My heart was thumping until Chestnut Knob Shelter came into view at the top of the ridge. It sat on a bald. We crossed the last open field, went inside, and set our gear down. The shelter was made of stone and had a wooden door. Pushing that door closed gave me a thrill; I felt protected after the longest half-mile of the day. I don't know how we missed the bear. Some hikers would be disappointed, but I felt relief. A bear is like a ghost on the trail. When you don't see it, the threat can weigh on your mind.

My feet were toast by the time we hiked the last six miles and pitched our tents at a campsite near VA 623. I was glad to see another tent even though its occupant, a male hiker, retired early. Miles and I had time to cook supper and hang our food bags before dark. We ate sitting on rocks near a curve in the two-lane road. No cars went by.

The next day we reached Bland, Virginia and checked into the Big Walker Motel, a long single-story brick building located on top of a steep hill. We took turns doing our laundry in the sink and hung it all on a clothesline behind the motel, banking on the remaining strength of the afternoon sun. It wasn't much of a laundry system for a hotel, but they had a heck of a hiker box.

We walked down the side of the road past the I-77 interchange to the Dollar General for resupply and carried our groceries back. We bought beer at a gas station and ordered a pizza for supper. All those things we did—the ones I learned on the trail, sometimes the hard way, back in the spring; the ones we repeated in every trail town—all of them were routine now.

I was no longer a rookie.

In the morning Miles and I caught a shuttle back to the trail. The driver, Bubba, had beautiful blue eyes I studied in the rear-view mirror from the back seat.

My feet hurt before we left the motel, so I started hiking with two Ibuprofen in me, making the morning a good one. The weather was beautiful. I led, and I had lots of energy until late in the afternoon. By then, having declared myself an ex-rookie, I shouldn't have been surprised that we climbed, descended, crossed streams, and climbed again—but I was. I expected to see our destination, Jenny Knob Shelter, around every curve. Would we ever reach it? On the *Guide* page the route looked easy: bumpy terrain, but no high mountain peaks. I grew impatient and wondered if we were lost. We were not; the white blazes didn't lie.

Both of us needed water, so we had to keep going. By the time we reached the shelter, my feet felt like two blocks of wood. I was thrilled to change my shoes, freeing my sandals from their strap on my backpack as soon we arrived, chose our tent sites, and set our packs on the ground. And then we began the routine of setting up our tents, fixing supper, eating, and hanging the food bags.

The next day's destination was Wapiti Shelter. It was a 14-mile hike with a break in the middle at Dismal Falls, a natural recreation area where Dismal Creek flows over multiple layers of flat rocks. Visitors can cool their feet, jump in where the creek pools at the bottom, or set up camp beside the water. Miles and I took a long lunch break at Dismal Falls. There was nothing dismal about the beautiful "can't-miss" spot 0.3 miles off the Appalachian Trail in the month of June. We waded in the cool, shallow water at the top and caught up with friends we knew.

I tripped on a root and fell on the side trail, on level ground where the path was thick with pine needles. That was the dismal part. The fall was quick and the needles were no cushion. I was not badly hurt, but another miracle outcome didn't spare me one second of embarrassment or disappointment. I took a few minutes to treat a wound on my left arm, and we hiked on. Hours later I was stiff and sore, glad tomorrow would be an "easy" eight miles to Woods Hole Hostel. The first two miles would be up a mountain. We would gain 1,200 feet in elevation and then hike over a few of what I called humps until descending to Sugar Run Gap. Piece of cake.

I put up my tent near Miles' on the flat ground outside Wapiti Shelter, having no knowledge that a brutal double murder happened there in 1981. A man named Randall Smith met his victims in the Dismal Falls area, hiked north with them along the AT, and killed them at the shelter the same night. If I had known, I might have been suspicious of the men we met there—for instance, the two middle-aged section hikers we met at Dismal Falls.

That would have been a shame. Locomo and Maps were kind and funny. They pitched their tents near ours that night. Miles and I were finding a new group of hikers, including a father and son we would continue to see on the trail. The boy was 11 years old, and he could throw a bear line every time. He loved helping us. He and Miles would look for a suitable tree. I contributed my cord, net bag, and a rock to put in the bag for weight. Not having to throw that line at night was bliss. As the first one up, I was glad to retrieve our food bags the next morning. It was a painless penance.

At dinnertime someone cooked enough hot dogs for a group. By then I was operating alone, one of the last to get my tent up and hike down the hill for water. Miles was the social one. She ate a hot dog in the shelter and learned everybody's trail name.

In the days after we left Turtle, I was feeling tension between Miles and me. It was crazy; I knew both of us wanted to get along. Who wouldn't on a 2,189-mile journey? We wanted to have fun together, but our personalities didn't get the memo. After we packed up to leave Wapiti Shelter, we had an argument. It was about something I brought up—no doubt, some minor complaint—and instantly regretted. I have forgotten the subject of that exchange; but whatever it was, we had not hiked out before discussing it, so those remaining within earshot heard us.

I was no longer a rookie on the trail, but I had achieved limited success communicating with my partner. Our exchanges of the sort we had that morning were seldom productive.

"I'm not a deep thinker," Miles would say, needing to disengage. I used too many words to suit her. I was too vague and too negative. To top it off, my timing was bad. Miles didn't care for early-morning discussions. She would lose patience and cut the conversation off.

The hike to Woods Hole Hostel wasn't easy after all. It wasn't because of the mountains, or even my shoes; it was because the day started on a bad note. I was sure Miles was furious, and I was frustrated. Why couldn't she listen? Our arguments solved nothing and led to hard feelings.

That wasn't all. I was spooked after falling the previous day. My caution was obvious as I led the way over the first mountain. I realized I needed to get back in touch with the trail. I needed my mojo back.

Negative thoughts invaded my mind as I walked. I replayed the argument and knew I was again preoccupied with Miles and missing my own hike. *No.* I couldn't allow her in my last private space—my head.

Get her out, get her out, get her out! I said it to myself every time I caught my thoughts drifting in the wrong direction. That soothing message cleared my mind.

We hiked in silence for a while, and then she spoke from behind me. "I'll say one thing. You sure know how to f--- up a Sunday morning."

We were each other's nightmare; how else could I put it after that?

Get her out!

At least it kept my mind off my feet.

Chapter 50
Eh?

After a storm comes a calm.
—Welsh author Matthew Henry

Woods Hole Hostel, a mountain retreat in southwest Virginia, sat a half-mile off the Appalachian Trail, 621 miles north of our official starting point at Springer Mountain, Georgia.

We arrived at the hostel on June 14. Since the end of March we had hiked less than one-third of the Appalachian Trail. When I thought about where we were versus the 1,568 miles that lay ahead for Miles and me, I wondered if I could do it.

I knew I could do the hike—the 621 miles of wild, rugged, twisting trail behind me proved that—but could I endure the turn our relationship had taken? I appreciated Miles's hiking experience and admired her determination to reach every goal, but would she ever let up on me?

Her attention to my communication skills was heating up. The issues were a combination of my hearing difficulties and our opposing discussion styles, including Miles's insistence on "direct answers."

At times I couldn't hear her if she spoke from too far behind me or in front on the trail. I had to ask her to repeat what she said. We would stop hiking and face one another, an annoying process that resulted in less progress, thus less talk.

When I did hear Miles, being unable and unwilling to limit my responses to one or two words, I took a moment to shape my answer. As I thought through the possibilities, she would interpret my silence to mean I hadn't heard her and would come close and repeat the question at a higher volume. What must have sounded like arguments to others were often Miles's attempts to make herself heard.

Taking too long to answer a question can be a sign of deception. In my case it wasn't; I was no more interested in deception than I was in discord, but my aversion to confrontation made me a victim. It was easier to let Miles think what she would than to argue.

She watched my face. "Do you know you look to the right when we're talking?"

I didn't know it, but so what? Eye movements, or "tells," have been documented. Looking to the right and up means a person is assessing logic. Looking to the right at ear level indicates the person is processing sound. I could have been doing either.

I found this in a police novel: "When lying, people take pains to avoid direct answers." Miles thought I was being dishonest because my replies didn't fit her definition of a direct answer. Maybe I *was* evasive. It had never bothered anyone else.

Woods Hole Hostel was an oasis despite the fact that Miles and I were avoiding each other. In addition to the main house, which was a bed and breakfast, the hostel included a separate bunk house and bathroom facilities for hikers. The property included vegetable gardens. Goats roamed the hillside.

After we took adjacent beds on the upper floor of the bunk house, we took turns cleaning up and turned our soiled clothing over to hostel personnel. Having someone else do the laundry was a treat. We visited on the bunk house porch with Maps, Locomo, and other hikers we knew. I was glad to see familiar faces and have a diversion. Maybe no one noticed how little Miles and I said to each other.

I left the bunkhouse to sit at a table on the porch of the main building. I rented a laptop computer to access the internet, planning to order a gift. Miles's birthday was coming up in the next two weeks. In spite of our tension today, I wouldn't ignore her birthday. By then this morning's argument would be forgotten.

I was up and running on the laptop when Miles came across the yard and sat down with me.

"What are you doing?" she asked. I knew by her tone she was making up.

"Just going online to check my e-mail," I said.

We ordered smoothies and drank them together on the porch. I would tell her later about intending to order the birthday gift and she would shake her head and say, "No presents." Fine; the rule would also apply to my birthday in a few weeks.

After a wonderful breakfast, we finished our chores and left Woods Hole Hostel for Pearisburg, 12 miles away. We hiked with

Locomo and Maps. The trail rose as we left Sugar Run Gap. Locomo, the fastest hiker, got ahead. Miles was second. I followed her, and Maps was last.

We worried about Maps. He would become short of breath and fall behind. Maps would stop to rest and Locomo would be drawn back to wait, either for him or with him. "I'd settle for a saddle," Maps said during a break, referring to the flat gaps between mountains.

The four of us sat down for a one-hour lunch break along the trail and then continued over the longest mountain. Miles and I lost the men around Angel's Rest, the highest point. We made the long descent and waited at the bottom, listening for voices or footsteps, but the woods were quiet. After a while Miles made an arrow on the trail with sticks to indicate we had gone on. We didn't see Locomo and Maps again, but we would hear from them later and know they were well.

A female hiker was sleeping on the ground where we exited the AT. Once we emerged from the woods, there was no shade. We walked on paved roads to the streets of Pearisburg, Virginia, where the sun was on us like a broiler. The outskirts of town seemed deserted, the way a place can be on a hot, still summer day.

We checked into our hotel in a rundown section and ate dinner at the Mexican restaurant across the street. We walked to the strip shopping center behind the restaurant and resupplied at the local Food Lion, which bore a sign informing customers it would be closing for good.

After shopping, we returned to the hotel. I was glad the walking was over for another day. Evening brought with it a physical and mental letting down. We gathered our laundry and took it to the washer, taking advantage of the convenience despite starting the day in clean clothes. In the room I spread out my groceries for the inevitable sorting. Miles sat on the balcony at twilight and called home.

Hiking with a partner can be compared to marriage in that it is 24/7 and guaranteed to be imperfect. Miles and I were learning firsthand that the trail itself wasn't the only source of ups and downs. In the quiet of that night, I wondered: Could we hike together for another 1,555 miles?

Chapter 51
Hey, Wild Bill!

Hey, Wild Bill, wait for me!
—Portly, gap-toothed actor Andy Devine as Jingles,
sidekick on the TV show
"The Adventures of Wild Bill Hickok," 1951–58

After leaving Pearisburg we skipped our next destination, Rice Field Shelter. The shelter was a mere six miles north on the trail—too few for our ramped-up daily goal—but distance wasn't the reason.

Miles and I were climbing the steepest incline of the day when we passed a male hiker resting against a tree.

"If you meet my hiking companion ahead, tell her I'll be along," he said, saying her name. "My name is Tom." What was it with men named Tom? We had met so many on this trip. It reminded me of the Year of the Jims.

As a divorcee in the early 1990s, I was a regular on the singles scene. The Internet had yet to bloom as a dating option. I attended dances at hotels and singles meetings held in the basement of a nearby church. Over the course of a year, I dated three men named Jim.

That fall my friend Lou and I flew to Minnesota to do our holiday shopping at the mammoth Mall of America, which opened in Minneapolis in 1992. We spent a night in a nearby Holiday Inn. The hotel was hosting a singles dance, so Lou and I joined the party. We had fun dancing and mingling with the local crowd, particularly two men we met—both named Jim.

Miles and I were hiking in a section of Virginia where water was rare. Many sources were dry. We stopped at a mountain stream with a reduced flow and had to wait in line to fill our bottles. A woman was bent over the water, taking her time. It was no surprise to find out the woman hogging the stream was the same one who had left Tom beside the trail.

When we reached Rice Field Shelter at the top of the mountain, we heard her inside dominating a conversation. Holding court.

"Let's hike on," Miles said. "I can't stay here with that obnoxious woman."

Instead of beginning a steep descent after we passed the shelter, we climbed over a wooden stile to follow the trail into Rice Field. We took in a panoramic view of blue sky, rolling Virginia hills, green-and-brown valleys far below us, and in the distance the purple mountains of West Virginia.

"Woo hoo!" I said as we passed the sign indicating the long view to my home state.

The terrain flattened to gentle bumps for the next few miles. Miles led the way past power lines and over balds to a campsite where we ate, hung our food bags, and spent the night. The bugs were bad, signaling possible rain.

I didn't question Miles' desire to hike beyond Rice Field Shelter that day; when someone makes us uncomfortable, it's the smart thing to do. She and I agreed on that point before we left home. There were other days when I wondered what she was thinking.

We varied our speed and distance depending on the terrain and weather, as any hikers would, but rarely on our whims—with one exception: moseying. On Sundays, on days of extreme heat and humidity, or "just because," we set a slower pace. It was Miles' idea to mosey, a hiking equivalent of sleeping in or lingering over the newspaper in regular life. Our moseying days often followed aggressive ones in which we'd exceeded our daily mileage goal.

We would start later than usual and, true to the definition of *mosey*, would aim for a leisurely pace instead of the brisk march we were used to. Slowing down was attractive in theory, but Miles's moseying speed was faster than mine. In fact, it was faster than my hiking speed.

"I'm not in any hurry," she would say when we set out, and I came to recognize that as the signal I would soon be left behind.

"This isn't personal," she said one day from behind me, "but I'm tired of looking at your backpack. I'm going to hike ahead." I didn't take it personally; being behind a slower hiker is a bit like driving behind a semi. You long to speed up and you have no view until you pass.

When Miles pulled ahead on the wooded trail, she was like a wraith in a ghost movie. I would watch the distance between us lengthen and the figure of Miles grow smaller, glimpsing bits of her as she rounded a curve or disappeared behind a stand of trees. It was comforting to catch a flash of her red coat ahead or spot her silver-colored pack and know she hadn't disappeared, but I wondered why she suggested slowing down and then did the opposite.

One morning we were hiking along a rocky ridge where the trail dipped and rose. She was in front. Suddenly I was on the ground. Falling was always so fast. I'd slipped on a rock—or was it the wet grass?—landed hard and skinned my right arm and one of my knees deeply enough to draw blood. I don't recall Miles saying a word after turning to see me sprawled among the rocks. By then the surprise had gone out of my falling, but she was gentle and patient in bandaging my wounds. It pains me to say this next part.

"I was trying to keep up with you," I whined. "I can't do it!"

The whining is the part I hate to admit. It was childish, and my outburst prompted another awkward exchange.

"I'm done," Miles said, putting her hands up as if to stop me from sputtering another pathetic syllable. Done with what? Done talking? Done with me?

How could the gentle person dressing my wounds be the same one who had so little patience with me five minutes later? She and I had survived the "big talk" at the NOC, but that was two months ago. Was every negative feeling between us going to return? Was hiking ahead her way of leaving me again?

It seemed our fragile partnership was cracking apart and our plans might be doomed, but I was tired of being wrong. I was tired of being too slow or too clumsy or too poor a communicator.

I missed the days of Ms. Rabbit, when I was alone but my own person. Her voice had grown faint along with mine.

I decided to stick to my own hiking speed, even if I fell behind. Asking Miles to slow down wasn't the answer. She had to hike her own hike, too.

Over time I came to believe she intended to slow down on those designated days but was incapable of following her own suggestion. Anyone whose favorite expressions include "Let's get 'er done" is going to have a difficult time moseying along the Appalachian Trail.

We hiked on, together or a half-mile apart, but always meeting at the end of a day. I continued to fall from time to time despite my efforts to prevent it by watching my feet. Looking down at my boots was a habit guaranteed to slow me down, but I knew from experience how a fall would wreck my self-confidence. I had been lucky, landing time after time on my soft backpack. That's not to say it would always be the case.

On June 17 we packed wet tents and left our campsite for Bailey Gap Shelter, 14.9 miles north. We were back to our aggressive daily schedule. The first few miles took us along a flat ridge. We were "hiking our own hike," which meant Miles was hiking at her quicker pace. The first couple of times she got ahead she stopped and waited for me, using the time for a break. After a while we abandoned that plan as inefficient and agreed to meet at Pine Swamp Branch Shelter for lunch.

She was soon out of sight, but I maintained a respectable pace until I stepped onto a rock the wrong way and hurt my right knee. I didn't fall; at least I had that.

The pain was tolerable on the flatter stretches, but by then those were few. The trail rose and plunged and rose again, slowing my progress and providing a means of torture. I could hardly walk on the uphills, and my trekking poles offered no relief. I took a few Ibuprofen and tried to phone Miles, not to call her back to help me but to let her know I would be late. My phone had no service. I typed a text, sent it, and hoped to pass a spot on the trail where the phone would work for a few moments so Miles could receive the message.

Once I made it to the lunch spot, we took a long break. I removed my boots and socks for a while and rested my injured leg. A stream ran near the shelter where we ate, and I splashed the cool mountain water on my sore knee.

We hiked the last four miles to Bailey Gap Shelter in the afternoon. It may have been located in a gap, but that gap was near the top of a mountain. Sweat poured off us. As soon as we arrived we had to follow a side trail downhill to replenish our water. The filtering, cooking, and other evening rituals took the edge off the day, and I settled into the dusky wooden hold of the shelter. Tomorrow was another day.

PART 4
WINDS OF
CHANGE

Chapter 52
At a Crossroad

If you come to a fork in the road, take it.
—Yogi Berra

Miles developed an uneasy feeling after we left Laurel Creek Shelter on June 19. I've had feelings like that, hard to explain but as real as a toothache.

We had been carrying wet tents and sleeping in the shelters since leaving our campsite two days before in a morning rain. We planned to hike 12.4 miles that day, but as the result of Miles' feeling—one of resistance, if not dread—we skipped a 26-mile section of the trail.

We didn't realize we would miss three famous landmarks—Keffer Oak, the second largest oak tree on the AT at 18 inches around; the Audie Murphy monument honoring the most decorated American soldier in World War II; and the stone monolith called Dragon's Tooth—as we descended through a pasture to stand at the edge of VA 630 and thumb a ride to our new destination, Four Pines Hostel near Newport.

I was as unassertive hitchhiking as I was in any other situation.

"Stick your thumb out," Miles said.

Traffic was sporadic, but fast on the two-lane. Pickup trucks—maroon, white, red—whizzed by us.

"Should we start walking toward town?" Miles asked, waiting for a yes or a no. Hell, I didn't know what we should do. I did know she would favor continuous forward motion.

Get her out.

"Let's walk," I said. It was better than standing still on the narrow strip of wet grass.

"A woman will pick us up," I said as we came to a church parking lot. We didn't have a prayer with the pickup trucks.

"You were right!" Miles said moments later as a female driver slowed and pulled onto the blacktop in front of us.

Our rescuer, an environmentalist, was on her way to meet friends for a hike. She had a big dog in the car, but she made room for Miles and me, our backpacks and trekking poles. As it turned out, we had been hitching in the wrong direction for the hostel. She couldn't take us there, but she dropped us off at the Newport Post Office.

The late-morning sun was warming Newport, Virginia as Miles and I hauled our packs from the P.O. to the Super Val-U Grocery and gasoline station next door. We leaned our packs against the front wall of the store while we shopped for drinks and snacks. What fun it would be to unpack at the hostel later and hang my tent and damp sleeping bag out to dry!

Miles got the number from her *A.T. Guide* pages and called the shuttle for Four Pines. "We're at the Super Val-U at the intersection of Route four-sixty and the Blue Grass Trail," she said into the phone. To me she said, "They'll pick us up in an hour."

We were not in a town, but at a crossroad. We waited on the platform of an outdoor sign by the highway, eating snacks and drinking orange juice until the ants found us. We grabbed our food bags and moved beside the Super Val-U, where we shared a strip of shade with a black pickup truck.

That was where we decided to leave the trail.

"I miss my family and you shouldn't be on the trail," Miles said, facing me. She was referring to my numerous unexpected encounters with the ground.

So, I'd fallen a few times. I wasn't the only hiker to lose footing on the Appalachian Trail, and the cause wasn't my age or gender. According to the online blog *The Trek*, "Injury in the backcountry . . . is anecdotally one of the major sources of ended thru-hikes." The number from one survey of PCT hikers was 25 percent. Young people fell. Men fell. What about Flashback, who blew out his knee the first week? Some who fall are hurt so badly they must leave the trail. I kept going, every time.

I disagreed with Miles—whether I belonged on the AT was *my* call—but I didn't respond because I heard something deeper in her words. She wanted to go home.

So, did I, and I didn't care what face she put on it. Whatever reason we gave the world, the time had come to end this hike.

For me it had been difficult for a while. I don't mean the usual hard parts: climbing mountains, sleeping on planks or dirt, wondering when a 300-pound black bear would amble out of the woods to eat me. I mean the hard personal part, the part that's too long and relentless and intimate not to provoke hard feelings. Miles must have felt the strain, too; how could she not? We were mismatched companions with different personalities and skills, each one thinking she knew more than she did. Our idea was not to leave the trail that day; we were talking about skipping the south-bound portion of our thru-hike and coming home after our time in Maine.

Maine was a done deal. By then I didn't want to go—didn't care about summiting Mt. Katahdin—but we had agreed with Mr. M that the three of us would go to Maine in July, no matter what. He was still working at his job and looking forward to the vacation. I felt I had to see it through.

Miles and I put a tentative time frame to the rest of the hike. We could summit Katahdin on July 7 as planned and be home by the 10th. Three more weeks.

We had expected—then hoped, then hoped against hope—to be in Waynesboro, Virginia now, 186 miles north of where we stood. By the time we reached Waynesboro I would have 800 miles and three months of spring and summer behind me. It was a long time to be on the trail.

We weren't going to make Waynesboro in 12 days on foot at our current pace, and we couldn't change the target again—too chaotic— but we would find a way to arrive there on time. Mr. M would meet us at our trail angel Judy's house and drive us to Maine.

We were wrapping up our discussion when we saw the Four Pines shuttle coming. Who could miss it? The aging van had been painted by hikers. It was blue with a large, winged dragon along each side, the tails curling up to the roof. The back panel bore the name DRAGON WAGON, a friendly dragon face, mountains, and a yellow sun.

In minutes the crossroad was a vanishing point behind us. I settled into the Dragon Wagon and knew I would count down the remaining 21 days. Miles and I didn't announce our new plan. It was too soon. As far as anyone else knew, we were on track to complete the Appalachian Trail.

Chapter 53
Now I Lay Me Down to Fight Bugs, Smell Chickens, and Worry About Being Murdered

Where did you sleep?
—Everyone

Over the next nine days Miles and I slept in a barn, a hotel, four shelters, two campsites, and a campground. The campground was a mistake, and the last campsite had us preparing for "fight or flight."

At Four Pines Hostel we set up in a barn at the top of a hill rather than in the hostel itself, which was grimy looking and full of young people. It was also home that night to Baltimore Jack, who turned up a few times in our travels.

We staked our tent pieces on the grass to dry, and I flung my sleeping bag over a nearby fence to air out before I walked down the hill for a shower in the main building. I was lucky I'd bought a lightweight towel in Damascus, as Four Pines Hostel did not furnish towels. How can a hostel expect its customers to air dry? The tiny, steamy bathrooms guarantee your clothes will stick to you even if you have a towel.

Baltimore Jack was reading a book when I walked outside. Other hikers were standing in the pasture with their cell phones. I wanted to call Joe but could not get enough bars for reception anywhere on the property.

For dinner, 13 of us jammed into the Dragon Wagon and were driven to a restaurant. Later, back in the barn, I took my shoes off and said, "My feet are swollen."

"It's a lack of potassium," Miles said.

With that, we climbed into the bedding we had spread out on wide shelves of plywood and slept. A few feet below us chickens could wander in and out of the barn, leaving souvenirs on the dry dirt.

The next day we slack-packed from VA 311 to Daleville. After the van driver let us off by the road, he took our backpacks to the Daleville Howard Johnson's and we hiked with light day packs that held only our lunches, water, toilet paper, and a few emergency supplies.

We took our first break at the famous McAfee Knob, watching braver hikers pose for pictures at the unprotected edge of the high rock. I could not go near it and was relieved when we returned to the path in the woods that would take us past another stomach-dropping view at Tinker Cliffs.

We ate lunch at Lambert's Meadow Shelter amid posted warnings of bear activity. I watched the high grass for movement and later kept a 360-degree vigil as we got water from a stream near the shelter.

It was one of our best hiking days. Miles and I were in synch. We made great time, completing 21 miles of trail despite two afternoon rainstorms, countless mountaintop boulders, and four towers of power lines rising from a bleak, otherworldly section of ridges under a threatening sky. I wondered if the last mountain would ever let us go.

We arrived at HoJo's at 7:00 p.m. to claim our backpacks in the lobby, clean up, eat out, and sleep in real beds.

The next day, June 21, was a Sunday—Naked Hiker Day, not that we planned to celebrate it. The temperature reached 91 degrees, forcing both of us to hike at a moderate pace. When we came to a stream we soaked our bandanas and wiped our faces, necks, and arms with the cool water. Our destination was Fullhardt Knob Shelter, located on top of a mountain five miles from Daleville.

I didn't cook that night. With no source nearby, we had to conserve our water supply. Miles called it dry camping. The sky was a picture of rain on the way. We heard from another hiker that a bad storm, "Tropical Depression Bill," was due that night, so we stayed in the shelter for safety. The storm did not come.

I couldn't hear out of my left ear. It had been stopped up for weeks, so I took my hearing aid out. Why run the battery down?

"I'll change my left wax guard again," I said to Miles, who must be tired of raising her voice. "But I'm almost out of blue wax guards."

"Are the red ones and the blue ones different?"

"Just the color," I said. "Red for right, blue for left."

"Then why can't you use a red one if you run out of the blue?"

Could I? The color-coded wax guards were a way to tell the hearing aids apart, but so was their design. Each one fit only one ear. *Thanks, Miles.* Why didn't I think of that?

With nine days to get to Waynesboro, we left Fullhardt Knob Shelter at 7:00 a.m., hiked 6.2 miles to the next shelter for lunch, and went another 7.3 miles to Bobblett's Gap Shelter for the night. Our hike took us near the Blue Ridge Parkway. The AT crossed the parkway several times, requiring us to walk onto pavement in direct sunlight after the shade of the forest. It was boiling hot, and we took frequent breaks. The shelter never seemed to get any closer, and I arrived hot and sticky.

We heard some friends say they were hiking to a swimming hole the next day. They planned to camp there, at Jennings Creek. Miles and I decided to join them. We hiked to VA 614 and stood beside the road in a dilemma.

The campsite at Jennings Creek was located near the same trail point as Middle Creek Campground. I had trouble with the difference between *campsite* and *campground*. The difference is this: A campsite is a clearing. It might include a few logs arranged around a fire ring. A campground is a managed facility where campers are charged a fee.

"Do you want to go to Jennings Creek or the campground?" Miles asked in typical Miles fashion. "Jennings Creek or Middle Creek?"

"Middle Creek," I said.

Instead of crossing to re-enter the woods, we began walking down the road. Middle Creek Campground was two miles away. It was another hot day, and we walked on pavement carrying our heavy packs. We turned onto a secondary road. Every curve of it presented a cruel reality: No, the campground was not just ahead. A few vehicles passed us, but no driver offered us a ride.

I chose Middle Creek expecting to find the swimming hole and the hikers we knew, but I was wrong. They had gone to Jennings Creek. By the time I realized my mistake—that we should have gone to Jennings Creek—we were there.

The campground was all but deserted. We chose a campsite and got changed for the pool. Our swimsuits were makeshift, sports bras and shorts. We would not create a stir in them; after a boy and his father left, the pool was empty. A plastic chair floated upside down in the water. Our swim was a silent experience for the most part, but the water was refreshing. After we showered and dressed, we got our supper from the snack bar and ate it on the patio studying our *Guide* pages to evaluate our chances of reaching Waynesboro by July 1.

Not so hot.

I needed to let Judy know we might need a ride and tell my brother the latest. Joe was driving from Ohio to meet us for a visit before we rode north. Phone reception would be helpful if I could find the right spot to stand on our vast planet.

The owner of the campground shuttled us back to the trail at 8:30 the next morning, along with a hiker named 44 who had camped beside us. It was June 24.

To reach our destination, Thunder Hill Shelter, we would hike over Fork Mountain, Floyd Mountain, and Apple Orchard Mountain. Floyd Mountain had, by my count, five separate peaks. The elevation gain to the highest one was over 1,800 feet—steep. The shelter was located on the far side of Apple Orchard Mountain.

Miles and I got into another heated discussion when we reached Cornelius Creek Shelter at the top of Floyd Mountain. We were five miles from our goal, but I was dripping sweat. My heart was racing, and I had to keep stopping on the way up the mountain. My lack of energy and rapid heartbeat scared me, and I didn't want to go up another incline that day to sleep in a shelter that had been placed on the bear-warning list.

"I'm concerned," I said to Miles, and told her my symptoms.

"What do you want to do?" she asked. "I want to hike on."

"I don't feel . . . ," I began. *When would I learn?*

"GO or STAY?"

We were now using our outdoor voices.

"I want to stay here," I said, noticing a male hiker seated a few feet away. He had an earful.

We stopped early for the night, and Miles made the best of it. When she gave in, she was a good sport.

The shelter had lots of flat acreage. We pitched our tents behind it, near the privy. At dinner we met a mom, her two daughters, and their hiking companion, who was considering whether to leave the trail. When the first three left her behind after supper, she decided to stay and hike her own hike.

The next night Miles and I camped on a flat, grassy site at Marble Spring after hiking more than 12 miles. We ate with another hiker sitting on logs. In the evening deer came to the edge of the woods to eat foliage. The bugs were bad, so I wiped myself down with Ben's Wipes and was in my tent by 7:30. I slept with the vestibule open to let in air. We were due for a resupply in the town of Glasgow. After walking across the James River Bridge the next morning, we came to a road. We hitched the seven-plus miles into town and had lunch with a few other hikers at a pizza restaurant on the main drag.

It started raining. Miles and I walked to the free hiker pavilion behind the restaurant, plugged in our phones, and left our packs there while we walked to the Dollar General to shop. Part of the pavilion was under roof. A picnic table sat outside, and an enclosed shower had been put in beside the main structure.

When we returned we sorted and packed our food at the picnic table and took showers, drying off with three-dollar towels we picked up at Dollar General. We left the towels for two other hikers, a couple. She cut his hair before they cleaned up.

Miles and I walked back to the two-lane road and stood in the sun with our thumbs out, hoping to get a ride back to the AT. When no one stopped, Miles suggested we start walking to the trailhead, but I resisted. Why walk in the heat when we could possibly ride, if anyone would take notice of two older ladies standing by the road wearing backpacks.

At last a red Cadillac SUV slowed down, pulled off the road, and glided toward us. Inside were a man and woman looking to be in their fifties. She had dark hair, dyed. His was gray.

He unlocked the tailgate and we shoved our packs and poles into the space. We sat in the back seat making conversation about why we were hitchhiking with the sun frying us in Glasgow, Virginia. It was all pleasant and I was grateful to be riding in a beautiful, air-conditioned car.

When we pulled over near the trailhead, he got out with us and pointed to a short cut he said would save us a mile. We thanked him but didn't take it, because purists don't deviate. We were hiking the AT, not some other path.

"She isn't his wife," Miles said as the couple drove away.

We spent the night in Johns Hollow Shelter, two miles in. For a while Miles and I were the only occupants, but other hikers arrived later. We aired out our tents, set them up, and hung our wet socks on a clothesline. When we were done it looked like rain, or worse.

Miles said, "If it starts to storm, we'll grab everything we can and run for the shelter."

"Why wait?" I said. "Let's take down our tents now and sleep in the shelter." It proved to be a good move; the rain came at 4:00 a.m.

June 27 was a Saturday. We hiked close to the group from the shelter, occasionally passing them or letting them pass us. After a couple big ups and a long downhill, we ate lunch in Punchbowl Shelter and watched the rain. By then our feet were soaked and wrinkled from walking in it.

We planned to camp that night at a site near the Pedlar River, but we couldn't find it. The *Guide* information was confusing, so Miles walked up and down the two-lane looking for the campsite with no success. When the others arrived, a male hiker from Germany found our site. Then he and the others hiked on.

The campsite was between the road and the Pedlar River. The road was not heavily traveled, so we felt safe setting up. It rained off and on. We cooked and ate supper outside, Miles sitting on a rock and me on a damp log.

While we were eating, a car crept by. It then came back the other way and stopped. The male driver called out the open window to Miles, "Do you like spicy food?"

What was that about?

"NO!" Miles said, and sat with her back to the road. The car drove on, but she was spooked. I had started to change into my camp sandals.

"Leave your boots on," Miles said. "I'm going to walk down the road and see if that car is parked. If it is, we're packing up and leaving, no questions asked."

I wondered where we would we go, how far we would have to hike. Besides being uneasy about the car, I was beat.

"We passed a campsite in the woods before we came to the road," Miles said, answering my unspoken question.

The car was gone. We stayed put but took precautions, first blocking the entrance to the campsite with logs and branches. We then took our hiking poles into our tents as potential weapons. I also laid two hefty rocks in my vestibule in case I needed to throw them at someone.

We were beside a rushing river, so any other noise was drowned out once we got into our tents. I was glad when it began to rain. This is what I told myself: *Who would go to the trouble to pursue campers on such a night?* No one, I hoped. By the time I fell asleep, it was late.

The morning light coming into my tent was a gift, as was my relief at knowing Miles and I had not been raped or murdered. We wasted no time packing up to leave.

Now we were four days from our new pickup point, the Visitor Center in Buena Vista, Virginia. I had reached both Judy and my brother, and they were coming for Miles and me on July 1.

Chapter 54
Three Months

**When you reach the end of your rope,
tie a knot in it and hang on.
—Thomas Jefferson**

Miles and I stepped over the pile of branches we'd placed at the entrance to our Pedlar River campsite, followed the two-lane road back to the woods, and hiked 7.7 miles north along Brown Mountain Creek. It was our last stretch of trail before we would trade our hiking boots and poles for a ride and two days of real-world living at the home of our trail angel, Judy, and her husband in Waynesboro.

Waynesboro would be a turning point. It would end our northbound hike. According to plan but 158 miles south of our original destination, we would flip to Maine. What we wouldn't do was hike for another three months. I had been counting the days since Newport when Miles and I decided to leave the AT.

Cheryl Strayed didn't walk the entire Pacific Crest Trail. She began at the beginning, as we had, and ended her hike at the Bridge of the Gods over the Columbia River between Oregon and Washington. Cheryl was on the trail three months. Miles and I hiked up Springer Mountain to the official beginning of the AT on March 30. Now we were approaching the end of June—three months for us, pure coincidence—and I was ready for a change.

I had never been to Waynesboro, nor had I met Judy in person. She and I attended the same high school in West Virginia too many years apart to meet. She knew my brother, and because of Joe and my AT hike she and I became acquainted on Facebook.

I tried to avoid that word—*Facebook*, still a prickly subject—when talking to Miles. She was not on social media and thus had not met Judy personally or in cyberspace.

The path along Brown Mountain Creek wound through what quickly became one of my favorite areas. The trail leveled out and passed excellent stopping points with views. Posted signs explained that a community of freed slaves had lived along the creek in the early 1900s.

We stopped for lunch at Brown Mountain Creek Shelter and decided to stay the night. The shelter was extraordinary for its peaceful setting. It was built on a hill above the creek with thick forest on the other side. We could hear the water moving. The shelter was deserted except for Miles and me. We spent the afternoon organizing our packs and drying our tents, sleeping bags, dry sacks, shoes, and socks in the sun. That process was a reminder it was time to get out of the woods.

I was almost out of food, and I knew my cooking fuel must be low; I'd been using the same 8-ounce can of gas since Pearisburg. One of my bags for unfiltered water was leaking around the opening, a no-no for the mess as well as the lost water. The rain cover for my pack was history. The snaps that held it on had rusted to the point I could not unsnap them to remove the cover, so I cut the elastic cords, which then disappeared inside their casing, leaving no means to hold the cover in place and keep out the rain.

While my gear and clothing were drying outside, I lay down on the shelter floor. I was surprised when I woke up and Miles told me I'd slept for an hour and a half. By suppertime the temperature had dropped, and I put on my orange quilted jacket. We had company for a while before a Canadian hiker called Pop Tart and the couple who joined us for supper hiked on.

Brown Mountain Creek was our last NOBO shelter. We left it on Monday, June 29 and hiked two miles to Rt. 60, where Miles called Three Springs Hostel for a ride.

Oma, owner of Three Springs, picked us up within 15 minutes of our call. We had lunch on the deck of the hostel, eating from our food bags, and then got cleaned up. It was a beautiful day with no noticeable humidity. We spread our funky things on the lawn and over the clothesline to let them air in the sun. We'd done that very thing the day before, but hiker funk is a hard smell to eliminate. It was in the fabric of every bag I carried: dry bags, sleeping bag, compression sacks, and the one that held them all: my backpack. Wood smoke, cooking odors, and sweat combined to permeate the material.

We ate dinner with the other guests on the screened porch at Three Springs, looking out toward a pond where wildlife gathered each evening and foxes chased deer past the house. While Miles and I were hiking, Judy had asked what we wanted to eat when we arrived at her house. Miles named four items she was craving: potato salad, watermelon, ice cream, and homemade brownies. If I had not been there, I wouldn't have believed she got her wish that night at Three Springs Hostel. All four items were included in Oma's menu for our buffet supper of hamburgers, chips, and the rest.

Miles and I had considered spending the next night at a campground, but we liked Three Springs Hostel so much we stayed on. Oma would drive us to the visitor center in Buena Vista on July 1, where we would meet Judy and my brother.

June 30 was our last day on the AT in Virginia, and I woke up wanting to relax. Miles wanted to hike. It was her birthday. I knew the date from the false birthday at Woods Hole Hostel where, in the aftermath of our fight, I had tried to order a present.

Per her wishes the occasion would go unobserved, but I could give her a day on the trail. I also did it for myself. Spending ten or more hours sitting on the deck of the hostel looking out over the yard and gardens might make a long day. Relaxing was good in theory after months of hiking, but not in practice.

"Miles, I'd like to hike today," I said. We were still in our bunks.

"Really?" She sat up in bed.

"It's nice out, and we can slack-pack southbound from Hog Camp Gap to Route Sixty, adding six miles to our trail total."

Hog Camp Gap was a short, bumpy ride uphill from the hostel. After breakfast Oma drove us the mile and a half and let us out with our day packs. We turned south toward Brown Mountain Creek, but not to retrace our steps; we would stop at Rt. 60 where Oma first picked us up. We could have started there that morning and hiked toward the hostel, but it would have meant climbing a huge mountain. By hiking south, we followed the trail down the steep mountainside instead of up.

We did the hike in three hours, including the 30 minutes we took for lunch at the top of Bald Knob. Miles and I sat on a large, flat rock to eat.

"You've been rough on me on this trip," I said.

"I have been rough on you, and I'll continue to be rough," she said.

The implication was there: . . . *as long as you need it.* That wouldn't be long. If our plans worked out, I'd be home in ten days. I could make it until then by holding my worst feelings inside. That was my way, right or wrong. I knew one thing: I could never tell another soul the truth about this hike.

Chapter 55
Waynesboro

Three things cannot be long hidden:
the sun, the moon,and the truth.
—Buddha

"She's a BITCH FROM HELL," I said, enunciating the last three words. "I don't want to go to Maine with them. I wish I could go home, but I can't. It's too late."

My brother and I were sitting in a bar in Waynesboro, Virginia with fresh draft beers in front of us. We had left the home of our trail angel to take a ride on a sleepy afternoon in civilization.

Keeping a secret is an awful burden. I wasn't planning to tell anyone the truth about my hike—ever—but one comment from the person who knew me best was all it took to break that promise.

"Let's have it," Joe said. "I know something is bothering you."

"My AT hike hasn't been the perfect experience reflected in those Facebook pictures," I said. "At times it was horrible. Miles and I are mismatched as partners. We have different goals and different hiking styles, but it wasn't just that. She was critical of me.

"I had a lot to learn when we started, and I think her mission was to make me over—which I did not want or need. Oh, pardon me; *think* is the weakest word in the English language. Did you know that? I wasn't just a bad trail partner; I didn't know how to communicate! She snapped at me, made snide remarks, and even threatened to leave me in North Carolina. And I'm such a wimp. All I did was try to please her so she would stop."

"It's our upbringing," he said. "Mom's drinking and verbal abuse made us this way. We go into survival mode."

"Well, I'm done," I said, remembering the times Miles cut me off with those words. "Except for the trip to Maine. And you can't tell anyone."

I didn't want our hostess to know Miles and I were at odds; Judy and I had just met. I didn't want our friends back home to know.

I was reminded of my grandmother's letters after I left home as a young adult. Even though we lived in separate states, Grandmama ended her notes with a warning—"Destroy" or "Burn this"—as if someone from our little town might discover she mentioned them or passed along a tidbit of local gossip.

"She doesn't like me either," I said. "She'd probably dump me over a cliff in a New York minute."

"Then why go to Maine?"

"I have to. We all agreed on it, and Mr. M has been so nice to me. I don't want to start something now. After Maine I don't have to see her again."

I'd entertained the idea of skipping Maine, of course. Maybe Miles had picked up on it. In the last few weeks of our hike she had talked of inviting other hikers to ride north with us. How was that going to work? The back of their SUV would be full of gear, leaving the two seats, and the two of them would take the front. One woman she mentioned inviting had a large dog. For me that ride would be a nightmare. Did Miles want me to back out of our remaining plans? If so, her message lacked the directness she advocated.

"She gave me an assignment!" I said. "I guess—oh, sorry, *guess* is another weak word—anyway, she must have given it to me because I'd contributed next to nothing toward planning our time in Maine. She said, 'I want you to research Baxter State Park and Mount Katahdin. I want you to tell me what trail you would recommend we follow to summit Katahdin.'"

"Did you do it?"

"I'm doing it, but I'm furious. I spent months planning my hike before she came on board and wanted to change it to a flip. By the time I reached Maine, I would have made my reservations like everyone else. I would have known what to do.

"Oh, well. I could go on and on," I said, "but I won't." And then I smiled because those were famous last words Joe had heard many times.

We spent two nights at Judy's. Oh, the luxury of it! My own room, hot showers, fluffy towels, tasty meals, and the lovely company of our hosts.

The first night they took us to a restaurant for dinner. Joe was in the restroom when our table was ready. In his absence Miles turned to me and asked, "Do you want me to sit on the end so that you and Joe can sit together?"

Instead of giving her the immediate answer she craved, I thought it through. That was my downfall.

"YES or NO?" Miles said through gritted teeth. I wasn't going to change her and wasn't trying, but she was determined to change me.

The next day Judy took us on a tour of her city. Waynesboro, population 21,500 (est.), is an official Appalachian Trail Town located at the foot of the Blue Ridge Mountains about two miles from the trail entrance. It offers hikers a place to rest and resupply in Virginia's gorgeous Shenandoah Valley by providing a campsite on the South River, free showers and shuttle services, and a printed guide to local businesses and medical facilities. Enhancements include hotels, hostels, restaurants, galleries, and stores—including an outfitter. Thanks to Judy and her pride in her city, Waynesboro would become a stop on all my trips.

In addition to having Miles, my brother, and me as houseguests, Judy generously invited two others to lunch: my friend Ellen, who lived nearby, and the Canadian hiker Pop Tart, whom Miles and I had met at Brown Mountain Shelter.

The invitation to Pop Tart came about suddenly as we were riding through Waynesboro near the trailhead at Rockfish Gap. Miles spotted him walking, lowered her window, and yelled, "Pop Tart!" When he turned and recognized her, Judy stopped the car and Pop Tart piled in. He spent the afternoon with us while Judy put his hiking clothes and sleeping bag through the laundry.

The time for our flip to Maine came quickly, and Mr. M arrived in the early afternoon of July 3rd to pick us up. While Miles and I got our things together for the trip north, Judy showed him her gardens and then the three of us rode off for the next phase of the journey: our Maine vacation.

I wondered how much he knew, probably everything.

I had pictured myself in Maine when I was packing my outfits at home. I imagined it was evening. I was wearing a long skirt to dinner at a rustic restaurant in a quaint village with water nearby. Music wafted from inside. The other tourists were similarly dressed. I knew we would be hiking, but my hiking clothes were not present in that fantasy. In addition to those well-worn items, I packed good shoes, a couple nice tops, and the long skirt.

Millinocket: It sounded like New England. It sounded like a resort community in New England. After hiking over 800 miles of the AT, I could use a bit of resort living: wine, nice meals, relaxation, and regular clothes that held no funky scent of woods and camp food.

I disliked Miles's insinuation that I was uninformed and ill prepared for Maine, but I was about to discover the truth about that.

Chapter 56
One More Mountain

Hiking's not for everyone.
Notice the wilderness is mostly empty.
—Sonja Yoerg, *The Middle of Somewhere*

Miles, Mr. M, and I arrived in Harpers Ferry as the July 4th weekend was beginning. Before we checked into the EconoLodge on Union Street and went out for dinner, we stopped at the Appalachian Trail Conservancy Headquarters and Visitor Center on Washington Street.

Because the ATC office is located there, a stop in Harpers Ferry is a ritual for those intending to complete a thru hike. Every hiker poses for a picture on the porch and thus is entered into the official registry before continuing north or south.

Intent is a key ingredient; with more than 1,000 miles to go in either direction, some hikers will leave the trail without finishing. Technically Miles and I—registered as Nos. 849 and 850—were still thru-hikers, but by then we did not intend to finish the Appalachian Trail that year. When we stood together for our ATC photo, I felt like a fraud.

After dinner the three of us drove through town twice but did not park because of the holiday crowds and lack of parking space. We went back to the hotel and I was asleep by 9:00 p.m.

I woke up around 5:00, glad not to worry about disturbing anyone. I fixed a cup of coffee in my room and added Godiva cocoa mix, which I learned to do on the trail. At 7:00 I met Miles and Mr. M for breakfast in the hotel, after which we began the day's drive. He drove, and she navigated. I did nothing from Harpers Ferry to Freeport, Maine but sit in the back seat and consume an occasional snack.

I hoped to glimpse the Statue of Liberty from I-95 when we passed New York City, but my view of Liberty Island was blocked by a section of New Jersey.

As we rode north I thought about the research I'd done at home, looking up all the lakes and huts along the AT in the New England states. From my reading of memoirs and trail journals, I knew about the landmarks: Mahoosuc Notch; Upper Goose Pond Cabin, where I'd hoped to stay; Hanover, New Hampshire—home of Dartmouth College; the top of Mt. Washington, where hikers like to moon passengers on the Cog Railway train; the 100-Mile Wilderness; and more.

Years ago, I lived in New Hampshire and Connecticut. I'd been to Maine once in my twenties. We drove up the coast, stopping at Ogunquit to spend a day at York Beach lying on a blanket and braving the icy waves of the Atlantic. It was a far cry from hiking the Appalachian Trail. I certainly had not thought of the AT; thus, "Maine" was an unknown, the way the Presidents were unknowns except for my reading and pictures I had seen.

I had not been to Freeport, home of the L.L. Bean flagship store. Freeport is a gorgeous paradise of cute shops and outlets. We had dinner there at a place called Gritty McDuff's Brewing Company: lobster rolls, chowder, and beer. It was my New England fantasy come to life, and we were still 183 miles south of Millinocket.

We got the last two rooms in the local EconoLodge, and after breakfast on the 4th of July we shopped before driving on. We had lunch in Bangor, where Miles and I took pictures of each other beside a 31-foot statue of the fictional lumberjack Paul Bunyan. That afternoon we arrived in Millinocket, where one can drive down a road and behold the granite monolith that is Mt. Katahdin dominating the view from 60 miles away.

Millinocket is an old mill town—oh, *Mill*-inocket; got it—with roughly 3,000 inhabitants. The town slogan is "Now the mill's closed, it's just Nocket." We drove through the outskirts and then downtown, past homes and businesses that had seen better times. The memories were sharp and familiar; I had been in mill towns before. This was not a quaint resort. In Millinocket I would not need my long skirt.

We stayed in one of eight Katahdin Cabins, roadside wood structures painted yellow. Plastic Adirondack chairs in solid colors of lilac, peach, and turquoise were placed outside. Inside, our cabin had two bedrooms with a narrow hall between them and a bathroom at the end of the hall. There was no kitchen, but my room had a microwave and theirs had a refrigerator. We ate out and brought in beer and snacks.

On Monday we took a ride to Baxter State Park. It was July 6, one day before our scheduled summit of Katahdin. We stopped at a Ranger Station and then walked to the edge of Katahdin Lake to look at the mighty mountain across the water. I could see what appeared to be a rock slide around the middle but I figured Katahdin, like every other mountain we had climbed on the AT, was achievable.

That day we did a ten-mile hike in the park. Mr. M dropped Miles and me off at Abol Bridge and we entered the AT there, hiking north. He drove to the opposite end of the trail, parked, and hiked south to meet us. The trail was easy, flat terrain winding along a rushing stream, so I was shocked when I tripped on a root and landed hard on the brown pine needles. My face hit a rock. My good glasses dug into my nose and scratched it on both sides. The left earpiece bent out of shape. The glass didn't break, so after Miles patched me up I put the damaged specs back on and continued to hike, crushed that I had fallen on a flat section of trail when I was about to climb the highest mountain in Maine.

I was not in love with Maine. It was too wild for me. The water was too choppy, the forests were too dense, and the summer wind was too chilly. Big animals lived there, in acre upon acre of remote woods. When Cheryl Strayed hiked the Pacific Crest Trail and the heat became too much, she wanted to be in Alaska. Maine reminded me of Alaska, and I *didn't* want to be there.

We were climbing Mt. Katahdin in the morning. The northern terminus of the Appalachian Trail is 5,269 feet high. Hiking it is not a casual pursuit. We were taking the Hunt Trail, which follows the AT. A park ranger described the trail to us as starting out gently but eventually turning into a boulder scramble. That meant we would need to put away our trekking poles in order to use our hands to climb the boulders, he said. Hunt Trail is 5.8 miles one way and rated "Very Strenuous" in terms of difficulty. Eight to ten hours of hiking are required to reach the summit and then return.

The day of the Big Climb arrived. Miles was more excited than I was; that is the story of our whole hike. Of the three of us planning to summit Katahdin, she was the one who most wanted to do it. Any excitement I felt was balanced with apprehension. I would be glad when we were back down the mountain.

Mr. M had made a reservation for us. We had to be at the park gate between 6:00 and 7:00 a.m. I rose at 5:00 and woke the other two a bit later. It was already light; Maine is so far east the sun rose at 4:53 that day, as opposed to 5:32 in New York City and 6:19 in Cincinnati, Ohio.

We waited in line at the gate, got in, and parked at Katahdin Stream Campground. After a visit to the privy we were in the woods, climbing Hunt Trail. The ranger had told us the trail would not be particularly challenging until we got above tree line and began the boulder scramble. Maybe it wasn't challenging for him, but he was speaking to three people in their sixties! The trail began gently as promised, but it quickly turned into a riot of roots and rocks. The rocks got larger and seemed to multiply. It was like hiking up an avalanche.

Mr. M led the way up. I was in the middle, and Miles was last. Other hikers passed us all morning. I remember a male in shorts who climbed around us, his legs covered in bites from black flies. We were a bit early for the end of black fly season in Maine, so the dreaded insects snacked on me as well.

When we reached the boulder scramble, I went first. I climbed onto a flat rock where I would have to stand in order to continue the climb. I looked to my left and saw past the unprotected edge to the ground far below. What if I fell? My life would be over.

"I can't do this," I said from my prone position on the rock. What would Miles think of me now?

"My knee went out," she said. "I can't go any farther. I have to turn around."

An injury on the trail is more than painful when it means you're done. After all the planning, spending, travel, hard work, and anticipation, your hike takes a crushing turn. I was not crushed by our failure to continue to the summit; I was relieved, but I felt bad for Miles. She was in physical pain, and I knew her disappointment at not summiting was far greater than mine.

We struck a victory pose below the boulder scramble and Mr. M captured it with our phone cameras. Being in that place was our accomplishment. Miles' tenacity might bring her back one day for another attempt, but I knew I would not return.

I would never reach Baxter Peak, the high point of Katahdin and location of the famous weather-beaten wooden sign where climbers who summit pose for photos. I would never be photographed raising my arms in victory behind that sign.

So be it.

Chapter 57
After-Effects

Returning home is the most difficult part of long-distance hiking;
you have grown outside the puzzle and your piece no longer fits.
—Author and adventurer Cindy Ross

Miles, Mr. M, and I spent the remainder of our Maine vacation reading in plastic Adirondack chairs and eating out. Their preference would have been to hike. Mine was not; thanks to the combination of my earlier fall and our day on Katahdin, I didn't care to set one foot on a hiking trail. I offered to stay behind and let them spend a day together, but they said no.

The three of us ate a picnic lunch by a lake with the wind whipping up whitecaps and blowing our Subway wrappers off the table. The mood was cordial, the undercurrent from my perspective a held breath. Tension was alive in the cabin, too, or at least within the walls of my room, fighting for domination with the double bed, dresser, microwave table, and television set already touching like chain links in the small space.

We left for home two days after our attempt to summit Mt. Katahdin. Every time Miles and I got out of the car, we experienced what is known in the trail community as hiker hobble—stiffness and pain from sitting after so many weeks of being on the move. We took our first few creaky steps toward every restroom and restaurant like a couple of zombies or people older than ourselves.

Before leaving the state we stopped again in Freeport for a few hours of shopping. I found myself staring at my feet as I walked through the outlet malls, the way I had on the trail when I was watching for dangerous rocks and roots. I had to stop before I ran into someone or fell down a flight of stairs.

We bought souvenirs for our families and then returned to the car for the trip to Cincinnati.

My biggest and most immediate task upon arriving home was to retrieve my car from its temporary home in Georgia. After the long ride from Maine I wished it were not so, but I couldn't be without a car.

Joe drove me to Atlanta. We got my car, spent the night in a suburban hotel, and left for Cincinnati in the dark the next morning. I could see the headlights of Joe's little Miata behind me. Twenty minutes later, when his car broke down on the interstate during rush hour, I drove on, unaware.

I was out of the city by daylight. A look in my rear-view mirror revealed my brother's absence. Where was he? Something must have happened.

A huge traffic jam on the other side of I-75 prevented me from turning around, so I exited the interstate and called Joe, who had pulled over safely and was by then awaiting the diagnostics result at a nearby Mazda dealership.

"I can't get back into the city," I said. "Southbound traffic is backed up for miles, but I hate to leave you."

"Go on home," he said. "There's nothing you can do here. I'm fine. If the repairs take another day, I'll get a hotel."

I did as he suggested, arriving at my house after a full day of driving. The sheer luxury of my own bed, a house with doors that closed, electric lights, privacy, a hot shower every morning, and multiple kitchen appliances was hard to beat, yet readjusting to my suburban life was a bumpy process. I was reconciling trail habits with a new reality.

I had lived simply for more than three months with only the possessions I could carry. I saved money by being on the AT, where everything was stripped down to need. I had become a skinflint! I thought nothing of repeating my outfits, a choice that would have horrified me before I hiked ten weeks wearing the same clothes. Now I didn't want to shop. I didn't want anything. I wondered if that state of mind would wear off, no pun intended.

Buying groceries was complicated as I transitioned from trail food. My eating habits had to change now that I was no longer burning thousands of calories each day. It is impossible in real life to duplicate the kind and duration of exercise one experiences on a long-distance hike. Afterward, weight gain and muscle loss are constant threats.

At home I saw an alien face in the mirror. I couldn't remember what cosmetics I wore before my hike. I had reverted to my natural, unassisted appearance on the trail. People told me I was beautiful that way. I appreciated the compliments, but slowly I returned to my beauty routines—haircuts, pedicures, and later hair color and fingernail polish—because I was no longer living a primitive life.

I washed my hiking clothes and cleaned up the gear I had carried through the woods for months, hoping to rid my pack, tent, and sleeping bag of the funky smell of thru-hiking. But did I really want to remove all traces even if I could? I stored my leftover food packets in the basement. Would I ever use them?

I continued to go to bed at hiker midnight for the longest time. I had trail dreams night after night. Sometimes in the dreams I was lost.

After a daily routine of cooking, eating, and hiking I returned to a lack of structure. No demands were made on my time. Like many others after a long hike, I lapsed into a vegetative state, at first recovering and later plagued by confusion and depression. I was lonely. I lingered on the sofa, watching TV and having little ambition. I was dissatisfied with returning to my previous life and habits but did not know what to do instead.

Both Miles and I suffered body damage. Both of us underwent physical therapy after the trail. In my case the diagnosis was biceps tendinitis, described as an overuse injury. Most likely it was the repeated hoisting of my backpack that affected my left arm and shoulder to the point I could not raise my arm to use an ATM from my car.

Eventually I lost four toenails. I blame the replacement shoes I bought in Hot Springs. The experience of losing each nail was not at all like the lost-toenail scene in *Wild*. In a far more palatable scenario—one I did not notice in the early stages—each of my nails was pushed out painlessly by a new one growing in. When it was time to alert me, they wiggled and I pulled them off—no big deal.

I came home with scars on both shins and huge calluses on my feet. The balls of my feet and the undersides of my toes were puffy and sensitive. Some areas were numb. None of it has changed with time. I say it every time I have a pedicure or buy a pair of shoes: *My feet will never be the same.*

People at home wanted to know about my hike, but most didn't really grasp what I had done. How could they without a similar experience?

I lost track of most of the hikers Miles and I met. Rose left the AT before we did. K and C completed their thru-hike and sent us pictures of themselves in a victory pose at the summit of Mt. Katahdin. Pop Tart made it as well. Turtle and I e-mailed each other. I kept in touch on Facebook with the few hikers whose real names I knew.

I used the U.S. Mail to settle up with Miles for the costs we split on the trail. I settled in at home and looked forward to the perspective that would come with time and my return to civilization.

Chapter 58
A Priest, a Bear,
and a Handyman

I've been absolutely terrified every moment of my life—
and I've never let it keep me from doing
a single thing I wanted to do.
—Georgia O'Keeffe

I went back to the trail twice that year. The first time I went alone, pulled back by an e-mail from Miles. We had been home 19 days, and I was still recovering from our hike.

Miles was returning to Great Smoky Mountains National Park to make up the miles she missed in April when she was called home. I didn't need to sit in my house while she was hiking through the Smokies; I could make up a section we missed in Virginia when we ran out of time. The 49 miles from Hog Camp Gap to Waynesboro seemed ideal.

My decision was made simple by Miles'. I could go back to the trail without agonizing over whether to invite her. Would I be lonely? I couldn't be any lonelier than I was at home. Besides, I had Ms. Rabbit for companionship.

A piece of glass with a rabbit etched into one side wouldn't protect me from real wildlife. When my pre-hike jitters returned, I bought a pepper gun at a local firearms store. It was lighter than a bear spray canister but designed for the same effect. I still had my whistle, too. Would I be safe on the trail? It was always a question, always a haunting worry, but I went ahead.

After a night at Three Springs Hostel and the bumpy uphill shuttle ride, I entered the trail at Hog Camp Gap. I didn't intend to hike 14.3 miles, but at lunchtime I changed my destination from an easier target to The Priest Shelter, named for the mountain on which it was built. Fourteen miles was an insane distance for my first day, but presumably I still had my trail legs and had not gone soft over the last three weeks.

Wrong.

It felt like starting in Georgia again. I was on the trail nine hours, including all of my breaks—two "pack-off" breaks and lunch. I had to make frequent stops on the uphill climbs. After struggling up the final hill, I arrived at the shelter at 5:15. Two Ibuprofen pills had made it possible for my aching feet to get me that far.

Before turning in I added my comments to The Priest Shelter register, where hikers are encouraged to make their entries "confessions" because of the name. I wrote the truth: I had nothing to confess.

Thanks to my initial ambition, my body was a wreck by my second day of hiking. My right knee was especially troublesome as I picked my way down the long side of The Priest.

Hiker and author Zach Davis, writing for REI, called The Priest one of the seven hardest day hikes on the Appalachian Trail: "[It] showcases central Virginia's steepest climb with more than 3,000 feet of elevation gain over the 4.3-mile one-way trek." That would be hiking from north to south. As a northbound hiker, I went down that 4.3-mile stretch instead of up. The descent was another kind of agony. My boots pinched my feet, my toes were jammed against the fronts, and my left shoulder hurt from the weight of my food bag. I fought to keep my balance.

My fantasy all morning was of going to Crabtree Falls Campground and calling Judy to come and get me, but I reached the bottom of The Priest and stopped for lunch near the Tye River. After taking my third Ibuprofen of the day to dull my knee pain and doing my part to lighten my load by eating a pack of tuna salad on a tortilla, I decided to press on.

At 2:00 I arrived at Harper's Creek Shelter. My body was rebelling and the shelter was lovely sitting there in the sun with only the moving creek water breaking the deep silence. I had the place to myself. That would be a good thing for the next several hours until—gulp—dark; but at least the shelter was in a valley. The trail was visible on the other side of the creek, and if it was light, I could see anyone—or anything—headed my way.

I unpacked and, in the process, found three cans of Bud Light in the shelter. I laid them in the creek to cool while I gave myself a sponge bath, filtered water, and found a tree for my food bag. Why had someone left that beer behind? It could be trail magic, intended for the next shelter occupants, or it could be a smart move to eliminate 2.5 pounds of pack weight. Either way, I was going to have a beer with my supper.

A bit later I was sitting in the shelter reading a novel with my new pepper gun beside me when a shirtless man came down the trail toward the creek crossing. He carried a wooden walking stick with a bandana attached at the top like a hobo in the comic strips, but he was clean. He had a wholesome look and a friendly face. I put my pepper gun away when he wasn't looking.

This newcomer's first words to me were, "Are you Early Bird?" Did this guy have ESP? "I am, but how did you know?" I said. "I read your entry in the trail register last night. I'm Mister Fixit." "Nice to meet you. What do you fix?" "Back home, I'm a counselor." "So, you fix people. That reminds me of that Jimmy Jones song, 'Handyman.' He fixed broken hearts." He laughed. "I wouldn't go that far, but I do my best to help people." "I have two beers cooling in the creek," I said. "You're welcome to one of them."

We decided to hike together the next day, provided we could keep a compatible pace. The next shelter on the trail was 6.2 miles away, too short a distance for a long summer day, but the one after that was a whopping 22 miles away—too far. The *A.T. Guide* showed one campsite between the two shelters, and that site—14.7 miles ahead—became our goal.

It was August, and it was hot. Mr. Fixit was looking forward to a stop at Humpback Picnic Area, which I pointed out was 0.3 miles off trail. The extra distance didn't bother him. "We can clean up in the restrooms there," he said, "and have our supper at a picnic table instead of sitting on a log or the ground. When we get to the campsite, all we'll have to do is put up our tents." That part sounded good.

By the time we reached the blue-blazed side trail, evening had come, and we were tired. Our feet hurt. The sun had not set, but the woods grow dark before the open areas do. I worried about the fading light; once we'd taken the time to freshen up, cook, and eat, what time would it be?

We realized we could cut a mile off our evening hike by camping near the picnic area, so that became the plan. We had spotted one possible campsite in the woods.

After we had eaten and packed our gear, Mr. Fixit left to clean up. When it was my turn, he watched our packs. I returned from the restroom to learn that in my absence a couple in a car had cruised the picnic area looking for bears and deer. It was a favorite pastime of theirs. They had offered Mr. Fixit a ride.

"I told them no, that we are hiking. The man said this area was recently closed because of bear activity. Oh, there's a bear now."

"Right." I didn't even look.

"No, see for yourself. It's over there."

A black bear was ambling through a stand of trees on all fours about 20 yards from our picnic table. I watched its flat profile come alive as the bear emerged into the light and turned toward us. Had I been alone, I hope I would have had the presence of mind to unzip the pocket that held my pepper gun and take it out, because I didn't move. Mr. Fixit began to shoo the bear away, and the animal reacted to his deep voice by crossing the road and walking a short way into the woods. We could still see it.

"What direction did that bear come from?" I asked.

"The restrooms."

"Do you mean I was walking parallel to a black bear when I came back to this table just now?" He didn't have to tell me yes; it was obvious.

Now the idea of camping nearby was out. Our only choice was to proceed to our original target: the campsite near the top of Humpback Mountain, more than a mile away—and now we were in a hurry. Both of us had changed into our camp shoes at the table. His Crocs and my Teva sandals were comfortable, but not ideal for hiking; however, they would have to do.

We crossed the road, passing the bear at a distance, and re-entered the trail back to the AT. By the time we had covered the 0.3 miles to the main trail, light was seeping out of the forest.

"What time is it?" Mr. Fixit asked.

I checked my wrist watch. "Ten after eight." It would be dark by 9:00.

Would the bear follow us? Would we even see it? To add to the evening's challenges, most of our hike to the campsite was uphill. The incline would slow *us* down, but how fast could a bear run up a mountain? Could we even find the campsite in the dark?

I was sure I was radiating fear. Mr. Fixit began spouting positivity as I followed him up Humpback Mountain close enough to be annoying. By then I was looking behind me every few seconds for signs of the bear. I could imagine its stealthy gait, its growl, and the sharp smell of its fur. "We'll be fine," he said. "Have faith. Even if we need to hike after dark, we both have headlamps."

"Let's get them out now."

"We have plenty of time," he said. "Let's keep going."

Plenty of time? The trail and surrounding forest were growing darker by the minute! I had never made such progress up a mountain. If I stopped, Mr. Fixit got farther ahead; thus, I did not stop to rest, but after a while I began to relax. So far, so good. I had seen no evidence of the bear we'd encountered at the picnic area. If it followed us, I still had hope: my pepper gun, the weapon I had ready at my side the evening Mr. Fixit walked down the trail to Harper's Creek Shelter.

The weapon I had never fired.

When we neared the top of Humpback Mountain, we could see the sky, and it was not black, but blue. There was hope. Mr. Fixit spotted the clearing right away. "I think this is it," he said, and we slapped our tents together in the remaining light.

"Will you please put your tent close to mine," I said, and he did. Our stakes were not two feet apart. I left the rain fly off my tent to allow a breeze and hoped not to see a dark, furry face looming over the netting at me.

In the morning I was surprised to wake up feeling safe in our little campsite. The sun was coming up and the woods around us were peaceful. I had slept soundly, undisturbed.

Now I had a fierce need to pee. No way would I have left my tent during the night. I got up and grabbed my pStyle. Mr. Fixit was sitting up in his tent. "Turn your back," I said as I ran behind a tree.

In my haste, I misused the pStyle and gushed urine all over myself. It soaked my shorts and underwear and ran down both legs. I screamed, and then I laughed. Too bad we were 22 miles past The Priest; now I had something to confess!

"I've had an accident," I said. "Please don't look," and I stumbled back to my tent to clean up and change.

It was our last day on the trail, and we had a 12-mile hike to the trailhead at Rockfish Gap. With every mile I wanted to toss my ill-fitting shoes; but after a couple nice descents, a lunch stop at Paul C. Wolfe Shelter, and a change of footwear, we ended on a long, flat stretch and emerged from the trail in mid-afternoon. He had a car waiting. I had Judy's telephone number.

After we shared a quick parting hug, he said, "Now you can say you've seen a bear up close."

I smiled. "Yes, and you can say you hiked with a sixty-nine-year-old woman who wet her pants!"

Chapter 59
Oh, Shenandoah!

The second time I returned to the AT, it wasn't the mountains calling; it was Turtle. Sometime after Miles and I left her in Marion, Virginia, she had changed her trail name to Fern to avoid further attention from a persistent male hiker. Fern invited me to hike the length of Virginia's Shenandoah National Park with her. We would meet at Judy's in Waynesboro and enter the AT at Rockfish Gap, the trailhead where I'd finished my hike with Mr. Fixit. Fern and I would hike north to Front Royal, a distance of 107.7 miles.

I wanted to do the hike with Fern, but I was wary. I feared she and I would not be compatible, only because discord had dominated my first and longest hike. I couldn't bear to have another relationship sour on the trail.

Despite my misgivings, I accepted Fern's invitation and left home on October 11, 2015. I looked forward to seeing my friend and getting outside again, yet I was nervous. In addition to snakes and bears, I worried about the short days of autumn and my ability to hike the required miles before dark. I feared I'd be stiff and sore and out of shape when Fern—who had already been hiking—was raring to go.

I knew what to expect from the trail, but I could not stop creating scenarios in my head. The wilderness scared me, but I was more anxious about the hike straining our friendship. Maybe I was cursed. Maybe Fern would have preferred to be with Miles, discussing literature and putting their heads together over the nuances of the *A.T. Guide*.

"I invited *you*," Fern said when I brought it up. I felt better hearing her verbal italics. I was not the consolation prize, but the person she wanted for a companion.

The morning of our hike I woke up at 3:45, my mind racing. My sleep schedule was always a problem on the trail, but more so now. In the fall, nights on the AT are 12 hours long. That translates to a short time for hiking and a long time to be in a sleeping bag. If Fern and I followed nature's cycle after a day on the trail, we would slip into our sleeping bags before 7:00 p.m. and get up after 7:00 a.m.

Judy drove Fern and me to the trailhead and hiked with us until she was called to duty by a group of southbound hikers who needed a ride into Waynesboro. Fern and I continued on, breaking for lunch at the summit of Bears Den Mountain. Moments after we stepped back onto the trail I fell, landing on a thorn bush and bending my glasses. I was not hurt and Fern was solicitous, but I couldn't help thinking of Miles. If I kept falling, would Fern grow tired of my clumsiness or come to expect it?

It was hard to be negative with Mother Nature preening all around us. Her finest season brought crisp mornings; warm, sunny afternoons; and good sleeping weather at night. I would start each day in a sweater and shed it as the temperature rose. Each day was glorious; the sun illuminated all the trees in their prettiest outfits. Fern and I hiked and chattered under miles of bright leaves: red and purple, yellow and orange, gold and green. Muted versions made a different palette on the path, where fallen acorns and apples lay among the leaves and we had to be careful not to slip.

I had never been so immersed in fall. I had experienced 70 previous autumns, but none were like that one. And my time together with Fern was restoring the self-confidence I had lost with Miles.

One day Fern said, "I have a friend who wants to hike with us for a day. Would you mind?"

"No, of course not."

"Her trail name is Katydid. I'll tell her to meet us on Saturday."

As it turned out, forecasters were predicting a cold snap for the weekend. Fern and I didn't want to be in the mountains during the expected frost, and it was more than a preference. Plunging temperatures could be dangerous. My sleeping bag, for example, would be ineffective below 32 degrees. We decided to leave the park on Saturday afternoon, spend two nights at Judy's, and return to the trail on Monday.

We kept our plans with Katydid, and on Saturday she met us in the park. Having two cars there allowed us to place one at each end of our hike. The complex process of shuttling vehicles made it possible for us to cover more AT miles; instead of doubling back to a parking lot, we could hike in a straight line from Point A to Point B.

The three of us met in the morning at Bearfence Mountain trailhead. We left my car there (Point B) and drove Katydid's south to Point A, where we entered the Appalachian Trail to hike north, back to my car. At 14 miles, it would be the longest hike of the week. We would need to be mindful of the time. Fern and I were expected at Judy's at 6:00 p.m. for dinner.

Fern and Katydid hiked at the same pace, which was faster than mine. I didn't mind being left out of their conversations; it gave me time for my own thoughts. I wasn't worried when they hiked ahead—until late afternoon, when I realized I might be too slow to reach my car in time.

The wind was picking up and the temperature was already dropping by the time we reached Lewis Mountain Campground. We had hiked 12 miles, and the car was another two.

"I don't think I can make it," I said. "I'm beat."

Katydid's energy was flagging along with mine. She had not been hiking for weeks the way Fern had. The three of us stood looking at one another. All I wanted was to get out of that park, but the last thing I wanted to do was hike the next two miles to make it happen.

"Give me the car keys," Fern said. "I'm fast. I'll hike to the car and drive it back here."

I knew she was capable. In the weeks prior to our SNP hike, Fern had been hiking a section of Virginia alone when Hurricane Joaquin collided with a cold front, producing a week of high winds and rain and prompting the governor to declare a state of emergency. She survived by navigating flooded creeks and huddling alone in the shelters.

"Here, take my daypack, too," I said, reaching for the nylon bag I carried for town use. "Leave your backpack with us."

Fern hurried back to the trail and in moments had hiked out of sight. Katydid and I settled at an empty picnic table to wait, but soon moved into the ladies' restroom with our gear. The air was cold inside, even after we closed the windows, but at least the walls protected us from the wind.

When Fern drove my gray Elantra into the campground and pulled off the blacktop, I was warmed by my own gratitude.

"You were heroic," I said.

We passed the rest of the weekend cleaning up and reorganizing our supplies at Judy's house. Monday morning she drove Fern and me back to the park. As we rode past frost-covered fields before sunrise, I shivered in the front passenger seat, dreading our arrival at Bearfence trailhead and the moment I would have to get out and hike. It was time for Fern and me to continue north to Front Royal.

Good weather returned to the park that week. Fern and I had fun stopping at waysides to eat cheeseburgers and drink blackberry shakes. We slept in shelters called huts and camped in the woods. We saw bears crossing Skyline Drive in the distance. We took pictures and talked about the books we would write. We summited mountains and marveled at the tiny towns spread over gorgeous autumn valleys below us. After a week we reached Front Royal, where we spent a night at the home of a trail angel Fern knew called Slingshot.

My hike was over after we reached the northern boundary of Shenandoah National Park, but Fern had more hiking to do. We drove her car from Slingshot's to Judy's the next day and left it there. We got into my car at Judy's house and drove 84 miles south to Daleville. On the way we told stories and laughed until we cried. I thought I might lose control of the car.

That was friendship. All of it was friendship: Fern and Katydid, Judy and Slingshot with their ready hospitality, Fern's heroic two-mile hike to the car, and our laugh-fest on the way to Daleville.

One day I would have to make up the two miles I missed that Saturday. Completing a thru-hike might not be possible or desirable for me, but I was a purist about where I'd walked. I didn't like breaks in the solid line marking my time on the Appalachian Trail.

After two successful weeks hiking with Fern, I had proved one thing to myself: I could have—and be—a friend on the trail. I *was* slow, but I was not cursed or a bad risk. Fern and I had a few negative memories, like the time I fell on the thorn bush or the time she uncovered three dead mice in a fire pit, but most of our memories were good and we became closer because of our hike.

We spent the night at Howard Johnson's, and in the morning I dropped Fern at the trailhead to spend another ten days on the AT. It was the 25th of October, almost Halloween. The leaves would fade and fall; the air would turn cold again soon enough. I was ready to be home.

Chapter 60
The Apology

Don't over-expect.
—Sheriff Andy Taylor to Gomer Pyle
on *The Andy Griffith Show*,
Episode 105, "A Date for Gomer"

In early December Miles invited me to meet her at a restaurant for lunch. We had not seen each other since our return from Maine in July. The winter sun felt good eight days before Christmas.

"I didn't think you'd come."

I hadn't wanted to, but I'd turned down one invitation already. When this one came, I said yes but put her off a week because I was on a diet.

I was on my guard as we ordered, picked up our food, and sat down at a table for two. After a few minutes Miles looked across the table at me and said, "I want to apologize to you."

Those six words shocked me; I had not expected an apology. My hope had been for a peaceful lunch.

"I was really hard on you," she said. "I'm sorry for being so bitchy and critical on the trail."

I couldn't argue. By the end of our aborted thru-hike, I didn't care if I saw her again and thought she must feel the same way about me. Otherwise, why had she suggested other people I might hike with if I decided to continue on the Appalachian Trail?

Miles's acknowledgment of her behavior meant a lot to me. I felt an instant softening, although her apology did not wash the last few months away.

"Neither of us will defer to the other" was one of her declarations during our planning sessions for the trail. Six months later, the AT had shown us we were not two peas in a pod; far from it. At first I thought it was me, and it was; I was a rookie making rookie mistakes. Later I thought it was her, and it was; in whatever spirit her advice was offered, it translated to criticism. We disagreed.

By the time we did our flip to Maine, both of us were exhausted and ready for a break from hiking. We didn't say we were ready for a break from each other, but I believed that to be the real issue.

"After we got back," Miles said between bites, "I read a book by the Barefoot Sisters. They argued, too. During one of their fights they refused to continue hiking together. That book showed me that other trail partners—even relatives—have their tense moments. They disagree and get sick of each other."

She was relieved at her discovery upon reading the book. "Things happen," she said. "I think it's normal."

"*Think* is the weakest word in the English language." By then I could say it with a touch of humor.

Miles was right that spats and bad behavior could be the case for any two people spending three and one-half months together in a challenging situation. The stress has to go somewhere. She and I were constant companions after having little contact for the previous 15 years. Did we know each other? Had we conveniently forgotten what we didn't like about the other person? The trail was sure to bring it out.

I apologized to Miles for being an inadequate boss all those years ago. As with her apology, it likely failed to address specific issues, e.g., any she had retained in the interim, but it made me feel better.

"I've been working on my AT book," I said. "I tried to leave you out or make you a shadow figure to avoid exposing our difficulties, but it didn't work. People will want to know how we got along. I'm struggling with that. How do I tell my story?"

"I don't care what you write," she said, "as long as it's true."

We talked about our climb halfway up Mt. Katahdin. "That boulder scramble was so scary," I said. "After seeing so many mountaintops, I didn't realize I was afraid of heights."

"I thought you turned around because of me," Miles said, "because my knee gave out."

"No, don't you remember? I was terrified the minute I crawled onto that first exposed rock. I couldn't stand up, let alone continue climbing."

"I dislocated a shoulder that day," she said. Had she known it on the mountain? It was news to me.

Miles had explained our failure to summit beautifully to our friends: "The trail gods spoke to us. They said, 'Your challenge is over. Your climb ends here. Your Appalachian Trail trials are over, and you can go home now.'"

After the bombshell of her apology at lunch, she brought up the second item on her agenda: She wanted us to continue hiking the AT together the following year. I had expected it, but I had not prepared an answer that satisfied me. I didn't want to hike with her, but how could I tell her? As it turned out, our meeting was such that I could have been blunt, but by the time the topic came up I wasn't ready to tell her no.

"I'll think about it," I said. There was that word again.

Six months earlier beside a grocery store in Newport, Virginia, Miles had told me I didn't belong on the trail. Now she was asking me to return to it—as her partner.

The Appalachian Trail was created for anyone who wants to hike it. Sometimes I wanted to, and sometimes I didn't; but I belonged all right, along with the thousands of others—young, old, fit, weak—who have walked the AT. No one could take that away.

Would I go back? Maybe I would one day, but I wanted to be home the following year. I wanted to experience the spring and summer walking in my neighborhood and sitting on my deck by the water. I wanted to write my book. I bought patio furniture with my trail savings because I wanted to be outside. That's "o-u-t . . ."

So, I e-mailed Miles, preferring that method to a phone call, and told her as much. I wished her well if she chose to go back to the AT. Since then we have returned to our previous state: cordial acquaintances who cross paths once in a while.

Epilogue

It's when you are safe at home that you're having an adventure.
When you're having an adventure you wish
you were safe at home.
—Thornton Wilder

Some things look better from a distance: bears, snakes, rock fields, open cliffs, boulder scrambles, black mud, drenching rain, and a certain skinny dirt path that follows 2,189 miles of the Appalachian Mountains from Georgia to Maine.

I didn't expect a perfect experience on the AT, but the ways my hike wasn't perfect surprised me. I didn't expect the trail to be so difficult, or my pace to be so slow. I didn't think I would have physical issues like falling. I didn't dream I'd be a rookie after reading 43 books, or become the underdog of my own hike.

I did expect to walk all 2,189.2 miles wearing the same clothes every day, eating instant meals sitting on a rock or wet log, and carrying my belongings in a backpack.

In *Wild*, Cheryl Strayed was pursued by a reporter from the *Hobo Times* despite her repeated insistence she was not a hobo. On a recent summer morning, Fern and I had to walk beside a highway to reach a store for resupply. Except for a few toots from passing drivers, no one bothered us, but I texted my brother that we felt like hobos.

"You're not hobos. You're *fauxbos!*" Joe said. I might be a fauxbo, but I'm a real hiker. My 1,195 miles on the trail prove it.

People ask what I learned in my time on the AT. From my initial hike and three repeat trips to the trail, I learned to cut myself some slack. I'm adventurous and willing to take reasonable risks. To my friends I am amazing, a hero.

I've unlearned negatives from my first hike. I'm not a poor communicator; I have my own style that may not work for everyone. I'm not a bad trail partner; all of us are rookies sometime. I can be a friend out there. I've learned to say no when my gut tells me to.

I now see "Hike your own hike" as appropriate advice for many life situations.

What would I change if I could? I wish I'd had more of a how-to. I didn't try to be a bad trail partner to Miles, but I now realize I didn't fully know how to be a good one. My reading didn't spell it out. Miles and I didn't spell it out, and I needed it spelled out. As it was, I learned some of those lessons after I failed to do something right—or do it at all. It was reminiscent of my childhood in an alcoholic home; the teaching came after the mistake. My childhood wasn't Miles' fault, but every instance of that kind of correction on the trail stole a bit of my self-esteem.

The times I liked best on that first hike were the times Miles and I were in sync: when our communication was uncomplicated and our steps and goals aligned; when all we had to do was hike. On our best day we covered 21 miles, some of it in thunderstorms. We were soaked. I wiped raindrops off my glasses again and again just to see the trail. Some of the route was over mountaintop boulders that went on forever; some of it was through areas with posted bear warnings. None of that mattered because we kicked butt. Together.

I wondered how hiking the AT would change me. I changed physically, losing fat and gaining muscle. When I came home, my clothes fit and I felt like a million dollars. Being in shape is one reason I am tempted back to the AT.

I don't like loose ends, which is another reason I keep going back to the trail. I want to fill in the gaps left when I skipped sections for lack of time or fear of danger or injury; but I won't return to them all. Knowing the difference between bravery and stupidity is important.

The quiet of the woods and the simplicity of routines on the Appalachian Trail combined to clear my head. That clarity didn't last, and recapturing that calmer state as part of a simpler life is another component that calls me back to the trail.

I have new scars from every hike. The trail beats me up. I'm lucky to have good health at my age and to emerge in one piece from so many hard miles.

All of the small changes contributed to a whole. I see it now, four years after I first picked up *Wild*. My transformation from retired book editor to AT hiker was the equivalent of Clark Kent rushing into a phone booth and emerging as Superman.

I could hike up a mountain without stopping. I could put up a tent in the rain and be inside before the sprinkles became a downpour. I could hike vast stretches of backcountry alone, with a partner, or with a glass rabbit for company—all because another woman's story yanked me out of my comfort zone.

Wild was my phone booth.

The trail lets us explore other parts of ourselves in virtual anonymity, to become someone else for a while and shed our real-life identifiers for a trail name. Occasionally under that cloak of anonymity life on the trail answers our deepest questions regarding who we are.

Some people look better from a distance. Maybe I do, but the trail made me appreciate my imperfect life. In hiking, you spend 12 to 14 hours a day putting one foot in front of the other and another two or three hours completing the related chores: setting up camp or settling into a shelter, getting water, preparing food, storing scented items beyond the reach of bears. When you return home, you might take some time to adjust, or feel depressed, but eventually you move on to a different routine. At home I make plans that are so antithetical to hiking, it's as though I have a dual personality. The trail becomes the thing it was in the beginning: a dream without sound or feeling, a vision only. Maybe I am that spoiled suburbanite Miles suspected was hiding under my hiking clothes. If that's the case, I'm fine with it.

In June of 2016 Judy and her family stopped in town on their way west, staying at Miles' for a night. I joined the two families for dinner at a restaurant and we had a wonderful time. Months later I got a message from Judy, who knew Miles and I had our strained moments on the trail.

"She thinks she saved you," Judy wrote. Her words released more of the hurt and animosity I had harbored for months and replaced them with wisdom.

When my friend Anita came through town, I tried to return Ms. Rabbit to her. "You keep it for now," she said. "You might need it again on the trail."

Maybe.

On my 70th birthday my brother and I watched *A Walk in the Woods*, the movie based on Bill Bryson's best-selling book, which is also the best-known book about the Appalachian Trail. I still read about hiking. I hike local trails in good weather, and sometimes when a breeze carries the complex scent of dirt and rotting leaves and new green plants, I'm right back on the AT in my mind.

I spent 2016 traveling in the spring and staying home in the summer. I did not hike. Katydid and I made up the two skipped miles from Lewis Mountain Campground to Bearfence trailhead in Shenandoah National Park on May 17, 2017. Fern and Judy hiked with us.

Fern and I returned to the AT in 2017. We spent three weeks hiking in Maryland and Pennsylvania until a fall forced me off the trail. Will I go back? You never know. It always looks better from a distance.

Some things are better as wishes or dreams, not to be confused with real life. Hiking the Appalachian Trail wasn't—isn't—my life; it's something I did based on a book I picked up in a second-hand bookstore.

Something *wild*.

THE END

Author's Comments

Everyone shines, given the right lighting.
—*Quiet* Author Susan Cain

Thank you for choosing *How the* Wild *Effect Turned Me into a Hiker at 69.* It is my third book and the one with the longest title. I wanted to call this book *TAME*, the opposite of *Wild* and perfect for a senior citizen's adventure. However, the word itself was deemed too tame to have commercial appeal.

The "why" of a long-distance hike or any such endeavor is important, but identifying and expressing it can be a challenge. Do we always know what drives us?

I know what called me to the trail, but knowing it was Cheryl Strayed's memoir did not keep me from wondering at times if I had lost my mind. I was afraid on my hikes—of heights and storms and wildlife. I fell multiple times: slipping in mud, tripping on roots, missing a step in a boulder field, or doing an unexplained face-plant on a bed of pine needles. I've been cold and wet. My body is marked—maybe forever—with scars and bruises. My feet are still calloused.

The *Wild* Effect must strike randomly. My book club read this manuscript and *Grandma Gatewood's Walk*, yet none of those women raced to the outdoor store afterward.

I learn from every adventure and every book I write, usually in a flash of insight sometime after I have typed "THE END." For me there is always another layer to be found. It comes from that other journey, the one I didn't expect to take.

A few weeks after I finished writing this book, I came upon an article titled "12 Things Introverts Absolutely Need to Be Happy." The author was Jenn Granneman, a *Psychology Today* blogger and advocate for introverts like herself. Granneman hosts a web community called *Introvert, Dear.* Her article and later the book, *The Secret Lives of INTROVERTS: Inside Our Hidden World*, were the equivalent of lightning bolts to my brain. They provided a larger picture and answered some of my questions about myself, Miles, and our trail exchanges.

Why did I retreat to my tent or sleeping bag at the end of a day instead of engaging with others? Introverts can get "peopled out"; we need down time. *Why was I so passive when Miles was angry?* It is a characteristic of introverts that we would rather not engage with an angry person. *Why couldn't I produce a "direct" answer when Miles wanted it?* Unlike extroverts, introverts need time to process our responses.

I had attributed our differences on the AT to our being "wired" differently or having different personalities. I was close, but I did not name the thing I now believe was a source of our contentious times on the trail: different *temperaments*.

According to Granneman's book, introversion and extroversion are not personality traits but temperaments, encoded in our DNA from birth. Temperament and experience combine to shape each person's behavior and personality. We are not at fault for being who we are.

If you are fascinated by the prospect of learning more about your makeup and that of others, check out *The Secret Lives of Introverts*, *Quiet*, and the many other materials that address introversion and extroversion.

I hope you enjoyed this book. As noted earlier, some names and attendant facts have been changed to protect individuals' privacy. Most of the dialog is taken verbatim from my trail notes. In a few cases I created the wording—mine or someone else's—from memory. I apologize for any errors or misinterpretations.

Questions for Discussion

1. Could you do what the author did? What experiences have taken you outside your comfort zone?

2. Did a character in the book remind you of someone in your own life: a friend, family member, boss, or co-worker? Who and why?

3. What feelings did this book evoke in you? Was there a chapter or passage that stood out or gave you an "a-ha" moment? Can you recall a scene that struck you personally, for instance, one in which you would have behaved differently?

4. Did the characters' experiences cause them to grow? If so, how?

5. How did the book expand your range of experience or challenge your assumptions? Did reading it help you to understand another person better, or even yourself?

6. Are you an introvert, an extrovert, or possibly a "brave introvert" like Turtle? If so, in what way?

7. Setting can be a backdrop or a major character in a story. To what degree did the locations in this book color the telling of the story? How did setting affect the central characters?

8. Name something you learned about hiking that could apply to many life situations.

9. This book offers a look inside another culture: the culture of the trail community. What is different from your own culture? What do you find most surprising, intriguing or difficult to understand? Is that culture something you would like to experience?

10. What do you think the author's purpose was in writing this book? What ideas was she trying to get across?

11. If you had the chance to ask the author one question, what would it be?

12. What surprised you most about the book?

13. Peek into the future: What relationship do you see between Miles and E. B.? Who do you think will return to the trail?

14. How was this book like or different from others your club has read? Did you have expectations of this book? If so, did it live up to them?

15. Were there any particular quotes that stood out for you? What were they?

16. Would you recommend this book or give it as a gift? Why or why not?

17. What did you like best about this memoir, and why? What did you like least about it, and why?

18. What impact did the structure and writing style have on your enjoyment of the story?

About the Author

Jane Congdon grew up in the mountains of West Virginia. After graduating from Concord College (now Concord University), she made a career of words, working as an English teacher and a newspaper reporter before finding her niche as a textbook editor in Cincinnati, Ohio. She retired in 2009 after 30 years to write and take on selected editing projects.

At age 59, Jane followed Dracula's footsteps through Transylvania, resulting in the memoir *It Started with Dracula: The Count, My Mother, and Me* (©2011). She then co-authored her brother's memoir, *Mr. Joe: Tales from a Haunted Life* (©2013). Both books were published by Bettie Youngs Book Publishers and are available from Amazon and other outlets.

At age 69, Jane returned to the mountains as a backpacker. To date she has hiked 1,195 miles of the Appalachian Trail in 7 of its 14 states: Georgia, North Carolina, Virginia, West Virginia, Maryland, Pennsylvania, and Maine.

She is a member of West Virginia Writers. Visit her website at www.janecongdon.com.

Reading List

Allen, Amy. *Summoning the Mountains: Pilgrimage into Forty.* Deadwood, Oregon: Saille Productions, a Wyatt-MacKenzie Imprint. Amy Allen, 2012.

Alt, Jeff. *A Walk for Sunshine.* Cincinnati, Ohio: Dreams Shared Publications, 2009.

Amparo, Daniel (Lt. Daaan!). *An Adventure on the Appalachian Trail.* Self-published by Daniel Amparo, 2013.

Appalachian Trail Conservancy. *Appalachian Trail Thru-Hike Planner.* Harpers Ferry, West Virginia, 2012.

Appalachian Trail: Women's Group, closed online group, Facebook.

Blanchard, Dennis R. *Three Hundred Zeroes: Lessons of the Heart on the Appalachian Trail.* Sarasota, Florida, 2010.

Bond, Gary. *Rethinking Life on the Appalachian Trail.* Paperback: CreateSpace Independent Publishing Platform, 2013; Kindle version, Amazon Digital Services, Inc., 2012.

Merit Badge Series. Backpacking. Irving, Texas: Boy Scouts of America, 2007.

Bryson, Bill. *A Walk in the Woods.* New York: Broadway Books, 1998.

Callaway, Robert A. *Slow and Steady: Hiking the Appalachian Trail.* Highland City, Florida: Rainbow Books, Inc., 2014.

Clapper, Craig. *Legging It: Life Lessons Learned Thru-Hiking the Appalachian Trail.* Xulon Press (no city given), 2014.

Croteau, Terry. *Footpath My Ass!* Xlibris Corporation (no city given), 2009.

Davis, Jennifer Pharr. *Becoming Odyssa.* New York: Beaufort Books, 2010.

Davis, J. *Called Again.* Beaufort Books, 2013.

Davis, Zach. *Appalachian Trials.* Self-published, 2012.

Fulton, Kathryn (Ed.). *Hikers' Stories from the Appalachian Trail.* Mechanicsburg, Pennsylvania: Stackpole Books, 2013.

Grylls, Bear. *The Kid Who Climbed Everest.* Guilford, Connecticut: The Lyons Press, 2007.

Hare, James R., Editor. Emmaus, Pennsylvania: Rodale Press, Inc. *Hiking the Appalachian Trail, Volumes 1 and 2,* 1975.

Hill, Jim. *Appalachian Adventure.* Self-published, 2013 (no additional information available).

Homan, Chris. *A Door into Another Land: Appalachian Trail Memoirs.* Lexington, Kentucky, (self-published), 2014 (no additional information available).

Irwin, Bill with David McDasland. *Blind Courage: A Blind Man's 2,000-Mile Journey of Faith on the Appalachian Trail.* Waco, Texas: WRS Publishing, 1992; 1993; revised 1996.

Letcher, Lucy and Susan (the Barefoot Sisters). *Walking Home (Adventures on the Appalachian Trail).* Mechanicsburg, Pennsylvania: Stackpole Books, 2010.

Luxenberg, Larry. *Walking the Appalachian Trail.* Mechanicsburg, Pennsylvania: Stackpole Books, 1994.

Mass, Leslie. *In Beauty May She Walk: Hiking the Appalachian Trail at 60.* Harpers Ferry, West Virginia: Appalachian Trail Conservancy, 2009.

Maxwell, Megan ("Hashbrown"). *The Appalachian Trail Girl's Guide: Part Memoir, Part Manifesto.* Self-published by Megan Maxwell, 2014. Sold by Amazon Digital Services, Inc.

Miller, David. *AWOL on the Appalachian Trail.* Boston/New York: Mariner Books, a division of Hougton Mifflin Harcourt Publishing, 2011.

Miller. *The A.T. Guide (2014 Northbound).* Titusville, Florida: Jerelyn Press, 2014.

Montgomery, Ben. *Grandma Gatewood's Walk.* Chicago: Chicago Review Press, 2014.

O'Bannon, Allen and Mike Clelland (illustrator). *Allen & Mike's Really Good Backpacking Book*. Guilford, Connecticut: Globe Pequot Press (a FalconGuide), 2001.

Pugh, Michelle ("Brownie"). *Love at First Hike*. Self-published, 2013.

Quinn, Carrot. *Thru-Hiking Will Break Your Heart: An Adventure on the Pacific Crest Trail*. New York: Penguin Books, 2014.

Ray, Michelle. *How to Hike the Appalachian Trail: The Nitty-Gritty Details of a Long-Distance Trek*. Mechanicsburg, Pennsylvania: Stackpole Books, 2009.

Reisinger, Nan ("Drag'n Fly"). Trail journal online at www.kickngliders.org/private/ NanReisingerAppalachianTrailJournal.html. 2014.

Roberts, Suzanne. *Almost Somewhere: Twenty-Eight Days on the John Muir Trail*. Lincoln and London, Nebraska: Bison Books (Outdoor Lives Series), 2012.

Rogers, Susan Fox, Editor. *Going Alone: Women's Adventures in the Wild*. Emeryville, CA: Seal Press, 2004.

Shaffer, Earl V. *Walking with Spring*. Harpers Ferry, West Virginia: Appalachian Trail Conference, 2004.

Smith, Dave. *Don't Get Eaten*. Seattle: The Mountaineers Books, 2003.

Smith, D. *Backcountry Bear Basics*. The Mountaineers Books, 2006.

Strayed, Cheryl. *Wild*. New York: Vintage Books, a division of Random House, Inc., 2012.

Stolz, A. Digger. *Stumbling Thru, Book One: Hike Your Own Hike*. Niantic, Connecticut: Follyworks Publishing LLC, 2013.

Stutzman, Paul. *Hiking Through: One man's journey to peace and freedom on the Appalachian Trail*. Grand Rapids, Michigan: Revell, 2010; 2012.

Tilton, Buck, and Rick Bennett. *Don't Get Sick*. Seattle: The Mountaineers Books, 2002; originally published in 1995 as *Camping Healthy: Hygiene for the Outdoors*.

Walker, Bill. *Skywalker—Close Encounters on the Appalachian Trail*. Macon, Georgia: Indigo Publishing Group, LLC, 2008.

Other Books by Jane Congdon

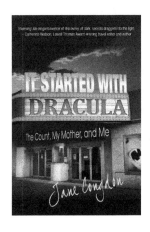

It Started with Dracula:
The Count, My Mother, and Me

The terrifying legend of Count Dracula silently skulking through the Transylvania night may have terrified generations of filmgoers, but the tall, elegant vampire captivated and electrified a young Jane Congdon, igniting a dream to one day see his mysterious land of ancient castles and misty hollows. Four decades later she finally takes her long-awaited trip—never dreaming that it would unearth decades-buried memories and trigger a life-changing inner journey. A story of hope, love—and second chances.

TRAVEL / MIND • BODY • SPIRIT / MEMOIR / DRACULA
ISBN: 978-1-936332-10-6 • eBook: 978-1-9-36332-11-3
6 x 9 trade paper • 330 pages • $15.95

"Unfinished business can surface when we least expect it. It Started with Dracula is the inspiring story of two parallel journeys: one a carefully planned vacation and the other an astonishing and unexpected detour in healing a wounded heart."
—Charles Whitfield, MD,
bestselling author of Healing the Child Within

"Elegantly written. Cleverly told. Electrifying."
—Diane Bruno, CISION Media

"Thrilling! Dracula fans will love the movie references and devour the adventures of one of their own in Romania."
—C. Dean Andersson, author, I Am Dracula

"A touching memoir filled with hope, forgiveness, and the audacity to follow your dreams."
—Bram Stoker Award-winning author, Michael Knost

"Stunning! An elegant memoir of discovery, of dark secrets dragged into the light."
—Catherine Watson, Lowell Thomas Award-winning
travel editor and author

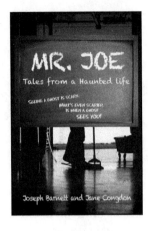

Mr. Joe: Tales from a Haunted Life
Joseph Barnett and Jane Congdon

Do you believe in ghosts? Nor did Joseph Barnett until the winter he was fired from his career job and became a school custodian to make ends meet. The fact that the eighty-five-year-old school where he now worked was built near a cemetery had barely registered with Joe when he was assigned the graveyard shift. But soon, walking the dim halls alone at night, listening to the wind howl outside, Joe was confronted with a series of bizarre and terrifying occurrences.

It wasn't just the ghosts of the graveyard shift that haunted him. Once the child of a distant father and an alcoholic mother, now a man devastated by a failed marriage, fearful of failing as a single dad, and challenged by an overwhelming illness, Joe is haunted by his own personal ghosts. The story of Joseph's challenges and triumphs emerges as an eloquent metaphor of ghosts, past and present, real and emotional, and how a man puts his beliefs about self—and ghosts—to the test.

RELATIONSHIPS / MIND • BODY • SPIRIT / MEMOIR
ISBN: 978-1-936332-78-6 • eBook: 978-1-936332-79-3
6 x 9 trade paper • 360 pages • $18.95 US

"This is truly inspirational work, a very special book—a gift to any reader."
— Diane Bruno, CISION Media

"Thrilling, thoughtful, elegantly told. So much more than a ghost story."
— Cyrus Webb, CEO, Conversation Book Club

"There are no lucky breaks, no sudden miracles here, but there is redemption. Love and perseverance can win. Read Mr. Joe!"
— Jack Rogers, Executive Director (retired), West Virginia Public Defender Services

"The Fabulous Book Babes will definitely read Mr. Joe as a selection."
— Fabulous Book Babes, Mason, Ohio

"This well-crafted memoir will be a gift to you. Mr. Joe tells a powerful story of personal enlightenment and transformation. Its theme of haunting proves irresistible."
— Anita Phillips, life coach and fitness trainer

BETTIE YOUNGS BOOKS

We specialize in MEMOIRS
. . . books that celebrate
fascinating people and
remarkable journeys

Visit our website at
www.BettieYoungsBooks.com

To contact:
info@BettieYoungsBooks.com

CPSIA information can be obtained
at www.ICGtesting.com
Printed in the USA
FSHW01n0723070718
49931FS